Two-Way Street in Art Education
Cross-Cultural Research

Akio Okazaki

Two-Way Street in Art Education
Cross-Cultural Research

by
Akio Okazaki

This edition published by BookWay
Printed in Japan

ISBN:978-4-86584-424-5

Cover Design: Rie Okazaki
Cover Illustration: *Surface to Reverse-2014-* by Akio Okazaki, 2014, acrylic on canvas, 182×228cm, collection of the Institute of Art & Design, University of Tsukuba
Printed in Japan

《 正 誤 表 》

本書に下記の通り間違いがありましたので、
お詫びして訂正致します。

	誤	→	正
P.ⅲ　16行目	Noe	→	Naoe
P.ⅲ　17行目	Shingo	→	Kir

Acknowledgments

I was interested in creative writing in high school. I did write some pieces of poetry, and hoped to become a poet. An art teacher diverted my interest toward visual arts. Upon graduating from high school, I enrolled as a student in the four-year art teacher training program at a college of education. After completing a bachelor's degree, I taught visual arts at a junior high school in Kobe. I also obtained a master's degree in art education. I have worked in the fields of art and art education for 40 years. My experience as a painter and a teacher of art has influenced much of my cross-cultural views in art education.

For the development of this book, I owe a debt of gratitude to many people. Some of them are painters whose work has influenced my works of art. I owe my artistic debt to Kyu Tanioka, Motonao Takasaki, Hiromichi Tsutsui, Kazuo Misaki, Jinichiro Tashiro, and Shinichi Tamagawa. In the field of art education in Japan, I am indebted to Minoru Keitoku, Sadahiko Naka, Motoki Nagamori, Tomotoshi Shiomi, Yukio Iwasaki, Yasuaki Okamoto, Kinichi Fukumoto, Hiromitsu Fukuyama, Mituie Nagamachi, Takeshi Ishikawa, Kazuo Kaneko, Osamu Miyawaki, Toshio Noe, Naoki Mizushima, Kazuhiro Ishizaki, Rikako Akagi, Norihisa Nakase, Akira Maemura, Asahiko Yamaki, Kazumi Yamada, Shingo Masuda, Takaaki Okumura, Tetsuo Arai, Kazuyo Nakamura, and Yasuyoshi Saito.

In the field of art education in Britain and North America, I also owe a lot to many scholars. David Thistlewood, Mervyn Romans, Elliot Eisner, Stephen Dobbs, Lary Kantner, Alexander Wilds, Frank Wachowiak, Gilbert Clark, Robert Ott, Brent Wilson, Kenneth Beittel, Albert Anderson, Paul Bolin, Harlan Hoffa, William Bradley, Patricia Amburgy, Mary Stankiewicz, Ronald MacGreger, Graeme Chalmers, Mary Foster, Mary Stokrocki, Stanley Madeja, Ralph Smith, Heta Kauppinen, Read Diket, Pradeep Dhillon, Peter Smith, Foster Wygant, Kery Freedman, and Doug Boughton are among those to whom I owe my cross-cultural debt.

I wish to thank Pennsylvania State University, the National Art Education

Association, the United States Society for Education through Art, the University of Illinois Press, the National Society for Education in Art & Design, Art Education Australia (formerly known as Australian Institute of Art Education), and the International Society for Education through Art for their assistance in publishing my papers in their journals and books, or in presenting them at the society's conferences.

I especially want to express my appreciation for Christos Meskos, Lewis Crowl, Keiko Maeda, and James Chambers who read the manuscripts of the earlier versions of the chapters in this book.

Finally, I express my deepest gratitude to my wife, Chiyoko, for encouraging me not only to work on painting but also to make papers on art education throughout my career.

Contents

List of Figures

Introduction

Fig. 0.1 Sculptures,
College of Education,
Pennsylvania State
University. Photo:
Akio Okazaki (1984).

Fig. 0.2 Memorial Plate of Viktor
Lowenfeld.
"The Sculptures, Plantings and
Seating of This Courtyard Where
Placed Here in Memory of Viktor
Lowenfeld."
College of Education,
Pennsylvania State University.
Photo: Akio Okazaki (1984).

Fig. 0.3 Japanese Edition (1963) of
Creative and Mental Growth (3rd ed.) ,
(Lowenfeld, 1957). K. Takeuchi,
T. Horiuchi, & K. Takei, trans.

Cross-Cultural Research

The chapters that are included in this book reflect my work in cross-cultural research in art education. When I started my journey in the field of art education in the 1980s, my goal was not cross-cultural research methodology. Earlier (in chapter 1), I have described in detail the brief history of school art and art teacher training, the prevailing open system of pre-service education, art teacher certification, and a preparation program offered in colleges in the 1990s. In the early 1980s, the Japanese art education at a higher level had not yet developed its own research field. Only eleven universities offered a master's program in art education. None of the Japanese professors of art and art education in the school of education had a doctor's degree because they were not required to have it in order to become a faculty member of a university.

The Japanese edition (1963) of Viktor Lowenfeld's *Creative and Mental Growth* was in its fortieth reprint in the 1980s. However, the Japanese interest in American art education was theoretical, and not practical. For those who were concerned with research in art education at a higher level in Japan, the only things that they could learn from Americans included matters such as the publication of the specialized research journals like the *Studies in Art Education* and the *Journal of Aesthetic Education* and the offering of doctoral courses in art education. I believe that this expansion in the field of American art education, particularly in the 1960s and the 1970s, should have served us well as then we made a choice of making a future in Japanese art education.

While a vast ocean separates Japan and the United States, there can also be a bridge by which eastern and western worlds encounter each other and integrate. Japanese art educators have compared American and Japanese ideas in more than a century (see chapter 3). American art educators have, similarly, synthesized the Japanese and American art cultures in their theories on art education. This book portrays the process of cross-cultural interpretation as a way of making sense of one's world in relation to those of others (Mason, Nakase, & Naoe, 1998; Naoe, 2003). A "communication network among scholars interested in cross-cultural research in art education needs to be established" (Eisner, 1979, p. 34). I find that cross-cultural research in art education is a "two-way street."

A "Two-Way Street" Approach
This book discusses obvious examples of what Japanese art educators have learned from Americans in more than a century. It also provides detailed instances of what American art educators have learned from Japanese. For example, the cases of both Akira Shirahama (see chapter 5) and Arthur Dow (see chapters 8-10) are interesting because they illustrate the gap between what was learned from others and what was realized in modernist art education. Their cases are also typical of a "push-and-pull" situation between traditionalism and modernism, nationalism and cosmopolitanism, and liberalism and conservatism in the changing attitudes of art educators toward modernism in their nations (see chapters 6-7).

Chapter 8 was originally included in the *InSEA 30th World Congress Proceedings* (1999) and reprinted in the ERIC database (2000). The document resume abstracts:

2

A U. S. art educator, Arthur Wesley Dow, synthesized Japanese and U. S. culture in his philosophy of art education. This paper portrays the process of cross-cultural interpretation as a way for an individual to make sense of his or her world in relation to those of others. The paper seeks to explain Dow's legacy in terms of the Oriental cultural tradition of art, noting that it is because his ideas were derived from his views regarding the nature of art rather than from a particular conception of children's artistic development that a multicultural heritage of art education is exemplified in Dow's interest in Oriental art. The paper discusses Dow's contribution to U. S. art education and considers interpretations of his transformation of Oriental art, speculating on spirituality and Hsieh Ho's first canon, ch'i, and notan. (BT, 2000, p. 1)

Dow's "turning the East" (Boyle, 2013; Williams, 2013; Battiata, 2014) model is parallel to Shirahama's "turning the West." This approach "might be to map the complex web of influences from Western to the Pacific Rim and tricontinental countries, and, in some cases, back again" (Stankiewicz, 2007a, p. 7). There is no doubt that both ways will make us richer in art education (Masuda, 1992, 2003). On September 19, 1903, "Dow departed San Francisco for Yokohama on the first leg of an around-the-world journey" and arrived in Yokohama, Japan, on October 7. "Of his three months in Japan, six weeks were spent in Tokyo, the remaining time at the port of entry, Hakone, Niko, Kyoto, Nara, Kobe, and Nagasaki" (Moffatt, 1977, pp. 100-101). In December of that year, he addressed Japanese audiences three times in Kyoto.

Shirahama left Yokohama in late February 1904, and arrived in Boston on April 6. During his study at the Massachusetts Normal Art School (Smith, 1924; Stankiewicz, 2016) from 1904 to 1905, Shirahama (1908) was able to attend to Dow's lecture at Teachers College, Columbia University, where Dow used a projector to show the Italian works of art, and provided a comparison of the works with Japanese color prints in order to describe color in Italian works.

Shirahama (1907) says, "To draw models, to study nature and to appreciate works of great masters' art make children understand what composition is by the building up of harmonious beauty through color, shape and space relation" (p. 44). It is clear that Shirahama's interest was not in the Japanese foundation of Dow's *notan* (a dark-and-light pattern) but in Dow's design methodology. Meanwhile, *notan* had become highly acceptable in the field of American art education. Indeed, the term "value" appeared too much of the traditional scientific scheme in the western world at that time.

Surely a "two-way street" approach was needed between the American and Japanese art education for enrichment of both and for achieving a cross-cultural understanding in art education (Wang & Ishizaki, 2002; Ishizaki & Wang, 2003). Davenport (2000) says, "Just as artists can learn to draw more precisely by attending to the spaces between shapes, so too might art education benefit from attending to the spaces between cultures where interaction takes place" (p. 372). Thus, the "two-way street" approach between cultures in art and art education is wide open. The extensive work of Shirahama or Dow in the earlier decades of the 20th century serves as a bridge in the "two-way street" of cultures through which cross-cultural researchers in art education on each side have to pass. It also becomes a gate to an alternate path for inquiry into art education through which multicultural researchers have to pass.

Transformation of Globalization

Chapter 2, which originally appeared in the (International) *Journal of Art & Design Education* (1991), describes modern art education in Europe and Japan. Just as the Japanese art had influenced the "impressionism" and "postimpressionism" styles, the idea of European modernism influenced Japanese artists and art educators. European artists had turned to Japan to find something that European art had lacked. In a similar way, Japanese artists and art educators later turned to Europe to find those elements missing from their current practices (Okazaki, 1991).

The story of the introduction of the European modernism into Japanese school art practice was reviewed by British and American art educators. Thistlewood (1991), the editor of the journal, reviews:

as Akio Okazaki informs us, the importation of exotic, western modernism has been a deliberate tactic of educationalists in his country, aimed at counterbalancing a normal tendency to didacticism. The national respect for regulation, and imported concepts of individual creativity, in effect counterbalance one another in dynamic tension. In historical terms, for example the *Japonaiserie* of the late nineteenth century, that so invigorates creativity in the west. (p. 128)

Romans (2005) edited *Histories of Art and Design Education: Collected Essays,* in which my paper of 1991 is reprinted. He introduces:

Section six is concerned with British/European influence in art and design education abroad. The two essays included here look at British art education in nineteenth-century Canada, and influence of European Modernist Art on Japanese art education in the early twentieth century. ... Coming full circle, as it were, Akio Okazaki's essay 'European Modernist Art into Japanese School Art: the Free Drawing Movement in the 1920s' begins by discussing the translation of the kind of nineteenth century British drawing manuals discussed by Rafael Cardoso, into Japanese. Okazaki shows that the export of the South Kensington system was not confined to British colonies, but introduced to Japan by Japanese art educators who had travelled to America and Europe experiencing versions of system first hand. Key elements of the system were incorporated in Japanese art education by the first decade of the twentieth century in the *New Textbooks of Drawing*. The backlash came with the short-lived Free Drawing Movement. Okazaki places the development of the movement in its wider socio-political context in Japan. In a carefully balanced account he shows how it was that European ideas of child-centred art education fused with exposure to European modernist art seemed a much more attractive approach and eroded interest in the official national textbooks. (pp. 16-17)

Adams (2006) reviews Romans' book, and writes:

> The essays that deal with art education outside of England, such as those by Chalmers and Okazaki, are refreshing reminder that art education's histories have other formations in different cultures. ... Okazaki provides enthralling descriptions of Japanese art teachers' liberation from prescriptive state-controlled textbook education, towards a free drawing movement that resulted in masses of classes being taken for outdoor landscape drawing expeditions. (p. 242)

Stankiewicz (2007b) also reviews Romans' book. She says:

> ... essays by Canadian and Japanese authors examine international influences on art education in 19th-century Ontario and 1920s Japan. ... Okazaki takes British, North American, and European influences into the "liberal twenties" (p. 231) when a range of Western influences contributed to make Japanese society more open and democratic. He examines how Kanae Yamamoto developed free drawing as a way to overcome the dominance of copy-book instruction and introduce what Eisner would later identify as an "internal mode of curriculum development" (p. 234) for Japanese art education. (p. 75)

Four reviewers provide their own interpretations on one paper. "Engaging in a cross-cultural dialogue is a critical part," and "globalization and its effect on art education has become an important topic" (Nakamura & Okazaki, 2003, p. 2). Therefore, "Art education can contribute to transformation of globalization so that both existing human relationships and individual personalities can find places in a broader human landscape" (Nakamura, 2009, p. 440).

A Gradual Process

The story of modern art education in America or Japan begins with Shirahama; Dow continues into the present, but it is more than ever a "two-way street" as suggested by Beittel (1983):

> I know, as Cox (1977) pointed out in *Turning East*, that things Oriental pass through a prism that all but transforms them into their opposite. An irony abounds here. It is as though I have gone a Japanese way, but without the hierarchy; and Japan has gone the American way, but without the free spirit. (p. 13)

Stokrocki (1995) edits an anthology which is dedicated to the seminal work of Beittel (Fisher & Bickel, 2006). It begins with "Okazaki's hermeneutic interpretation of Beittel's legacy" (iii). She comments on a shorter version of chapter 12 (Okazaki, 1995a):

> Japanese author Akio Okazaki attempts to explain an American scholar in terms of Japanese cultural traditions, of which Beittel was fascinated. Hermeneutics is a process of translating a text or any cultural document through examining its sources of thinking. Beittel's written work becomes a text in which one can decipher various meanings. Okazaki finds Beittel's "pilgrimage to other" places, ideas, and frames of reference as remarkable. Okazaki believes that Beittel introduced new ways [waves] of thinking as well as methods, which are all part of a central unifying source. Beittel explains this center as "The Great Tradition of language and learning itself." Okazaki encourages all new researchers to read Beittel's work for research alternatives as well as for personal consolation along the lonesome road of intellectual pursuit. (iii)

The ambivalent perception of American and Japanese relationship illustrates the clash between two cultural values in art and art education. A good example of such a clash might be Christo's "The Umbrellas" project. Project of Christo opened for display on October 9, 1991, in two places. Seventy-five miles north of Tokyo, in Ibaragi, Japan, 1,340 huge blue umbrellas were settled in a 12 mile range. Simultaneously, 1,760 huge yellow umbrellas were settled in an 18 mile range, north of Los Angeles. The project was exhibited for 18 days and about 540 thousand people enjoyed it in Japan alone ("Kurisuto no anburera purojekuto" [Christo's umbrella project], 1991; "Kurisuto Ten" [The Exhibition of Christo], 1991).

Experiencing the project helps us to see a "figure-ground relationship" of ambivalence in three ways. First, it makes viewers of both countries aware of natural and human-made environments. Viewers find themselves wrapped by huge umbrellas while they suddenly see land. Second, it provides a dynamic tension of the modernist and postmodernist forms of art. Viewers can enjoy it as a non-artistic event while they change their conventional ideas of modern art in order to recognize it as art. Last, it reflects on the seemingly incompatible foreign cultural value of art. Japanese viewers welcomed it while they were reminded of their culture of art in contrast to it. In these ways, the project forced viewers to redefine environment, art, and cultural value, by providing Rubin's famous "double representation" figure of the philosopher's cup as a kind of relationship between positive and negative spaces (Okazaki, 1995b).

Chapter 4, which was originally included in *Trends in Art Education from Diverse Cultures* (1995), indicates "the significance of the continuing cross-cultural exchange in the progress and renewal of art education" (p. 141). Kauppinen and Diket (1995) review:

Akio Okazaki uses the allegory of ambivalence in figure-ground relationship presented in Christo's projects of huge blue umbrellas on the land of Japan to illustrate the clash between two cultural values in art. The scene symbolizes the Japanese cultural history in art and art education, which has continually taken and transformed diverse influences from other cultures. In Japan, textbook-based art instruction and the centralized educational system are essential in transforming and assimilating cultural influences. The texts are revised every 3 years and renewed every 12 years. Okazaki argues that Japanese art education system has benefited by periodically discarding old practices and introducing new ones through the nationally distributed text. A method of art instruction through the fourth grade is "play activity." It uses body movement, material assemblage, space transformation, earthworks, formative plays, thinking, and planning in various locations of the school and playground. Okazaki sees cross-cultural influences as a two-way street. Just as Japanese art influenced Impressionism and Post-Impressionism, European modernism influenced Japanese artists and art educators. (p. 143)

The transformation of seemingly incompatible foreign cultures into art and art education is a gradual process (Yamada, 1992, 1995, 2003). Yet, to have continually taken and transformed diverse influences is a unique achievement (see chapters 11). Without diverse influences, no country has its inherent cultural values as pearls in an oyster (Stanley-Baker, 1984). Diverse influences from abroad (Ueno, Iwasaki, Okazaki, Okumura, & Hino, 2007; Akagi & Yamaguchi, 2019) provide a prime field of cross-cultural and multi-cultural research in art and art education.

Chapter 1

Originally published in the *INSEA News*, Vol. 1, No. 3, pp. 13-16, 1994.
Reprinted with permission by the Publications Board of InSEA.
Reprinted from ERIC database (ED 385 477).

Art Teacher Training in Japan

Fig. 1.1 Critical discussion of woodcut prints by 7th grade student, Laboratory School of Utsunomiya University (Japan).
Photo: H. Akutsu (1985).

Fig. 1.2 Clay sculpture (Japanese grappling *Sumo*) by 3rd grade students, Laboratory School of University (Japan).
Photo: M. Watanabe & T. Kobayashi (1985).

Fig. 1.3 Brent Wilson observed on a demonstration lesson at the Laboratory School of Utsunomiya University (Japan) in 1989.
(Wilson, 2008).

* Figures are not included in the originally published paper.

This chapter provides information about the past and present of art teacher training systems of Japan. It is not a discussion of problems of deciding how to prepare teachers of art that have to do with the conception of what art education is for, but rather, a description of the preservice education system in universities and colleges in Japan. In Japan, there are a number of schools, students and teachers. There are currently about 15,000 preschools, 25,000 elementary schools (grades 1-6), 11,000 lower secondary schools (grades 7-9) and 5,000 upper secondary schools (grade 10-12). Most of elementary and lower secondary schools are established by local public (prefectural and municipal) bodies. They are responsible for compulsory education. Preschools enroll about 2 million children, elementary schools 10 million, lower secondary schools 5 million, and upper secondary schools 5 million. The number of teachers employed is about 100,000 at the preschool level, 500,000 at the elementary level, 300,000 at the lower secondary level, and 300,000 at the upper secondary level. In 1990, 56.3 percent of elementary school teachers, 34.6 percent of lower secondary school teachers and 19.6 percent of upper secondary teachers were female (Ministry of Education, Science and Culture, 1994).

Teacher training is one of the most important tasks in education in general and art education in particular. Preparation of teachers of art in Japan goes back to more than 120 years, from when Japanese formal art education started.

School Art in Japan

In 1871, the Japanese Ministry of Education was established with a mandate to create a nationwide school system under its authority. Japanese art education within schooling started in 1872 when the first educational system was established. The turn of the 20th century was a remarkable period for building the Japanese compulsory education system. For example, in 1887 elementary school attendance reached only 45 percent. By 1897 it was 66 percent and jumped to 97 percent by 1907. Drawing became a required subject in grades 3 to 8 while manual arts was an elective subject. Since then, both drawing and manual arts, as parts of general education, were teaching subjects provided in elementary and middle schools until 1945 (Okazaki, 1991).

In the postwar period, the two separate subjects, drawing and manual arts, within school curricula were combined and "art and handicraft" became a required subject and established in the national guidelines for elementary and secondary schools in 1947. The Ministry of Education replaced "art and handicraft" with "fine arts" in secondary schools on the late 1950s. In the upper secondary schools (grades 10-12), the separation still remained. Students take fine arts, crafts production, calligraphy or music as one of the courses in the subject of "arts." Our national curriculum of art prescribed by the Ministry of Education is temporary. It has been revised and renewed in every 10 year (Okazaki, 1985b). In the Japanese national curriculum of art in 1990 for elementary and secondary schools, "expression (production) and appreciation are treated equally. But actually they are not. Exclusive appreciation class hour is one tenth of that production" (Nakase & Murakami, 1994, p. 14). This is due to the preservice education of art teacher and the teacher certification system in Japan. In their preparation, art teachers received lessons on more studio work than on art criticism, aesthetics, and art history. The overemphasis on studio production in art teachers training programs has a history.

The Prewar System of Art Teacher

Training Teachers training in Japan also started when the government established the Tokyo Normal School in 1872. Japan was divided into the 47 prefectural and local governments. They had established their normal schools responsible for training elementary classroom teachers in their schools. Prospective teachers took the studio work of drawing and the methods of drawing education. Secondary school teachers of art were trained mainly in the two institutions, the normal program at the Tokyo Fine Arts School and the drawing and manual arts program at the Tokyo Higher Normal School. These two programs were established in the opening decade of the 20th century by the central government for special purpose of training art teachers for secondary schools such as middle school, girl's high schools and normal schools.

For example, the normal program of the Tokyo Fine Arts School required 3 years. The curriculum was as follows: pedagogy and the art of teaching; aesthetics and the history of fine arts; anatomy (general outline of skeleton and muscles); designing (plane design with a small amount of solid design); freehand drawing (with charcoal, pencil and Japanese brush); mechanical drawing (plane, projective, geometrical and perspective drawing); handicrafts (clay, paper, wood and metal work); and practice of teaching (blackboard exercise, preparation of plans for elementary and secondary schools and student teaching experience). Among the various subjects in the normal program, the subject of freehand drawing was the one most emphasized. About 19 hours per week in each of 3 years was devoted to the study of freehand drawing. In the third year of the normal program, special emphasis (10 hours per week) was placed on student teacher as well (Okazaki, 1985a). The graduates of the normal program were granted certificates as secondary art teachers by the Ministry of Education. The Tokyo Fine Arts School and the Tokyo Higher Normal School had only two comprehensive programs of art in education at the higher level in the prewar period (Okazaki, 1992) while the number of higher institutions involving art teacher preparation program increased after the war.

The Present "Open System" of Teacher Preparation

The teacher training system in Japan underwent tremendous change in the postwar period. In 1946, the United States Education Mission to Japan advised the following two points regarding the teacher training in Japan: "one was that the curriculum for teacher training should comprise 3 areas—General Education, Teacher Education and Professional Education" and "the other was that normal schools should be reorganized into 4-year teacher's colleges and teacher training programs could be carried out in regular universities" (Committee for Facilitating Research, 1986, p. 13).

The old normal school system was discarded and the present new system of teacher training was established in accordance with the Education Personnel Certification Law in 1949. It incorporated the teacher education into the university system. The Japanese term this approach the "open system." It means that "faculties or departments in universities other than colleges of education and institutions without colleges of education, even junior colleges, can develop and offer teacher preparation programs," and "more than 800 institutions involved in teacher preparation now graduate nearly 175,000 students annually with teaching credentials" (U.S. Department of Education, 1987, pp. 14-15).

Teacher training is not limited to colleges of education but widely opened to teacher preparation programs at higher institutions. By 1985, 95 (51 national, 4 local public and 40 private) universities were helping prepare elementary teachers, and 366 (73 national public, 26 local public and 267 private) universities were including lower secondary teacher preparations.

Therefore, the proportion of teachers who were not graduates of colleges of education increased with school level. They filled one-third of the numbers of

14

teachers at the elementary level, two-thirds at the lower secondary level, and nine-tenths at the upper secondary level (U.S. Department of Education, 1987).

There are 25 art institutes in universities of arts and 65 colleges of education in universities. Most art institutes and colleges of education develop and offer secondary school art teacher preparation program that satisfies the legal requirements for certification to teach "fine arts" in secondary school or "crafts production" in upper secondary school.

Teacher Certificates and Art

Teachers in preschools and elementary and secondary schools in Japan should hold relevant teacher's certificates. They are usually granted from prefectural and local boards of education on the basis of standards laid down by the revised Education Personnel Certification Law in 1989. There are three different legal requirements for certification to teach in Japanese schools (grades K-12). They are advanced class certificate, first class certificate and second class certificate, all of which are valid across the nation.

The basic qualifications and the numbers of credits in specialized subjects (professional education studies such as social and philosophical foundations of education, psychology of education, child psychology, moral education, teaching methods, etc.) and in teaching subjects (Japanese, social studies, science, mathematics, English, music, fine arts, physical education, homemaking, industrial arts, student teaching, etc.) required for the 3 class teaching certificates at each of the four school levels. How can teacher certificates be obtained? For example, students who want to have a first class certificate of elementary schools must acquire 18 credits for teaching subjects, of which 2 are devoted to art and handicrafts studio work. They also have to earn 41 credits for professional education subjects, of which 6 are for student teaching and 2 are concerned with the teaching method of art and handicrafts.

If students would like to become lower secondary art teachers holding a first class certificate of fine arts, they must acquire 40 credits for fine arts, of which 20 are minimum numbers of credits for certificate (4 or 6 credits for painting, 4 or 6 credits for sculpture, 4 or 6 credits for design, 4 or 6 credits for crafts, and 2 or 4 credits for theory and history of art). They also have to earn 19 credits for professional education subjects, of which 4 are for student teaching and 3 are for the teaching method of fine arts.

Students seeking a first class upper secondary art teacher certificate must acquire 40 credits for fine arts, of which 20 should consist of painting (4 or 6 credits), sculpture (4 or 6), design (4 or 6 credits) and the theory and history of fine arts (2 or 4 credits). They also have to earn 19 credits for professional education subjects, of which 4 are for student teaching and 3 are for the teaching method of fine arts.

Those who want to obtain a first class upper secondary craft teacher certificate should acquire 40 credits for art and crafts, of which 20 should consist of mechanical drawing (4 or 6 credits), design (4 or 6 credits), crafts (4 or 6 credits), and the theory of design and crafts (2 or 4 credits). They also have to earn19 credits for professional education subjects, of which 4 are student teaching and 3 are for the teaching method of crafts production.

Art Teacher Preparation at a College of Education
Among 65 colleges of education, 47 colleges are affiliated with national public universities which are established, funded and operated by the national government. These colleges, formally normal schools under the pre-war system, are located in each 47 prefectural and local districts and mainly engaged in preparing elementary and secondary school teachers for their districts. They produce about 20,000 graduates annually who majored in elementary or lower secondary education.

In our district, Tochigi Prefecture, 75 miles north of Tokyo, Utsunomiya University is a national public university, where I have been a faculty member of college of education since 1980 and engaged in teacher training programs for both graduate and undergraduate students. Our college of education has 100 faculties. We have about 1,550 graduate and undergraduate students, of which 800 major elementary education, 350 major secondary education, 100 major mentally retarded children's school teacher education, 200 are students not in preservice education and 100 are graduate students in masters program.

The 4-year course for elementary and secondary school education majors in our college of education at Utsunomiya University is a typical teacher training program in Japan. It required the following credits for graduation. Elementary education majors must earn 30 credits for general education, 20 credits for teaching subjects, 40 credits for professional education studies, 26 credits for minor subjects, 4 credits for further studies with their choices, and 6 credits for student teaching. Secondary education majors have to earn 30 credits for general education, 44 credits for their teaching subjects, 18 credits for professional education studies, 30 credits for further studies with their choices and 4 credits for student teaching. The requirement of our college for graduation is 126 credits.

The department of art and art education in our college has 7 faculty, 2 painters, a sculptor, a designer, a craftsperson, and 2 art educators. The enrollments in our art and art education program is 80 students (50 elementary education majors who minor art, 20 secondary education majors who minor art and 10 graduate students majoring art education). The minor subjects for elementary and secondary education majors consist of more than 40 classes (per 2 credits) such as drawing, painting, sculpture, design, crafts, aesthetics, art history, art education research, and so forth. Faculties of art education are responsible for teaching such classes as elementary art, teaching methods of elementary and secondary school art and art education research.

Minimum requirement of student teaching in our college are 6 weeks (6 credits) for the elementary program and 4 weeks (4 credits) for the secondary program, which is based on the prescribed number of credits for student teaching in the Education Personnel Certification Law of 1989. Our college students experience their student teachings in our attached laboratory schools (a preschool, an elementary school, a lower secondary school, and a mentally retarded school for children) where about 80 teachers are responsible for student teaching. Our faculties of education and laboratory teachers work together in the course of student teaching, and encourage students to experience what school is, how actual school life is going on, what children are, what and how to teach, and so forth.

After obtaining bachelor's degrees, our students submit applicants for the teacher certificates that they wish to have to the Tochigi Prefectural Board of Education where our college is located. On the receipt of valid applications, the board of education will grant them teaching certificates. They are valid across the nation because they satisfy the requirements for certificates in the Education Personnel Certificate Law by the Japanese Ministry of Education, Science and Culture.

If our students would like to obtain more than one teaching certificate, they must take more credits than the requirement of our college. For example, most of our graduates of elementary education majors who minor art usually can obtain three first class certificates; elementary school teacher certificate, lower secondary school art teacher certificate, and upper secondary school art teacher certificate. Those of secondary education majors who minor art are able to obtain first class lower and upper secondary school art teacher certificates and a first class upper secondary school craft production teacher certificate.

Examinations for Employment

Most public school teachers are prefectural and local government's employees. These local bodies play a significant role in the selection of teachers for employment. The applicants for the teacher certificates must take prefectural and local appointment examinations which help ensure that all applicants compete on equal terms for any reaching vacancies.

The examinations are given in the two stages the "first consists of written tests in general education and specialized fields and skill tests in such areas as physical education, music and art. All applicants for lower secondary teaching jobs are required to take a test in physical fitness. The second stage consists of interviews" (U.S. Office Education, 1987, p. 17). These two stages have not been changed until the present. Once applicants gain entry to the teaching profession, they are given lifetime employment. They are qualified to teach at any of the public schools in the prefecture or local district in the following year.

Art Supervisors, Art Specialists and Art Teachers

In 1992, each prefectural and local district had several supervisors of art. The total number of art supervisors in the prefectural local boards of education was 224 that represent about 5 percent of 4,654 supervisors in Japan. They were formally public school art teachers in their districts and are taking leadership for inservice education for art teachers.

Art specialist in elementary public schools are employed in only two large cities, Tokyo and Kobe. The Tokyo Metropolitan Board of Education employed about 14 hundred art specialists in 1992. Elementary public schools in other prefectural districts require classroom teachers to teach art and handicraft in two class periods for each week.

At the secondary level, there were by 1989, more than 10 thousand lower secondary public schools in Japan where 13,450 art teachers were employed. Art teachers filled about 5 percent of 275 thousand lower secondary public school teaching positions. At the upper secondary level, the proportion of art and craft teachers decreased. There were 2,160 art teachers and 94 craft teachers. They filled only one percent of 220 thousand upper secondary public school teachers.

While the proportion of 17 thousand public school art teachers in Japan still remains, the new employment of art teachers has decreased in each year. In our Tochigi Prefecture, for example, more than 20 applicants were appointed as public school art teachers in the mid 1980s, but the appointment in1994 are decreased to only 3. This has been due to "a decrease in elementary and secondary school enrollments in recent years and the resulting decrease in the number of teachers recruited" (Ministry of Education, Science and Culture, 1990, p. 40).

Conclusion

The problem of trying to decide what kind of educational program to prepare for those who are going to become art teachers has two aspects. One is that our view of teacher education is affected by the conception of art education which is formed in schools. The other is the source or location for the development of art teachers.

The preparation of teachers of art begins in the universities and colleges and is completed in the schools in which art teacher works with children to develop their consciousness of art, creative imagination, and skills for making something (Eisner, 1989).

There is not space to describe these two aspects. What I described in this chapter only had to do with one of location, preservice education in art in universities and colleges in Japan, which had implications for the preparation of teacher of art. The brief history of school art and art teacher training, the present open system of preservice education, art teacher certification, a preparation program in college, becoming employed as an art teacher, and statistical data of schools, art teachers and art supervisors were described and identified. I would be happy if information about art teacher training in Japan serves as food for thought on your professional education of teachers of art.

Chapter 2

Originally published in the *Journal of Art & Design Education*, Vol. 10, No. 2, pp. 189-198, 1991.
Reprinted with permission through Copyright Clearance Center's RightsLink® Service.

European Modernist Art into Japanese School Art: The Free Drawing Movement in the 1920s

Fig. 2.1 Lesson 24, *Shintei Gacho* [*New Texbooks of Drawing*], Grade 1 (1910), p. 48.

Fig. 2.2 Drawing by 1st grade student copying the *New Texbooks of Drawing* (Nakamura, 1979, p.141).

Fig. 2.3 Outdoor drawing by 4th grade student in 1924 (Nakamura, 1979, p. 2).

* Figures are not included in the originally published paper.

Introduction

In the field of art education in Japan, there has been a great deal of European art education literature which has been translated or introduced into Japanese. In the 1870s, for example, two British textbooks of Burn were translated into Japanese by Togai Kawakami. One is *The Illustrated London Drawing-Book* (1852), and the other *Self-aid Cyclopedia for Self-taught Students* (1863). Both were edited into one volume, and published in 1871. This Japanese edition, *Seiga Shinan* (*Guide to Western Pictures*), was recommended by the Ministry of Education in Japan (established on July 18, 1871) for use at the elementary level, in accordance with the regulation of the first modern comprehensive educational ordinance (issued on

September 8, 1872) (Okazaki, 1984). Rosenfield (1971) describes Togai:

> Togai's knowledge of European art was based on Duch texts of considerable age, well removed from the esthetic issues which were affecting contemporary European art. This situation was not really changed even in the latter 1860s when more up-to-date French and English books were imported. Among these was a drawing manual by Robert Scott Burn, a British writer who specialized in instructions for self-teaching of artistic and mechanical subjects. Togai translated it under the title *Seiga Shinan* (*Guide to Western Pictures*), and it was published in 1871. (p. 194)

Togai Kwakakami as a literati painter is one of early scholars of Western painting. Between 1856 and 1868 he worked at the shogunate school for the study of European science. In the Meiji Restraction (1868), "Togai was employed by the ministries of education and the army. He established a private art studio and school for the study of Western-style painting" (*Kodansha Encyclopedia of Japan*, vol. 4, 1983, p. 181). He instructed many Japanese who later became early leading masters of Western-style painting.

Comparing these original texts with the Japanese edition, Kaneko (1981) indicates that the translation of Burn's books can be seen as almost accurate, though with some additions and modifications of figures according to the translator's own interpretation.

Another example of British influence on Japanese art education in the 1870s can be found in a Japanese textbook, *Shogaku Hutsu Gagakubon* (*Drawing for Use in Elementary Schools*) of Miyamoto, which was published by the Ministry of Education in 1878. This textbook includes pictures which were reprinted from Walter Smith's *Teacher's Manual of Free-Hand Drawing and Designing and Guide to Self-Instruction* (1873). The influence of "the South Kensington System" of art education was not limited to American, Canadian, and Brazilian art education (Macdonald, 1970; Chalmers, 1985; Barbosa, 1984), it also extended to Japan through Miyamoto's textbook.

Apart from the translations of key textbooks, subsequent European influences are demonstrated by several Japanese art educators who made their survey trips to the Western world in the earlier decades of the 20th century. Among them was Akira Shirahama (1866-1927). He arrived in Boston on 6 April, 1904, entered the Massachusetts Normal Art School in May and graduated 22 June, 1905. He left Boston on 25 August of that year and arrived in London on 6 September. He visited France and Germany before returning to Japan on 21 March, 1907. In the same year, the Normal Course of Drawing was established at the Tokyo Fine Arts School with the special purpose of training teachers for secondary schools, and Shirahama was appointed chairman of the course. Shirahama trained many normal-school art teachers and teachers of art at the secondary level for twenty years until his death (Kaneko, 1978a). After coming back to Japan, he devoted himself to developing more modernized drawing curricula.

The turn of the 20th century was a remarkable period for building the Japanese compulsory-education system. For example, in 1887 elementary-school attendance reached only 45 percent. By 1897 it was 66 percent, and jumped to 97 percent by 1907. Drawing became a required subject in grades three to eight. At that time, the Ministry of Education defined the purposes of drawing in the elementary educational ordinance, as "to cultivate in children the faculty of perceiving clearly and drawing correctly ordinary objects, and to foster the sense of the beautiful" (Kikuchi, 1907, p. 186).

Corresponding to the extension of elementary-school attendance, the Ministry of Education desired to have a comprehensive textbook of drawing that was not a mere copybook but a systematically organized text, including such content as drawing, painting, colour theory, composition, decoration and design. The Ministry, therefore, issued new drawing books for each elementary grade called *Shintei Gacho* (*New Textbooks of Drawing*) in 1910. This set of drawing textbooks was the first modernized series in the history of modern art education in Japan. The content and organization of the curriculum in the textbooks were developed under Shirahama's direction (Okazaki, 1985a). Thus modern Japanese art education system was established around the year 1910.

In the 1920s, Shirahama was criticized by certain art educators such as Kanae Yamamoto, the leading advocate of the Free Drawing Movement in schools during the later half of the Taisho Era (1912-1926) in Japan. He claimed Shirahama was responsible for the remnants of copyism and the lack of expressive value in the new textbook of drawing. He began the Free Drawing Movement in December 1918.

Background

The Taisho Era in modern Japanese history is the period of Taisho Democracy. Politics were concerned with the rapid rising of parliamentary power and party leadership. Culturally, there was a broad range of liberalizing tendencies and the swing of the pendulum back to enthusiastic borrowing from the West. The tendency toward democratic style depended not only on the expansion of the Japanese economy during World War One, but on the Japanese enthusiasm for liberal Western concepts. Japanese people were indeed responding to the victory of the major Western democracies such as Britain, France, and the United States, and the defeat of the more autocratic nations such as Germany and the Austro-Hungarian Empire, in their image of the ideal Western democracy (Reischauer, 1981, pp. 171-172).

Western writers on modern Japanese history in general show that the democratic movement in the Taisho Era of Japan caught the imagination of the country. They also describe how these political, social, cultural, and educational innovations took place at that time (Beasley, 1982). In his 1919 article "Liberalism in Japan," Dewey reported the climate of the period:

> One heard the word frequently from the mouths of Japanese fellow travelers as one crossed the Pacific: De-mo-krasie. ... Autocracy out of fashion, democratic styles were in. ... The Change of fashion was a fact, was indeed a large part of the situation. But it operated mainly to depress the prestige of the reactionary bureaucrats and to increase that of the liberals so that men

were willing, and even glad, to listen to them. (pp. 283-285)

Beasley (1982), a British writer on modern history of Japan, refers to the second decade of the century in Japan as "the Liberal Twenties" (p. 214). Under the global democratic movement, the new wave of liberalizing ideas and ways from the West gave impetus to political changes. All adult males gained the franchise in the mid 1920s (Reischauer, 1964, p. 93). Eckroade (1979) identifies the relationship between innovation in the political system and schooling in the 1920s in Japan. Kobayashi (1976) points out the growing interest in democratic education among Japanese educators (p. 30).

The democratic orientation in education resulted in a new movement of education in the 1920s. We call it the *Shin Kyoiku Undo* (New Education Movement). Sugiyama (1983) describes the movement as an:

> Early 20th century educational movement emphasizing the individuality and initiative of the student in opposition to the standardized education of state controlled school system as it has existed since the early Meiji (1868-1912). The principles and methods espoused by the Japanese movement were those of the European and American progressive education movement that arose in the late 19th and early 20th centuries. (p. 121)

The free expression or self-expression movement in Japanese arts and aesthetic education also began in response to the liberalizing tendencies in education at the time. By 1920 elementary and secondary school curricula included drawing, singing, and manual arts. In addition, students received lessons in literary composition or writing within the Japanese language education programme. "In art[s] education, a movement that included free composition developed to promote self-expression by school children" (Japanese National Institute for Educational Research [JNIER], 1978, p. 7).

This movement aimed at promoting children's self-expression in school subjects related to arts. In children's literary composition, for example, this movement emphasized the children's free expression and the educative value of composition based on their experience. It also aimed to free children from the strictly standardized language curriculum prescribed by the Ministry of Education. Children wrote in response to their life and world. Teachers encouraged students to express their individual ideas freely through the arts (JNIER, 1978, p. 65).

> Emphasis on free expression was not limited to literary composition, but spread also to music, art and school drama exemplified in the children's song movement and the free drawing movement at the end of the second decade of this century. From such stimuli developed a movement for education through art. (JNIER, 1978, p. 65)

We call this movement for education through art *Geijutsu Kyoiku Undo* (Arts Education Movement) (Ueno, 1981).

The Free Drawing Movement

The Free Drawing Movement (*Jiyuga Kyoiku Undo* in Japanese) in the 1920s is a historic event in the development of modern Japanese art education. As already states, Kanae Yamamoto (1882-1946) was its originator. As a young man he had trained as an engraver of Western style line-blocks for book and magazine illustrations. He also graduated from Tokyo Fine Arts School in 1906, and later spent several years (1912-1916) in Europe (Sullivan, 1965, p. 145). On the way back to Japan, he had an opportunity to attend an exhibition of children's paintings in Moscow. The children's free expression in the exhibition impressed him, and on his return to Japan he proposed the idea of free expression in drawing education to Japanese art educators (Okazaki, 1984, pp. 86-87).

Yamamoto's book of 1921 expressed his idea of the *Jiyuga* (free drawing). Yukawa (1965) later summarized Yamamoto's great contribution to the innovation of theory and practice of Japanese art education:

After his return to Japan he advocated the idea that the teaching of "Drawing" should develop the creative, aesthetic ability of each individual child. For this purpose he suggested that the child should be released from copying textbooks and be placed in nature, which he should be encouraged to draw as he felt. He told Japanese teachers that they should believe in the natural aesthetic potentiality that would be inherent in every child. ... The idea of "JIYUGA" aroused an echo from young teachers, in spite of the opposition raised by conservative art teachers and educational authorities. Copying textbooks was rejected by many teachers, and children were seen everywhere—in field[s], forests and towns—drawing directly from nature. (p. 10)

Why did Japanese elementary classroom teachers soon accept Yamamoto's advocacy of free drawing? The answer to this question relates to both the positive and negative aspects of the national textbooks for drawing used in public primary schools. The Ministry of Education established *Shintei Gacho* (New Textbooks of Drawing) in 1910, and required that they serve as the only national textbook until 1931. They reflect the instructional, or practical, means of teaching art. They considered children's developmental psychology, and included design methodology as part of contents of a drawing programme. Teachers' manuals for each grade prescribed special teaching method in each lesson plan. However, there remained the over-emphasis on a strict instructional approach to teaching art. The textbooks ignored the expressive aspect of art while they contained copyist or imitative drawing (Okazaki, 1985a, p. 64).

Japanese elementary school classroom teachers neglected the positive aspects of the Japanese textbooks, and took the easy way of having their students copy from illustrations in the textbooks. Yukawa (1965) describes how the negative aspect of the textbooks was used:

This new series of textbooks was characterized by diversified contents, suggesting [that] the child ... copy, ... sketch, ... depict [from] ... memory, as well as ... make patterns and ... learn simple pictorial drawing. In these various activities it was suggested that pencils (both lead and colour), brushes and watercolours might be used according to the interests and needs of children of different grades. When these textbooks were put into actual use, however, many school teachers were not prepared to utilize them properly; the textbooks were used by children as a mere collection of pictures to copy. The idea conceived in the textbooks was little realized in classrooms. (p. 10)

Yamamoto was the first one to point out publicly the continuation of copy work and the lack of expressive value in the new drawing textbooks. He believed that the purpose of drawing in education was for children to express themselves freely in artistic activities. His philosophy of art education provided another way for elementary school classroom teachers to teaching drawing. Those who were critical of the *Shintei Gacho* were willing to agree with his proposal. Yamamoto's free drawing movement brought several innovations. It taught both teachers and their students the use of natural objects, out-of-doors, as the primary source of expression. Influenced by their environment, students produced drawings and paintings with spontaneously and with minimal instruction. European modernist art, especially French Impressionism, became an exemplar for this sort of school art practice. Dependence on the official national textbooks declined from 3.5 million distributed in 1921 to 2 million in 1926, while the distribution of teachers' editions declined from 75 thousand to zero in the same period (Kaneko, 1979).

Counterbalance to a State-controlled Policy
Yamamoto's movement only lasted for a decade but it clearly was appropriate for its time. He contributed to the decline of what Elliot Eisner (1984) has called the "external mode" of curriculum development, which "occurs in locations outside of the context in which the materials are to be used," and which "takes form most

often in textbooks" (p. 263). Instead, Yamamoto provided art teachers with an alternative approach—the "internal mode of curriculum development" (as Eisner has proposed)—where "art teachers have a professional responsibility to develop programs for the student they teach" (p. 263).

The free drawing movement, by providing a counterbalance to the state-controlled centralization of art education, had the effect of depressing the prestige of reactionary bureaucrats, and increasing the prestige of liberals (Dewey, 1919, p. 283). There have since been appeared many "counterbalances" (Dobbs, 1983), accounts of which offer an alternative to the official history developed by the Ministry of Education. The free drawing movement is thus the root of a modern tradition of holding state-controlled art education in check.

Some American art educators are interested in adopting such practices (Foster, 1975; Wachowiak, 1985). Others, however, perceive that Japanese educational systems "proceed vertically from a central power base" (Ott & Hurwitz, 1984) and this worries them (Carson, 1981; Dobbs, 1983). The balancing governmental and non-governmental systems, which now has a seventy year history, is not always obvious. In responding to American views in 1985, I wrote:

> The Japanese style of setting national standards by guidelines and counterbalances to centralization by non-governmental art educators, however, are ambivalent. We have profitable feedback systems for discarding old art education practices and introducing new ones though we also have dangerous forces that cause the Ministry to overemphasize one particular ideology. Our energies and inventiveness for future art education can be harmed, and our counterbalance can be destroyed. (Okazaki, 1985b, p. 9)

In short, the free drawing movement in the 1920s gave elementary school classroom teachers the freedom to develop their own curricula for the students they teach. It made Japanese art educators perceive necessity of using their energies and inventiveness for future art education through the "internal mode" of curriculum development in art education. It can be praised as the first counterbalance to state-controlled policy of art education in the history of modern Japanese art education.

Conclusion: Figure-ground Relationship

The Free Drawing Movement also changed attitudes of Japanese art educators from the limited view of industrial drawing toward the more modernized concept of art as individual expression. Gradually there appeared the new conception of art, and the old view of drawing for industrial use disappeared.

Yamamoto used the Japanese term *Jiyu* (free) to equate children's freedom with the individualism of artists (Yamamoto, 1921). His effort to replace the old concept of drawing with the new one, art, met with success. Both Japanese artists and art educators responded to works by Manet, Gauguin, Van Gogh, Renoir, Matisse, Cézanne, and Rodin. At that time Japanese art magazines provided information about European Impressionism and Post-Impressionism. Young Japanese artists returned to Japan after their study in Europe, and they produced their works of art in the style of modernism. "The point about Renoir, Matisse, Cézanne, Van Gogh, and Gauguin," says Kawakita (1974), "was not so much a matter of the variations in their artistic styles as the insistence of all upon individualistic expression." Kawakita concludes: "the individualism of these artists agreed with the newest trends in thought and literature" (p. 96).

With Yamamoto, Japanese art educators believed that any copied drawing was harmful to children. They recognized that the art teacher should encourage his or her children to create their own style or mode of artistic expression. They gave students the freedom to express themselves. Yamamoto recommended that teachers should encourage children to express their impressions out-of-doors like the French Impressionists. Such methodology continues to the present and gains in popularity. "At the zoo and in the parks in Japan one can see swarms of children with their teachers, painting and drawing" (Carson, 1981, p. 43).

Brent Wilson, after his lecture to Japanese art educators at a national conference of art education in March, 1989, asked whether Cizek's and other European teachers had influenced the movement in Japanese art education (Wilson, 1989). The answer is that there was no such apparent influence during the first half of the 20th century. We recognize Cizek as the father of child art through the Japanese edition of Herbert Read's *Education through Art*, available in 1953. Read (1945) mentioned twice Cizek (p. 204, p. 209) and also listed Viola's works (1936, 1942) in his bibliography (p. 312). Japanese art educators thus read Viola's texts, and were introduced to Cizek's ideas during the 1950s. For example, Shimoda (1959a) illustrated Cizek's view of child art in 1959, though the Japanese edition of Viola's *Child Art* (1942) did not became available until 1976.

It was Yamamoto who was the father of children's art in Japan, as Cizek was elsewhere. Indeed, he was the first modernist in Japanese art education. His ideas were extended in the 1950s by those he had helped towards an understanding of modernism thirty years earlier. They began the "Creative Art Education Movement," of which Shimoda (1959b) has written that it "advocates letting pupils develop their creative power by releasing them from repressions" and also by featuring "their free expression" (p. 230).

Japanese art educators translated such books as *Education through Art* by Read (1943), *Children as Artist* by Tomlinson (1947), and *Art and the Child* by Richardson (1948). These books were available in 1950s, and Japanese art educators could use them to support the creative art education movement. Such British sources helped them see their mission to reconstruct art education more clearly. They were able to reflect British ideas upon their own goals and methods because of their background of responding to the historic free drawing movement of the 1920s.

Just as Japanese art had influenced the Impressionism and Post-Impressionism, the idea of European modernism influenced Japanese artists and art educators. European artists had turned to Japan to find something that European art had lacked. In a similar way, Japanese artists and art educators later turned to Europe to find those elements missing from their current practices. Read (1974) describes the influence of Japanese woodcut prints on European painters (pp. 22-25). The story of the introduction of European modernism into Japanese school art practice therefore is reminiscent of what Eisner (1989) calls "the idea that requires contrast in order to ... have figure-ground relationship." It is a prime field of cross-cultural research in art and art education.

Chapter 3   Originally published in the *Journal of Multi-cultural Cross-cultural Research in Art Education*, Vol. 2, No. 1, pp. 82-95, 1984.
Reprinted with permission by the United States Society for Education through Art.

An Overview of the Influence of American Art Education Literature on the Development of Japanese Art Education

Fig. 3.1 John G. Chapman, *The American Drawing Book* (1847), p. 21.

Fig. 3.2 T. Kawakami, ed. & trans., *Seiga Shinan* [Guide to Western Pictures], Part 1 (1871), p. 3.

Fig. 3.3 Japanese Edition (1986) of *Educating Artistic Vision* (Eisner, 1972). N. Nakase, A. Maemura, K. Yamada, A. Okazaki, T. Miyazaki, N. Mizushima, et al. trans. Cover painting by 4th grade Japanese student.

Fig. 3.4 Elliot W. Eisner in his office. Photo: Akio Okazaki (1984).

* Figures are not included in the originally published paper.

Since Commodore Matthew Perry's squadron of ships arrived in Japan in 1853, Japan and the United States have interacted culturally with each other by way of the vast ocean which is regarded as the bridge by which Far Eastern and Far Western areas encountered each other and became integrated into one world. The field of art education is no exception to the long exchange between the two nations. For research in modern Japanese education in general, several comprehensive books are available in English, such as Anderson (1959), Passin (1965a), and Kobayashi (1976). Although these three writers provide their own view of the epochs of

Japanese modern education history, I would like to propose, following Anderson's book, three epochs in the development of modern Japanese education in general as follows: "(1) The introduction and development of modern education, hereafter referred to in the text as the *Initial Modernization Epoch* (1872-1937); (2) the conversion of education to the needs of a nation at war, or the *Wartime Epoch* (1937-45); (3) the building of a new democratized system, or the *Democratization Epoch* (1945 to the present)" (Anderson, 1959, p. 2).

In the field of art education in Japan, there has been a great deal of American art education literature which has been translated or introduced into Japanese during each epoch, except for the unhappy Wartime one. The purpose of this chapter is to trace the American influence on Japanese art education in each of these three epochs.

The First Influence of American Art Education

The British influence on Japanese art education in the earlier period of the first initial modernization epoch was as influential as it was in America, typically exemplified by the case of Walter Smith's great contributions to American art education in the 1870s. For example, the first translation of a textbook on art education, what we call the *Seiga Shinan* (Guide to Western Pictures), was translated by Togai Kawakami[1] and published in 1871. This book was suggested by the Ministry of Education in Japan (established on July 18, 1871) for use at the elementary school level, in accordance with the regulation of the first modern comprehensive educational ordinance[2] issued on September 8, 1872. It is an industrial and mechanical "drawing manual by Robert Scott Burn, a British writer who specialized in introductions for self-teaching of artistic and mechanical subjects." His book, *The Illustrated London Drawing-Book* (London, 1852), "contains lessons in pencil sketching, figure and object drawing, perspective and isometric drawing, sketching in crayons, and engraving in metal and wood." In addition, his *Self-aid Cyclopedia for Self-taught Students* (London, 1863) was translated and incorporated into the *Seiga Shinan*, plus some "essays on architectural, mechanical, and engineering drawing, ornamental drawing and design, mechanics, and steam engine design" (Rosenfield, 1971, p. 194). Yet, comparing the original text with the translated book, Kaneko (1981) indicates that the "translation of Burn's book can be seen as almost correct, though with some additions and modifications of figures" (p. 19) according to the translator's idea. One such modification of figures is the fact that an illustration of a student drawing some lines on a chalkboard, which is found on page 21 of Chapman's *American Drawing Book* (1847), was added to the opening page of the translation of Burn's book (Kumamoto, 1973; 1982). This is, I think, the first influence of American art education on Japanese modern art education.

During the Initial Modernization Epoch

However, the impact of American art education on the Japanese, from the end of the nineteenth century to the present, except for the Wartime epoch, has been more influential than that of other countries, especially in the practical aspects of teaching art. Let us examine the translation and the introduction of American art literature into Japanese. During the initial modernization epoch, Cross's *Light and Shade: A Manual for Teachers and Students* (Boston: Ginn, 1897) was translated by Akira Shirahama and contained in the appendix of his book (1904) entitled *Zuga Kyoju Ho* (*Methods in Drawing Instruction*). In this book, Shirahama also includes several pictures which were reprinted from Tadd's *New Methods in Education* (New York: Orange Judd, 1901) found on pages 72, 90, 124, 127, 160, 165, and 171 (Shirahama, 1904, pp. 82-92). A picture on page 160 in Tadd's book can be seen in the fine art education text by Chapman, *Approaches to Art in Education* (1978), on page 4, top. Tadd's work on art, real manual training and nature study, emphasizes, according to Belshe (1946), "the cultural value of arts in industrial training" (p. 61) and makes three suggestions: the correlation of drawing with all other objects, improvement of aesthetic taste by practice in art, and encouraging children to create design. It also provides that "a study of artistic objects would profoundly influence the aesthetic preferences of individuals" (p. 62). Tadd's influence was not limited to Japan; it also extended to Germany. Like the American researcher Smith (1982) who points out Tadd's impact on Germany, [3] a Japanese researcher of arts education, Seki (1925), also indicates the impact:

> ... Tadd proposes drawing with both hands and "rotation of the branches of work" [which means multi-media follow-through[4]] as a new method in which children in every grade not only draw but do such things as designing, modeling, and carving. As an example of work, children first of all draw a figure or form on paper, next they model it in clay and finally they carve it in wood. Tadd believes that drawing ability may be increased by clay-modeling, which in turn may be improved by wood-carving, and this designing may improve their creativity. This trend, which almost paralleled the British trend, contributed greatly to the innovation of German art education. (pp. 316-317)

Beyond the impact of Cross and Tadd on Japanese art education, subsequent American influences are demonstrated by the following: The first comprehensive modernized nation-wide textbooks of drawing in Japan were made in 1910 and depended partly on the six volumes of Froehlich and Snow, *Text Books of Art Education* (New York: Prang Educational, 1904-1905); Münsterberg's *The Principles of Art Education* (New York: Prang Educational, 1904) was translated into Japanese first in 1915 by Shimoda and second in 1921 by Nishimiya; and Bailey's *Art Education* (Boston: Houghton Mifflin, 1914) was also translated in 1917 by Shimoda. The above American impact on the Japanese is corroborated by Dobbs' article. He writes:

> ... In fact, the influence of the United States can be traced to before the turn of this century, when Professor Akira Shirahama at the Tokyo Fine Arts School studied the approach and materials of the Massachusetts Normal Art School, at which Walter Smith had created the first major public school teacher training program in drawing beginning in the 1870s. The Japanese art text of the early period also shows the impact of Prang's books and the manual arts heritage. Further influence can be traced to Ernest Fenollosa at the Boston

Museum of Fine Arts, Arthur Wesley Dow at Teachers College, and Henry Turner Bailey's *School Arts* magazine. (Dobbs, 1983, p. 8)

At the time, such writers as Shirahama and Shimoda contributed greatly to introducing American art education trends at the turn of the 20th century in Japanese. First, Shirahama was an expert Japanese-style painter, trained at the Tokyo Fine Arts School, now Tokyo University of Arts, and he was the first chair of the Normal Course of Drawing which was established at the Tokyo Fine Arts School in 1907 as the first comprehensive art teacher training division in Japan, much like the Massachusetts Normal Art School in the United States. Shirahama's American-European art education survey trip took over three years, from March 18, 1904, to March 21, 1907. He spent the first half of his trip in America, particularly in Boston at the Massachusetts Normal Art School. Kaneko (1978b) presumes that he enrolled in the fourth year and studied in the Teacher's Class of "Pedagogy and Supervision" which offered "methods of teaching and supervising drawing" (Bailey, 1900, p. 36) or else he studied in the fifth course which aimed "to prepare students to fill positions as supervisors and teachers of drawing in the public schools" and in which the fourth year of the course was devoted to "preparation for the teaching of drawing" (Buckley, 1908, p. 329). Although he spent the latter half of his trip surveying British, French and German art education, he was more impressed with American art education than that of other countries. What he learned from the Americans was, first, the public school teacher training program in drawing at the Massachusetts Normal Art School which he translated into the Normal Course of Drawing at the Tokyo Fine Arts School. Secondly, he learned the systematic approach to art curriculum in the public schools in the United States. Shirahama played a great role, with the support of other Japanese art educators, in developing the first modernized art curriculum for the public schools of Japan. His direction for a new curriculum development under the influence of the United States resulted in the publication of *Shintei Gacho* (*New Textbooks of Drawing*) which appeared in 1910 and consisted of a volume each for grades one to eight. This was prepared as the only national textbook for nation-wide use by the Ministry of Education in Japan. In making and writing the new curriculum of the textbook, Shirahama referred mainly to Froehlich's and Snow's *Text Books of Art Education*. It "contained illustrations to be reproduced with exactness as exercises in learning to draw" and was "often published in series with one volume for each grade level." This made it possible "to spread the teaching of art principles throughout the school years in a systematic way" (Belshe, 1946, p. 82).

What the *New Textbooks of Drawing* in Japan contributed to Japanese art education heritage is, first, the innovation of curriculum reform in the public schools of Japan. The textbooks offer a modernized scope and sequence of art curriculum based on a systematic and incremental content borrowed from American art education. Secondly, it swept away the "nationalistic reaction" in art education. This reaction in "the area of fine arts seemed to have reached a fanatical stage when, in 1885, the traditional techniques of brush and *sumi* [Indian black ink used in Chinese and Japanese painting and calligraphy] were restored in elementary art instruction, replacing the pencil drawing" (Haga, 1971, p. 235), which had dominated art instruction in the elementary schools of Japan in the 1860s and 1870s. In spite of Fenollosa's great contribution to the "nationalistic reaction" in both art and the art education field, it is a historical irony that modern Japanese art education was built up completely on the exemplary model of American art education.

There was also another ironical fact in that both Shirahama and Shimoda were interested in Dow's theory and practice of art education which was based on the traditional Japanese-style painting theory and practice that Dow acquired from Fenollosa. For instance, Shirahama reports that during his stay in America he had the experience of observing Dow lecture at the Teacher's College, using a projector to show Italian works of art, providing a comparison of the works with Japanese color prints in order to describe color in the Italian works (Shirahama, 1908). In another article, Shirahama offered a justification of art education which emphasized "creative imagination" and "composition." He writes:

Children naturally tend to have some aesthetic quality so that we should encourage them to develop their mental and aesthetic growth. In aiming for such an end, we need such materials as models and reproductions in artifacts and plants, animals, and landscapes in nature. It is a fine method that we show children many kinds of reproductions for the works of great old masters because these works not only represent natural beauty but express their ideas in which their own philosophy of humanities is symbolized by a sense of beauty, subtle imagination and great thought. To draw models, to study nature and to appreciate works of great masters' art is to make children understand what composition is by the building up of harmonious beauty through color, shape and space relation. As a result, children's intelligence and aesthetic ideas are developed. We must help them to be stimulated and to inquire into their work. It is the purpose of drawing as a regular subject within the school curriculum to make creative imagination available to children's minds. (Shriahama, 1907, p. 44)

It seems that Shriahama learned "creative imagination" from Froehlich and Snow's textbook in which many illustrations "appear to have been designed to stimulate both an interest in art activity and a sensitivity to the beauty of nature" (Silverman, 1982, p. 174) and also that he based his idea of "composition" on Dow's book *Composition* (1899). But the fact that his attention to both ideas remained only mere interest and has not developed fully is evidenced by the bad transformation of *Text Books of Art Education* into *New Textbooks of Drawing* because the former aims to help children perceive poetic imagination through "nature study" as "an integral feature of art education programs" (Dobbs, 1972, p. 51), whereas the latter offers children a strict, standardized teaching approach to "drawing education" (Kaneko, 1978c, p. 48). On the contrary, Shimoda in his book of 1924 applies Dow's "synthetic method" of art education (Dow, 1908) by proposing that drawing and manual works, both fixed within school curriculum as a regular subject at the time, should be integrated into one subject of fine arts education. Thus, he pointed out that the *New Textbooks of Drawing* traced only the surface of the *Text Books of Art Education* (Shimoda, 1972,

p. 37).

The Taisho Era (1912-1926) in Japanese modern history is the period of "Taisho Democracy" which is "not limited to political matters, but includes the broad range of liberalizing tendencies and the swing of the pendulum back to enthusiastic borrowing from the West that characterized the period" (Reischauer, 1981, p. 171). In the field of education in general, especially during the post-World War I period, "there was a revival of interest in democratic education. Some of the younger Japanese scholars studying in the U. S. observed progressive education and found in John Dewey's writings what they considered a systematic educational theory based on democracy. Several of the students translated into Japanese Dewey's books *School and Society, The Child and the Curriculum, Democracy and Education*, and *Reconstruction of Philosophy*. Twice Dewey was invited to Japan to lecture, first in 1918 at Waseda University, where he spoke on 'The Philosophical Basis of Democracy,' and again in 1919 at Tokyo Imperial University where he outlined his instrumental philosophy." As a result, the "influence of his writings and lectures could be observed especially in the higher normal schools. The Japanese also brought to Japan such persons" as Helen Dalton, William H. Kilpatrick and Carlton Washburne (Anderson, 1959, p. 14).

The Japanese art education field also responded to the liberalizing tendencies at the time. There began the remarkable movement of art education in 1919 which began to change art education philosophy. It was the "free drawing movement" in teaching painting. It was advocated by the insightful painter Kanae Yamamoto (1882-1946) who "was trained as an engraver of Western style line-block for book and magazine illustration, and later spent several years in Europe" (Sullivan, 1965, p. 149). On the way back to Japan, in Russia he had the experience of appreciating a children's creative exhibition of painting in Moscow. He was impressed greatly by the children's art at the exhibition so that when he came back to Japan, he proposed the idea of "creativity" to Japanese art educators, replacing "imitation" or "copy drawing" (Yamamoto, 1921). Keitoku, a researcher in Japanese art education history, regarded this movement as follows:

40

This movement, which was reported in newspapers and magazines, received great public attention and began to pervade the field of art education. This movement, advocating creativity in the practical field of teaching art, was the first comprehensive non-governmental movement in the modern history of Japanese art education, and although its contribution was great, the idea of free expression in drawing and painting was finally regarded as mere representative painting, because it emphasized the method of encouraging children to paint pictures out-of-doors and because it lacked the theoretical basis of child-centered education, as well as the methodology of how to teach children to draw and paint. The reason why the idea of creativity, based on Western individualism as emphasized in the beginning of the movement, dissolved to a mere representative mode in teaching art is partly due to the limitations of Yamamoto's character and thought, but mostly to the fact that individualism and the psychological point of view were not truly understood at the time. ... Therefore, it can be said that the introduction of creativity and self-expression into Japanese art education was not until after the war. (Keitoku, 1980, pp. 25-26)

For this reason, Dobbs concludes that the "ideas which were to profoundly affect American art education and to change its late nineteenth century industrial orientation to one based on child study and progressive education are absent from Japanese art education until after the World War and the impact of American Occupation" (Dobbs, 1983, p. 8). This is not entirely correct because it ignores the historical fact that there has been a free drawing movement during the period of modern Japanese history of art education which researched many theories of children's development of drawing in the context of psychological inquiry. For example, Mamoru Seki was one of the scholars who contributed to the study of child development in drawing and painting at the end of the initial modernizing epoch in the field of Japanese art education. Seki borrowed the idea of delving into the developmental stages of children's drawing from European and American psychologists. He dealt with Stanley Hall's view of children's drawing, citing Chapter XX of "Pedagogy of Drawing" in *Educational Problems* Vol. II (New York: D. Appleton, 1911), (Seki, 1925, pp. 379-383; Seki, 1931, pp. 349-357). At the same time he discussed many scholars such as Barnes, Brown, Buhler, Cooke, Kerschensteiner, Levinstein, Lukens, Rouma, Stern, and Sully. What he continually emphasized throughout his books (1928; 1931) is the idea of the function of "imagination" in children's drawings which would be the open door of art education. He points out the idea of drawing as an art based on imagination from the time of the Greek philosopher Aristotle to the present. Thus, "the teaching of art is regarded as the cultivation of the student's mind and is realized from encouraging them to continuous rebirth of spirit and internal growth on mind" (Seki, 1928, p. 237).

In addition to tendencies such as these in art education, i.e. the free drawing movement and child study, Japanese art education was affected by the modern design education system of the Bauhaus in the mid-1930s. But these three trends did not completely pervade as common ideas of art education until after the post-war period because Japanese art education during the Wartime epoch was concentrated on militarism and nationalism and, like American children, "made stereotyped posters for the war effort and they mass-produced patriotic mementos and decorative items for organizations" (Chapman, 1978, p. 15).

The Democratization Epoch
Except for the unfortunate wartime relationship between Japan and the United States, America's impact on art education in Japan after the wartime epoch has been great. Dobbs provides the information about reconstruction of Japanese art education in the earlier period of the democratization epoch. He writes:

> ... the first set of national standards in art education provides an excellent example of Japanese penchant for successful assimilation. It seems that during the American Occupation bureaucracy, a man was charged with setting rules for the art classrooms, as part of the larger effort to reform the

Japanese schools and provide a foundation for the development of democracy. This gentleman drew upon the curriculum of the state of Virginia, and thus "The Virginia Plan" was established for Japanese art education. Whether apocryphal or not, the story indicates the reliance which Japanese formal art education in public schools has had upon American writers, at certain points in its development. (Dobbs, 1983, pp. 7-8)

The story Dobbs describes is well-known to Japanese art educators because it was included in a comprehensive book of the history of Japanese art education written by Yamagata who had the main responsibility for setting up the first national standards, called "course of study" of art education, with the support of Civil Information and Education (CIE), which was a staff section of the General Headquarters of the Supreme Commander of the Allied Powers and which was responsible for educational matters (Yamagata, 1967, pp. 773-779). The CIE[5] indicated the need for a course of study that would "provide a detailed outline of pupil experiences and teaching materials for each course at each grade level, with suggestions to teachers as to the use of these materials and the guidance of pupil experiences" (CIE, 1948, p. 192). It also provided such subject titles in art education as "Practical Arts" at the secondary level and "Arts and Handicrafts" at the elementary level (CIE, 1948, pp. 196-197). The first exemplary model of the "Course of Study" in art education was set up April 9, 1947, whereas *Fundamental Law of Education* and *School Education Law* were promulgated March 31. Its course of study has been revised and renewed four times (1951, 1958, 1968, and 1976). In the earlier part of the democratization epoch, such American art education literature as Winslow's *Art in Secondary Education* (New York: McGraw Hill, 1941) and Ziegfeld and Faulkner's *Art Today* were influential in the Japanese art education field (Arai, 1948). The idea of "art for daily life" contributed to the reconstruction of Japanese art education at the time because the idea was reflected in the first exemplary model of "Course of Study" in which the aim of arts and handicrafts was to make children contribute to the improvement of their life style.

Since then, numbers of books and articles by American art educators have been translated and introduced in Japanese. Let us examine the translations and introductions of American art education literature briefly. Prior to the 1960s, the chapter "Individual Dynamics Expressed Through Color Usage" of Alschuler's and Hattwiek's *Painting and Personality* (Chicago: University of Chicago Press, 1947) was translated into Japanese in 1949 while other chapters, "Individual Dynamics Expressed Through Line and Form" and "Space Usage and Spatial Pattern," of their book were also translated in 1953. Lowenfeld's *The Nature of Creative Activity* (London: Routledge and Kegan Paul, 1939) was available in Japanese in 1959. His other book Y*our Child and His Art* (New York: Macmillan, 1954) was also available in Japanese in 1956. Lowenfeld's impact on Japanese art which was already translated into Japanese in 1953, became gradually apparent from the early 1950s. For example, Takeuchi attempts to sum up the content of Lowenfeld's landmark, *Creative and Mental Growth* (New York: Macmillan, 1947), in his articles which appeared in the journal *Biiku Bunka (Magazine of Art Education)* from the August 1952 issue to the May 1953 issue, this being an official journal of the Biiju Bunka Kyokai (Society for Art Education) in Tokyo. Takei also makes an effort to summarize Lowenfeld's thoughts on art education in his article which appeared in the October 1953 issue of *Kyoiku Bijutsu (Art in Education)*, an official journal of the Kyoiku Bijutsu Shinko Kai (Socity for Art in Education) in Tokyo. Fukamizu translated the 8th chapter of Lowenfeld's book into Japanese which appeared in *Art in Education* from September to November 1957. Other American art educators whose articles or books were translated into Japanese are Victor D'Amico and D. F. Johnson. A part of D'Amico's *Creative Teaching in Art* (Scranton, Penn. : International Textbook, 1955), focusing on the teaching of graphic art, was translated in the October 1957 issue of *Art in Education*, while his other article "Coming Events" appeared in the September 1958 issue of *School Arts* in the United States, and was also translated in the February 1959 issue of *Art in Education* in Japan. Johnson's "Creativity: A New Challenge" in the October 1958 issue of *School Arts* was translated in the January 1959 issue of *Art in Education* as well.

During the mid-1960s, *Art in Education* continually offered reprints of articles by American art educators : Lowenfeld's "The Adolescence of Art Education" (*Art Education*, Vol. 10, No. 7, 1957) in the June 1960 issue of *Art in Education* (Muro trans.); Eisner's "Imagination and Materials" (*School Arts*, Vol. 58, No. 7, March 1959) in the July 1960 issue of *Art in Education* (Ue trans.); Zeigfeld's address (presented in the INSEA Congress in Manila in 1960) in the February 1961 issue of *Art in Education* ; Lowenfeld's "Commentary" (*Research in Art Education*, ninth yearbook, 1959) in the October 1961 issue of *Art in Education* (Ue trans.); and Eisner's "Curriculum Ideas in a Time of Crisis" (*Art Education*, Vol. 18, No. 7, October 1965) in the March 1966 issue of *Art in Education*. Because of Japanese interest in the American art educator's focus on "creativity," Lowenfeld's *Creative and Mental Growth* (3rd. edition, 1957) was finally translated into Japanese by Takeuchi, Takei, and Horiuchi and published by Reimei Syobo in 1963. As a result, the idea of "creativity" was instilled in the field of Japanese art education from the 1950s to the 1960s, although there was a great deal of objection about "creativity" as a single justification for art education after the 1960s in the United States.[6]

For American art educators, it should be most interesting that Lowenfeld's landmark *Creative and Mental Growth* as well as Read's *Education Through Art* is still "the 'text' to be read by art educators" in Japan and is the "only manual" to be kept "in hand or on the shelf as one" experiences "the child and his art" (Beittel, 1982, p. 20) in the field of Japanese art education. One of the reasons why Lowenfeld's translation has been read by Japanese is that his book provides useful supports which justify the idea of creativity as the purpose of art education. During the 1950s, three major non-governmental associations which innovated Japanese art education were established. The first of these is the Sozo Biiku Kyokai[7] (Society for Creative Art Education) founded in 1952. Those who attended the Society promoted the idea of creativity in the field of art education which goes back to the "free drawing movement" in art education during the Taisho Era. In the 1950s, the contribution of the Society was so great that "art teachers are convinced that art can be something more than what they thought before" (Muro, 1957, p. 8). Japanese art teachers who attended the pilot seminar in 1952 held by the Society for Creative Art Education "met to exchange ideas and report on new experiments on the teaching of art." They agreed that "art is not only a subject in which pupils created art work but also a wonderful opportunity for enhancing their personalities" (Muro, 1957, p. 10). In the effort to change Japanese art educators' idea to a creative approach to art education, Lowenfeld's fine thought provided a theoretical foundation for Japanese art educators during the 1950s and mid-1960s. For this reason, the creative orientation to art education in Japan blossomed rapidly in the 1950s, and, concurrently, Japanese art educators' great attention to American art education increased quickly.

However, the great leadership of the Society for Creative Art Education which promoted creativity as a single justification for teaching art withered rapidly in the latter part of the 1960s because the Society overemphasized the so called "child centered" methodology. Instead of the Society, the Zokei Kyoiku Center[8] (Plastic Art Education Center), founded in 1955, initiated a trend of pre-war Japanese art education which emphasized a modern design approach to art in education derived from the German Bauhaus system, and thus dominated the leadership of Japanese art education during the 1960s. This was in response to the beginning of Japanese economic and technological development. The focus of the Center was to instill such concepts as line, color, mass, organization, surface, movement, space, construction, texture, and so forth in the field of Japanese art education. The approach to design education advocated by the Center was not so much an aesthetic or artistic one as an instrumental one corresponding to Japanese economic and industrial development. However, another association, the Atarashii Eno Kai (Association of Innovating Children's Painting), founded in 1959, criticized both the creative and design approach to art education and promoted socialism in art education which was "seen as a means of meeting" socialistic "needs, whether they be needs directly related to art or not" (Eisner, 1972, p. 8). As a result of this transition from a theoretical interest of Japanese art educators in the 1950s to a practical one in the 1960s, attention to American art education decreased after the Tokyo Conference of INSEA in 1965.

In the late 1960s, the new trends of American art education after the work of Lowenfeld were dealt with in a book by a Japanese art educator in which such American art educators as Burkhart, Eisner, and McFee, found in *Readings in Art Education* (Waltham, Mass.: Blaisdell, 1966), were discussed (Ue, 1967). McFee's "The Foundations of Art Education," included in her book *Preparation for Art* (San Francisco: Wadsworth, 1961), was translated into Japanese by Takei and published in 1968. Since then, Japanese art educators did not become interested in the trends of American art education again until the beginning of the 1980s.

After more than ten years' absence of American influence on Japanese art education, except for such Japanese translations outside the field of art education as Eisner's *Confronting Curriculum Reform* (Boston: Little, Brown, 1971) and Gardner's *The Quest for Mind* (New York: Alfred A Knopf Inc., 1972), and also others related to the field of art education such as Kellogg's *Analyzing Children's Art* (Palo Alto, Calif.: Mayfield, 1969) and Arnheim's *Visual Thinking* (Berkeley, Calif., University of California Press, 1969), "today the traffic in American art education literature is considerably heavier, and professors and graduate students are aware of such publications as the *Art Education Journal*" so that "it is clear that increased sharing is taking place" (Dobbs, 1983, p. 8) between Japan and the United States. For example, I have translated such articles, all of which appeared in the *Art Education journal*, into Japanese in *Art in Education* as Eisner's "The Relationship of Theory and Practice in Art Education" (1982), Beittel's "Lowenfeld and Art for a New Age" (1982), and Madeja's "Computer Graphics: The New Subject Matter for the Art Curriculum" (1983).[9] Furthermore, the Japanese translation of American art education literature is Brittain's *Creativity, Art and the Young Child* (New York: Macmillan, 1979), available to Japanese art educators in1983 under the title *Yoji no Zokeisei to Sozousei* (Nagoya: Reimei).

Conclusion

This extended account of the influence of American art education literature on the historical development of Japanese art education reveals only the surface of what Japanese art educators have learned from the Americans. The major American contribution to Japanese art education is that it has given us the impetus to modernize our art education system, even if the American and European tradition of scientific art teaching has uprooted our traditional art teaching, based on the training of Japanese-style painting, which Dow noted as "one of the forces tending to uproot our traditional scientific art teaching which does not recognize Dark-and-Light as worthy of special attention" (Dow, 1913, p. 53).

The Japanese edition of Lowenfeld's *Creative and Mental Growth* is now in its fortieth reprint. However, the Japanese interest in American art education is not a practical one but a theoretical one. For those who are concerned with research in art education at the higher level,[10] if there are some things that we can learn from Americans, they are such matters as the publication of specialized research journals like *Studies in Art Education* and *Journal of Aesthetic Education*, offering doctoral courses in art education, systematic curriculum developments like CEMREL's Aesthetic Education Program (Barkan, Chapman & Kevn, 1970; Madeja, 1977), continually holding large-scale conferences like that at Penn State in 1965, and the computer distribution system of information in art education like the ERIC Clearinghouses. This expansion of the American art education field should serve "as food for thought as we make choices for the future" (Carson, 1981, p. 46) in Japanese arts and aesthetic education.

I also believe that "a communication network among scholars interested in cross-cultural research in art education needs to be established" (Eisner, 1979, p. 34). And I would be happy if this chapter serves as food for American thought in cross-cultural research in art education.

Notes

1. His contribution to art education is described as follows: "The Meiji government used Togai's skills also in the Ministry of Education, where he and Takahashi Yuichi conducted research into methods of art instruction. Togai's translation of Robert Scott Burn's teaching manual appeared in 1871, and the next year he and Takahashi promulgated lessons for elementary schools based on careful descriptive drawing of

48

objects in a modified Western manner using pencils instead of inks und soft brushes. This system remained in effect until 1885, when Fenollosa, Okakura, and others forced the return to one based on traditional methods" (Rosenfield, 1971, p. 198).

2. Japanese art education within schooling started in 1872. "Since the establishment of the educational system in 1872, drawing, as a part of general education, has been reckoned as one of the courses of study to be provided in elementary schools. But it was not actually instituted until the issue of the Elementary School Ordinance in 1880. The regulations of that Ordinance provided that there should be a course of drawing in elementary schools, where the local circumstances made this desirable. Consequently, in a few schools this course was established, but most schools did not have it" (Ministry of Education in Japan, *Education in Japan: Part 8, Art Education*. Tokyo: Ministry of Education, 1910, pp. 19-20).

3. Smith pointed out: "The memory method may have been introduced to Kershensteiner by Johannes Ehlers, one of three remarkable art educators working in Hamburg as the nineteenth century merged into the twentieth. Ehlers claimed to have derived his ideas from a work published in Germany in 1899 under the title of *Neue Wege zue Kunstlerishen Erziehung den Jugent: Zeichnen-Handfertigkeit Naturstudium-Kunst*, which had been written by an American, J. Liberty Tadd, director of the Philadelphia Public School of Industrial Art, and originally titled *New Methods in Education: Art, Real Manual Training, Nature Study*" (Smith, 1982, p. 27).

4. Tadd states: "Perhaps one of the most radical features of my method, apart from those of ambidexterity and memory drawing, and one that must be understood as being applied in all our schools, is the rotation of the branches of work. The pupils do not take a course of drawing alone, or of modeling alone, to be followed with another course for a certain period, but in every grade from the lowest the children are required to work in the four departments of drawing, then in soft clay, and then in tough wood carving. By drawing all forms first on paper, then in soft clay, and then in tough wood, all the possible physical co-ordinations are acquired in the different materials. The work of making form in clay reinforces the drawing; carving in wood reinforces the modeling. Designing forms in clay and wood, as well as on paper, compels originality

and invention, or the exercise of creative capacity at every step of the work" (Tadd, 1901, p. 5).

5. An exhibition where CIE provides a number of American children's paintings for Japanese was held in Tokyo in 1947 (K. Masuda & Y. Murakami, *Bijutsu Kyoiku Shi Note* [Note of Art Education History], Tokyo: Kairyudo, 1983, p. 147).

6. Two vivid examples of criticizing for a creativity orientation to art education are shown in the following: "for teachers to say that they 'promote creativity' is inadequate justification for the practice of art education; for again ethical problems are buried under the apparent facts of creativity" (D.W. Ecker, "Some Inadequate Doctorines in Art Education and a Proposed Resolution," *Studies in Art Education*, Vol. 5, No. 1, 1963, p. 76); and "art education is not the only field of learning through which general creativeness might be cultivated. In this respect, it is not unique. The contribution of art experience toward the development of general creativeness should not be minimized" (S .G. Wold and W. R. Hastie, "From Research and Theory to Teaching Practice," in W. R. Hastie, ed., *Art Education. Sixty-fourth Yearbook of the NSSE*, Chicago: University of Chicago Press, 1965, p. 345).

7. This is the same with "the Creative Art Association which develops teaching materials" (Dobbs, 1983, p. 9), but its contribution to Japanese art education during the 1950s lay not in developing teaching materials but in changing Japanese art educators' ideas to a creative approach to art education,

8. Dobbs also describes "the Plastic Art Education Center, founded in 1955," which emphasizes "design, derived from the Bauhaus principles. It is no coincidence that Walter Gropius toured Japan in 1954" (Dobbs, 1983, p. 9).

9. Eisner's article (*Art Education*, 1982, Vol. 35, No. 1, pp. 4-5) was translated into Japanese by A. Okazaki and reprinted in the October 1982 issue of *Kyoiku Bijutsu* (Art in Education, Vol. 43, No. 11, pp. 20-28); Beittel's article (*Art Education*, 1982, Vol. 35, No. 6, pp. 18-21) was translated into Japanese by M. Nagamachi and A. Okazaki and reprinted in the October 1983 issue of *Kyoiku Bijutsu* (Vol. 44, No. 11, pp. 29-32); Madeja's article (*Art Education*, 1983, Vol. 36, No. 3, pp. 15-17) was translated into Japanese by A. Okazaki and reprinted in the January 1984 issue of *Kyoiku Bijutsu* (Vol.

45, No. 1, pp. 26-28).

10. Japanese art education at the higher level has not developed its own research field, because "Graduate programs in art education began to develop in Japan during the 1960's, but at the present time these are limited to masters degrees offerings. A few Japanese graduate students have completed work in the United States and returned to work in their country. Traditionally art education training has been the province of professors in related areas such as design" (Dobbs, 1983, p. 9), painting, sculpture, crafts, and theory and history of art. In the early 1980s in Japan only eleven universities have their master's program in art education, but all Japanese professors of art and art education in the school of education do not have doctor's degrees because they are not required to have it in order to become a faculty member of a university.

Chapter 4

Originally published in Heta Kauppinen & Read Diket, eds., *Trends in Art Education from Diverse Cultures* (pp. 175-160), Reston VA: National Art Educaton Association,1995.
Reprinted with permission by the National Art Education Association (NAEA).

American Contemporary Art into Japanese School Art: Play Activities in the 1980s

Fig. 4.1 *Apparatus* by
Motonao Takasaki, 2013,
White paper on black board,
14.8 x 10 cm, Coll: Akio
Okazaki.

Fig. 4.2 Play activity
(Tuita, Itarashiki, &
Iwasaki, 1978).

Fig. 4.3 Outdoor play activity
(Kurata, Hayasi, & Saikoji, 1989).

* Figures are not included in the originally published paper.

Figure-Ground Relationship: Huge Umbrellas on the Earth

Rubin, a Gestalt psychologist, presented the now famous "double representation" figure as the relationship of positive and negative spaces. If the white area is thought of as positive space, a vase can be seen against a dark background, but if the dark area is thought of as positive spaces, two profiles can be seen facing each other against a white background. Both perceptions can be discovered while viewing the figure, but not be simultaneously. The ambivalent perception of figure-ground relationship illustrates the clash between two concepts, between conventional and contemporary arts within one culture, and between two cultural values in art. A good example for such a clash might be Christo's earthwork. The Umbrellas Project of Christo opened for display in October of 1991 in two places. Seventy-five miles north of Tokyo, in Ibaragi, Japan, 1,340 huge blue umbrellas were settled in a 12 mile range. Simultaneously, 1,760 huge yellow umbrellas were settled in an 18 mile range north of Los Angeles. The project was exhibited for 18 days and about 540,000 people enjoyed it in Japan alone ("Kurisuto no anburera purojekuto" [Christo's umbrellas project], 1991; "Kuristoten" [The Exhibition of Christo], 1991).

The project was designed to helps us see "an enigmatic relationship" (Christo, cited in Garoian, Quan, & Collins, 1977, p. 19) of ambivalence in three ways. First, it made viewers of both countries aware of natural and human-made environments. Their attention was caught by huge umbrellas while they suddenly found the earth itself. Second, it provided a dynamic tension of modernist art and postmodernist art. Viewers could enjoy the display as a non-artistic event, while ideally, they changed their conventional ideas of modern art in order to recognize it as art. Last, it reflected on the seemingly incompatible foreign cultural value of art. Japanese viewers welcomed it while at the same time they were reminded of how their culture of art stood in contrast to it. In these ways, the project forced viewers to redefine what is environment, art, and cultural value by providing double representation in a figure-ground relationship.

Understanding Art through Christo-Like Projects

Christo's projects have been making an impact on the world of art. They have also been incorporated into school art practice in both United States and Japanese. American students respond to Christo-like projects not as creating art, but as understanding art. Borgmann (1986) of Indiana University, for instance, coordinated a program enabling students and teachers to deal with contemporary art. Christo was invited to this special Art-to-School Program, and public school students (K-12) and their teachers were involved. Transforming human-made and natural environments into aesthetic sites with wrapping, "Sixth graders gave keen insights into society, why man creates today, and what makes it art. They discussed materials, techniques, ideas, philosophies, and aesthetic effects, all on their own level" (p. 20).

Christo-like projects for children were used as texts of discourse to promote looking at and talking about art in the art room, which provided balance to the major conventional approach of making art in a studio. Seeing the old familiar object or space in a new context was of primary importance, while the end result of wrapping was secondary. Thus "the actual studio project was not necessary to promote understanding of Christo's work" (Borgmann, 1986, p. 20).

Experiences gained through Christo-like projects were important factors in developing dialogue in the classroom. These programs were also intended to expose both art teachers and classroom teachers to contemporary ideas in art through non-studio approach to art. Teachers are expected to teach non-studio disciplines in the curriculum (art history, art criticism, and aesthetics). Awareness of contemporary art is more focused than the invention of another earthwork. Raising questions on art and talking about art, therefore, became the prime concern for the Art-to-School program (Borgmann, 1986).

Christo-like projects are not ready to be incorporated into the daily art education practice of U. S. schools. They remain summer holiday art.

Play Activities in Japanese Art Textbooks
In contrast, textbook-based art curricula of Japanese elementary schools have included Christo-like projects since the 1980s. There are five versions of commercially developed art textbooks, all of which adapt to the national guidelines of 1977 (effective from 1980 to 1991). They are approved by the Ministry of Education. Yet, textbooks writers have responsibility for what content should be included in the art curriculum and for structuring learning activities from grade to grade. Art is a required subject (two hours per week) throughout the first 9 years of compulsory education. Each of the 476 school districts has the power to select one of the five versions. The government then purchases textbooks from publishers and distributes them free of charge to children across the country (Ministry of Education, 1989).

Foster (1990), describing one version of a 1986 edition, said that it "shows three categories for art lessons—'Drawing Activities or Making Pictures,' 'Making and Constructing Activities,' and 'Making functional Objects.' The third through sixth grade books have page-spreads developed to historical knowledge while the first and second grade books include an additional category of 'Playing Together and Making Friends'" (p. 12). The additional category belongs to Christo-like environmental projects through which students are encouraged to draw play activities with their friends.

The earlier (1980) version, *Zugakosaku* (*Art and Handicrafts*) (Kurata, Hayashi, & Saikoji, 1980/1983/1986/1989), which has supplied about 70 percent of the text market, first included six lessons on play activity. The first three, for the first grade, consist of "Play with Dirt" activities, in which children draw pictures with a stick or water on the playground of their school; "Paper Streamers," in which students think about interesting ways to play; and "Play by Arranging a Lot of Things" (making a circular castle with sand and sea shells). The latter three, for the second grade, include "Play with Grass," in which children think about ways to play with grass, fruit, and flowers (making a moustache or a flower crown); "Play with Newspaper," in which they think about interesting playful activities or games that they make up out of newspaper (making costumes with pieces of paper, flying paper in the sky); and "Stack Things," in which children think about playing on the classroom floor (making a mountain and playing with a rolling ball). These above six lessons were given minor revisions in 1983, 1986, and 1989.

Downsizing behind Nature
The prescribed outcomes of dealing with Christo-like projects in Japanese elementary schools are different from those of U. S. schools. Japanese teachers encourage their students in the early grades to invent spontaneous earthworks with emphasis on team effort, while U. S. teachers help their young students gain individual understanding of art in sociocultural context. Christo's projects are downsized to young Japanese early children's basic group play, while they are used to promote Getty Center's discipline-based art education programs in the United States.

The downsizing of Christo's projects reflects on Japanese attitude toward nature. Christo-like projects become catalysts that relate basic human activity to nature itself. Small Japanese landscape gardens, for example, contrasts to the huge Western gardens with geometric arrangement of objects. The scenic composition of Japanese gardens represents the concepts of "borrowed view" and "abstract symbolism," both of which make the garden master regenerate the inherent qualities of natural raw materials for use in downsizing real landscape.

Today's Japanese artists still regenerate these qualities in their own works. A college instructor of mine described how he created his work for the first Japan Art Festival of New York in 1966. He "cut large canvas into hundreds of square pieces and affixed them at the center onto a black plate, leaving the edges free to curve for themselves according to nature, in this case temperature, humidity, and ... the property of [the] ... painted linen [matter]" (Takasaki, 1980, p. 33). He envisioned that hundreds of white parabola antennas against the black plate would make viewers feel "as if for a moment he had been taken to another world" (p. 34).

Although the style of Takasaki's work reflects on American Minimal Art of 1960s, it still preserves the traditional concept of "reality/illusion" of Japanese garden. His contemporary work is reminiscent of the famous gray rock garden of Ryoanji Temple, Kyoto, in which five groups of rocks on fine white gravel symbolize the small islands in the water of the sea. We call its symbolization Mitate. It means "'as if' Play," which is the same as young children seeing a piece of wood as a train (Nagamachi, 1988, p. 119). Japanese teachers consider Christo-like projects not as fashionable contemporary art but as foundations for basic "as if" activities, so they have gained popularity in Japanese elementary school. The downsizing of contemporary U. S. art into Japanese school practices is consistent with earthworks of Japanese gardens behind nature.

Filling Gap: Project "Do"

Yet, Japan and the United States make similar efforts to include Christo-like projects in art education. Both have tried to fill the gap between real art world and conventional school art style, which can still be found in present-day artrooms. Japanese efforts to fill the gap became apparent in 1970s. There were several insightful young elementary school teachers in Osaka, the second largest city in Japan, who did not wish to follow the ready-made content in commercial art textbooks. Sharing a perception of the gap and an interest in contemporary U. S. art such as Pop, Op, Environments, Earthworks, and Happenings, they founded Project "Do" in 1972.

The declaration of Project "Do" clearly states their intentions to create a new foundation of art education: "Art education lets children act. Formative action starts from action and ends with action. ... Art education ... lets them acquire the ability to control the energy of their activities. It lets children be free from desk work and lets them see 'environment' and 'material.' Art education is ... for the art-making activity itself free from any traditional criterion of knowledge or art works ... We would like to be donors of time, space, and materials, rather than teachers" (Nagamachi, 1988, p. 217).

Such statements about the principles of art education enabled them to define their mission. In using every resource of school environments, they were able to create new teaching and learning methods: "digging holes" by students, "Cutting wood" of old electric poles, "covering a jungle gym with newspapers," "Drawing a big figure with water on the playground" using for school lunch kettles, "taking hens and cocks for a walk," "copying a newspaper," "gathering air" in a large bag made from newspapers, "floating a wire on water," "making a spider's web" with paper tape all over classroom, and "making the space of classroom like the inside of our body" with paper constructions (Nagamachi, 1988, pp. 218-219). The familiar old childish play was seeing in a new educational context.

Educators at all level recognize that turning theory into practice is not an easy task. Yet, Project "Do" has been meeting with great success since the 1970s. Christo was invited to the 10th Tokyo Biennial in May, 1970, and he presented a project of wrapping space. Japan had been experiencing the student power movement, oil-related economic depressions, problems of pollution, concerns for preservation of the environment, concerns for the ecology of natural resources, and the beginning of

58

global information science society. A variety of these outside factors contributed to the success of the project. Other important factors were the energy and inventiveness of the teachers of Project "Do." They had the insight to include supplementary teaching materials that enhance the content of the prescribed art curriculum. They were able to embrace the expansion of the contemporary art world, and they translated its artistic phenomenon into the art program. This new approach to art education was carried into the field through books, journals, magazines, conferences, and workshops. Similar efforts to create a variety of play activities also made their way across the country. The Ministry of Education, therefore, included the Project "D" activities in the 1977 edition of the national guidelines (effective from April 1980), and authorized them as new subject matter for art education in the first two grades.

Play Activity into the National Guidelines
The objectives of play activity are indicated in the guidelines of 1977. In the first grade, the objective is "to enable pupils to perform with pleasure formative activities, utilizing different materials" (Ministry of Education, 1983, p. 85). Three outcomes are prescribed: "to perform formative activities using the whole body, being familiar with materials"; "to have an interest in the colors and forms of natural and artificial materials, and to perform formative plays such as thinking of what they want to make out of them, and enjoying putting them on their bodies"; and "to perform formative plays such as arranging natural and artificial materials, piling them up and copying them by making a print" (p. 85). These objectives and the outcomes are advanced in the second grade.

In July of 1978, some of teachers of Project "Do" published a book on play activities (Tuita, Itarashiki, and Iwasaki, 1978). At that time, the 1977 edition of national guidelines was not yet in effect. Other textbook writers and classroom teachers were inexperienced in play activity. They welcomed the book as a useful reference because of its inclusion of hundreds of visual presentations with few descriptions. The book encouraged them to understand how body movement, material assemblage, space transformation, and earthworks were essential to play activity in such places as the classroom, the school building, the gymnasium, and the playground.

The 1977 version of the national guidelines for art education has been updated and appears in the July 1989 edition. It has been effect since April, 1992. This edition suggests that the content of the play activity be extended to the fourth grade. Several kinds of commercially developed textbooks are already slated for use. These include three lessons in each of the first four grades, responding to numerous past decades of practice of play activity across the country. The 1978 book by the teachers of "Do" is still invaluable in providing ideas for play activity.

Play activities in driving have become an important part of Japanese textbook-based art curriculum. This is validation of the insightful teachers who explore new frontiers to discover and translate ideas that will be found in future curriculums. Art textbooks are renewed every 12 years and are revised every 3 years. The Japanese art education system has profited by periodically discarding old art education practices and introducing new ones through nationally distributed textbooks. Yet, our guidelines for art education should be open to interpretation and constantly revised (Okazaki, 1985b).

Conclusion: Grains of Grit into Pearls

Cross-cultural research is seen as a "two-way street" (Okazaki, 1985a). "Just as Japanese art had influenced Impressionism and Post-Impressionism ... the idea of European modernism influenced Japanese artists and art educators" in the 1920s (Okazaki, 1991, p. 196). According to Thistlewood (1991), the importation of western modernism has been "a deliberate tactic" of Japanese art educators aimed at "counterbalancing a normal tendency to didacticism" (p. 128). This continues to the present (Shields, 1990). The regulation of guidelines for art education and the imported concepts of contemporary U. S. art effectively counterbalance one another.

The story of incorporating contemporary U. S. art in Japanese school art practice is reminiscent of Christo's project, the huge blue umbrellas on the land of Japan. This visual scene can illustrate Japanese cultural history of both art and art education, which has continually taken and transformed diverse influences from other cultures. New waves of art from the outside have challenged Japanese artists and art educators to find alternatives missing from their current practices. They are "no longer safe in the old and not yet fully adapted to the new" (Muro, 1953, p. 109).

The transformation of seemingly incompatible foreign cultures into art is a gradual process. "Japanese culture in general," according to Stanley-Baker (1984), "may be likened to an oyster, opening itself up to repeated onslaughts from the ocean and transforming grains of continental grit into pearls" (p. 7). Yet, without diverse influences as grains of grit, no country regards its inherent cultural values as pearls. They provide a prime field of cross-cultural and multi-cultural research in art and art education.

Chapter 5

Originally published in Brent Wilson & Harlan Hoffa, eds., *The History of Art Education, Proceedings from the Penn State Conference* (pp. 59-66), Reston VA: National Art Education Association, 1985. Reprinted with permission by the National Art Education Association (NAEA).

American Influence on the History of Japanese Art Education: The Case of Akira Shirahama

Fig. 5.1 Art room of the Salem Normal School (Shirahama, 1911, Appendix).

Fig. 5.2 Art room of the Lowell Normal School (Shirahama, 1911, Appendix).

Fig. 5.3 Massachusetts Normal Art School (Smith, 1924, p. 19).

* Figures are not included in the originally published paper.

In the Fall 1984 issue of the *Journal of Multi-cultural and Cross-cultural Research in Art Education*, I published a paper on American influence on modern Japanese Art Education. That account, an extended overview, lists only the most obvious examples what Japanese art educators have learned from Americans in more than a century. In this chapter I provide some more detailed instances of the American influence.

Just as Arthur Dow in America turned to the Japanese to find something not in American art education, Akira Shirahama (1866-1927) in Japan turned to America to find those elements missing from Japanese art education. This chapter examines (1) Shirahama's study in America in 1904 and 1905, (2) his transformation of the theory and practice of American art education into Japanese methods, and (3) the limitation of his transformation of American ideas in art education into Japanese methods.

Shirahama's Study in America

Shirahama was born in Nagasaki, and studied English at Nagasaki Foreign Language School during his teens. In 1884 he entered the preparatory course of Tokyo Imperial University, but in 1889 changed his mind and entered the Tokyo Fine Arts School. After graduating from the school in 1895 with a major in Japanese-style painting, he became an associate professor at the Tokyo Higher Normal School.

In 1901 he became a full professor of painting at the Tokyo Fine Arts School. Next year he was appointed a member of the Committee of Art in Education by the Ministry of Education. He was also a member of another committee that was responsible for writing the national textbooks of art education in 1903.

In 1904, two national textbooks for drawing were issued by the Ministry of education. One of them was a copybook of Western-style drawing with pencil, and the other presented Japanese-style drawing (sumi-e or ink-painting) with brush and ink (Yamagata, 1967, pp. 358-359). The fact that the Ministry of Education issued both textbooks, which were completely different from each other, suggests that there were conflicting views over the best way to teach drawing. The Ministry of Education was not satisfied with the drawing books, so Shirahama was sent on a three-year art educational odyssey to the West from 1904 to 1907.

Shirahama arrived in Boston April 6, 1904, entered the Massachusetts Normal Art School in May and graduated June 22, 1905. He left Boston on August 25 of that year and arrived in London on September 6. He visited France and Germany before returning to Japan on March 21, 1907. In the same year, the Normal Course of Drawing was established at the Tokyo Fine Arts School, and Shirahama was appointed chairman of the course. Shirahama trained many normal-school art teachers and teachers of art at the secondary level for twenty years until his death (Kaneko, 1978a).

Dobbs (1983) correctly describes the American Influences in Shirahama's case, when he writes, "Japanese art texts of the early period ... show the impact of the Prang books and the manual arts heritage" and "the influence of the United States can be traced to ... the turn of this century, when Professor Akira Shirahama at the

Tokyo Fine Arts School studied the approach and the materials of the Massachuetts Normal Arts School" (p. 8). Thus, Dobbs identified the three American influences on Japanese art education in its early period (1) the Prang books, (2) the manual arts heritage, and (3) Shirahama's study in America. Let me first examine the latter two.

The impact of the manual arts heritage can be found in Shirahama's book entitled *Zuga Kyoju Ho* (Methods in Drawing Instruction, 1904) before his trip to the west. In his book, Shirahama includes "several pictures which were reprinted from Tadd's *New Methods in Education: Art Real Manual Training, Nature Study* (1901) found on page 72, 90, 124, 127, 160, and 171. A picture on page 160 in Tadd's book can be seen in the fine art education text by Chapman, *Approaches to Art in Education* (1978), on page 4" (Okazaki, 1984, p. 83). Showing reprints of these pictures from Tadd's book, Shirahama describes both Tadd's new pedagogy, "Drawing should be used as modes of thought expression" (Tadd, 1901, p. 5). He also reports that Tadd's new method was applied in Shizuoka Normal School in Japan. Shirahama regarded Tadd as "a man who brought Michelangelo's idea into art education, 'We must carry our instruments of perception in the eye, not in hand'" (Shirahama, 1904, p. 84).

The appendix of Shirahama's book also contains the translation of the *Outline of Drawing Lessons for Primary Grades* (Cross & Swain, 1898). Shirahama provides a citation of the Cross' description of how to use the Cross Transparent Drawing Slate (Cross, 1896, Chapter Ⅲ) on page 109 to 116. The figure of Cross' Slate was reprinted on page 114 of his book. An illustration of the same figure can be seen in the text of American art education history by Wygant (1983) on page 117. The development of a sequential order of elementary-art curriculums in Cross' book impressed Shirahama greatly.

Shirahama was different from those Japanese art educators prior to the 20th century who only reprinted examples of geometric and perspective drawing from Chapman's *American Drawing Books* (1864) in their drawing textbooks for elementary schools (Kaneko, 1985). Shirahama, however, not only reprinted pictures or figures from American art education literatures but also provided the

Japanese with then-recent American ideas of art education.

I believe that Shirahama's decision to go to America was influenced by two things. One was Shirahama's understanding of Tadd's new pedagogy and methods, i.e., drawing as "a mode of expressing ideas," and activities like modeling, carving, woodworking, etc. as "a mode of applying ideas" (Baker, 1985, p. 81). The other was Shirahama's knowledge that "At the Massachusetts State Normal Art College, Anton Cross produced *Free-Hand Drawing*" (Wygant, 1983, p. 117). Shirahama's research on the works of both Tadd and Cross before his trip to America demonstrates that he had sensitive eye to perceive the new trends in American art education at the turn of the 20th century.

As I have mentioned earlier, Shirahama entered the Massachusetts Normal Art School in May 1904, and graduated June 22, 1905. It is uncertain what courses Shirahama attended in the school, but since he was an expert in Japanese-style painting and lived in Boston only one-and-a-half years, Kaneko (1978a) presumes that Shirahama might have enrolled in Public School Class (Massachusetts Normal Art School, 1904). This course was "devoted to methods of teaching and supervising drawing, with special reference to public schools" (Bailey, 1900, p. 36).

During his stay in the United States, Shirahama had opportunities to visit American schools in Massachusetts and observe practices of teaching art classrooms. The appendix of his book, published in 1911, after his return to Japan, contains eight pictures that show several kindergarten and elementary-school classrooms, a secondary-school auditorium, and art rooms of the Salem Normal School and Lowell Normal School. His book also includes five illustrations of art works by American children, especially at the elementary level: drawing, water color, designing, etc.

Providing these pictures and figures for Japanese readers, Shirahama made an effort to introduce an art curriculum that had sequential instruction and a continuity of content like that of grades one to nine in the elementary schools of Massachusetts. He points out that American art education, especially at the elementary level, emphasized children's spontaneity and their psychological development, the use of various materials in their artistic activities, and the relationship of art education to

66

the manual work. He also stresses that these emphases owed much to the Froebelian idea of child-centered approach in art education; consequently, the old strict Smith method of industrial drawing was fast disappearing (Shirahama, 1911, pp. 68-69).

In addition, Shirahama was able to hear Dow lecture at Teachers College of Columbia University, using a projector to show Italian works of art, and providing a comparison of the works with Japanese color prints in order to describe color in the Italian works (Shirahama, 1908). In another article (1907), shirahama says, "To draw models, to study nature and to appreciate works of great masters' art is to make children understand what composition is by the building up of harmonious beauty through color, shape and space relation" (p. 44). It is clear that Shirahama's interest was not in the Japanese foundation of Dow's *notan* (dark-and -light), but in Dow's "design methodology," which was made so acceptable in the field of American art education by the contribution of "Tadd's design-centered methodology" (Baker, 1985, p. 84).

Thus Shirahama learned from the Americans at the turn of the 20th century (1) the approach to training teachers at the Massachusetts Normal Art School, (2) art curriculum and materials at the elementary level, and (3) design methodology in the field of art education.

Shirahama's Transformation

One of the things that Shirahama learned from American art education was the systematic pre-service training program at the higher level exemplified by the Massachusetts Normal Art School. After coming back to Japan, Shirahama soon got the opportunity to transform the teacher-training program of the Japanese system.

When the Normal Course was set up at the Tokyo Fine Arts School in April 1907, Shirahama, as chairman, developed its curriculum. The normal curse required three years. The curriculum was as follows: pedagogy and the art of teaching; aesthetics and the history of fine arts; anatomy (general outline of skeleton and muscles); designing (plane design with a small amount of solid design); freehand drawing (with charcoal, pencil, and Japanese brush); mechanical drawing (plane, projective, geometrical, and perspective drawing); handicrafts (clay, paper, wood, and metal work); and practice of teaching (blackboard exercise, preparation of plans for elementary and secondary schools, and student teacher experience). Among the various subjects in the normal course, the subject of freehand drawing was the one most emphasized. About nineteen hours per week in each of three years was devoted to the study of freehand drawing. In the third year of the normal course, special emphasis (ten hours per week) was placed on practice-teaching as well. (Ministry of Education, 1910a, pp.18-19).

The normal course at Tokyo Fine Arts School was one of the institutions "established by the Government for the special purpose of training teachers for secondary schools" (Kikuchi, 1909, p. 300) such as middle schools, girls' high schools, and normal schools. The graduates of the normal course were granted certificates as secondary school art teachers by the Ministry of Education. At this time, the Tokyo Fine Arts School was one of two institutions able to offer secondary-school teacher-training program in art. The other institution to offer a special course (drawing and manual work) was the Tokyo Higher Normal School. The normal course at the Tokyo Fine Arts School was one of only two comprehensive programs of art in education at the higher level at that time. The approach to training art teachers at Massachusetts Normal Arts School was very helpful to Shirahama in developing a new curriculum for the normal course.

Another thing that Shirahama learned from America was how to develop a more modernized art curriculum for use by elementary schools; he based this curriculum principally on one of Prang's text books of art education.

The turn of the 20th was a remarkable period for building the Japanese compulsory-education system. For example, in 1887 elementary-school attendance reached only 45 percent. By 1897 it was 66 percent, and jumped to 97 percent by 1907 (Japanese National Commission for UNESCO, 1958, p. 70). In 1907 compulsory education was extended from four to six years and the population undergoing compulsory elementary education increased.

Corresponding the extension of elementary-school attendance, the Ministry of

Education desired to have a comprehensive textbook of drawing that was not a mere copybook of drawing but a systematically organized text, including such content as drawing, painting, color theory, composition, decoration, design and so forth. The Ministry, therefore, issued new drawing books for each elementary grade called *Shintei Gacho* (*New Textbooks of Drawing*) in 1910.

This set of textbook of drawing was the first modernized one in the history of modern art education in Japan. The content and organization of the curriculum in the textbooks were developed under Shirahama's direction. Shirahama's editorial policy of curriculum development in the new textbooks depended partly on the exemplary model of Froehlich and Snow's *Text Books of Art Education* (Books I-VI) published by Prang Educational (1904-1905). Although "the Prang textbooks were widely used in Canada" (Chalmers, 1985, p. 73), the impact of these textbooks were not limited to Canadian art education; it extended to Japan through Shirahama's translation of the Prang textbooks into Japanese.

These frequently used Prang textbooks were planned in a series of conferences and consultations with leading art teachers and educators. Published in a series with one volume for each grade level, these books contained "illustrations to be reproduced with exactness as exercises in learning to draw," and made it possible to "spread the teaching of art principles throughout the school years in a systematic way" (Belshe, 1946, p. 82).

A comparison of the *New Textbooks of Drawing* in Japan and the *Text Books of Art Education* in the Untied States shows that both sets were almost identical in such aspects as publishing one volume for each grade, including illustrations, and the teaching of art principles.

The context of art curriculum in the American texts is divided into these groups (1) Observational or Objective Group, (2) Subjective Group, and (3) Creative Group. The first group deals with "landscape, plants, life, and still life," aiming at "the study of things." The second group considers "the study of principles or laws of beauty," and presents "the principles of perspective, of industrial drawing, of color harmony, and the principles of pure design." The third group deals with "creative exercises in composition, in decorative design, and in many forms of manual training" (Froehlich and Snow, 1904-05, prefaces to Books IV, and V).

In the Japanese textbooks the three groups are incorporated. For example, the illustrations in landscape, vessels, implements, furniture, plants, figures, animals, birds, architecture and so forth. The principles of perspective are taught in grades from four to six, while the principle of color harmony is taught in grades five and six. The principle of pure design is taught through design work in all grades. The exercises in both composition and decorative design are given in grades five and six.

However, there are some differences between the Japanese textbooks and the American texts. Imitative or copy-drawing still remained in the Japanese textbooks. Imitative drawing, memory drawing, representative drawing, and design work are the four principle areas of study in the Japanese texts.

Another difference between the two texts lay in their basic approach to art. The American text offered a kind of "intellectual and instrumental approach to art" (Silverman, 1982, p. 174), whereas the Japanese text offered an instructional approach to artistic activity and provided a strict teaching strategy. For example, the lesson in Book I of the American text begins, "Great wide, beautiful, wonderful World, with the wonderful water round you curled, And the wonderful grass upon your breast, —World, you are beautifully drest!", and shows an illustration of a child looking out the window. On the following page of the American text: "Look out of the window! Look, look, look! Sky so blue, I see you! Grass so green, I see you! I see you and I love you, And so I will paint you" (Froehlich and Snow, 1904, Book I, pp. 1-2). The same nature theme was incorporated in the first lesson of drawing education for the first-grade Japanese children. (Student editions of the Japanese textbooks were not prepared for the first and second grades, but teachers' editions for both grades were available. Above grade three there were both student and teachers' editions.) The teachers' edition for Book I in the Japanese text (Ministry of Education, 1910c) states the objectives of the first lesson are to "encourage children to draw a landscape in spring, using colors, and to acquire the skill of drawing a horizontal line with a pencil" (p. 1).

The teaching strategy of the (Japanese) teachers' edition consists of two stages. The first stage is observation:

Teacher should encourage children to look out the window, to recognize the clear separation of land and sky, to see the greenness of the spring field, and to understand that, although the color of the sky on a very fine day is pure blue, it looks pale blue on ordinary days. Teacher should show the children green and blue paper and give them ideas about two colors. (p. 1)

The second stage is how to draw:

Teacher should draw a rectangle on the board and reproduce the illustration contained in the textbook. After that, teacher asks the children to draw a rectangle on their paper and make two dots a little below the horizontal center of the paper. Teacher should then help pupils to distinguish the two parts of sky and land by drawing a horizontal line between the two dots, and to paint the land green and the sky blue, using transverse strokes of the brush. (p. 1)

In addition to these stages, special teaching points were indicated: paying attention to painting the upper space dark blue and corresponding land space dark green; encouraging children to make soft pencil-line on paper; making suggestions as to what kind of posture is desirable and how to manipulate the hand in order to create a good work; and helping children distinguish the two colors of green and blue (p. 1).

These two different approaches to teaching can be found in another lesson (drawing and painting Japanese lanterns) provided in Book I of both texts. The American text contains this description: "paint pictures of Japanese lanterns. First, paint the beautiful shapes with water. Drop in the bright colors. Show the dark rims of the lanterns. You can make the dark color with red, yellow, and blue. What fun it is to paint lanterns!" (Froehlich and Snow, 1904, Book I, p. 47). The Japanese lesson, dealing with the same kind of pictures of Japanese lanterns, focuses on a form study on how to draw lanterns hanging above the child's eye (Ministry of Education, 1910c).

By comparing the above examples, one can understand the two approaches to the teaching of art. The distance between the American and Japanese texts might be due to a gap between what Shirahama learned from American art education and what he realized in modernizing Japanese art education, but it seems this limited translation of American ideas into Japanese art education was due largely to the necessity of compromising with traditionalists.

The Limitations of Shirahama's Transformation

After 1868 when the old Tokugawa shogunate was destroyed and the new Meiji government established, formal schooling in art education began, in accordance with the first modern comprehensive educational ordinance, issued September 8, 1872. For a time, Western and traditional systems coexisted. Eager to Westernize the educational system, the Meiji government adopted a policy of teaching mainly Western-style pencil drawing in elementary art classes.

This Westernization was, of course, not embraced without reservations; indeed, "nationalistic reaction in the area of fine arts seemed to have reached a fanatic stage when, in 1885, the traditional technique of brush and *sumi* was restored in elementary art instruction, replacing the pen and pencil drawing which had been practiced for nearly ten years" (Haga, 1971, p. 253). Fenollosa, his aide-de-camp Okakura, and others took the lead in this strange regressive movement. Owing to their enthusiasm to revive interest in Japanese art, "the Ministry of Education reversed its earlier policy concerning art classes in elementary education" in 1885 and replaced "pencil-drawing with brush-and-ink painting in Japanese style" (Shively, 1971, pp. 115-116).

As a result of these two opposite forces in Japanese art education, there were, during the opening decade of the 20th century, conflicting views over the best way to develop an art curriculum at the elementary level, whether to follow Western art or Japanese. A temporary solution was the publishing of two kinds of copybooks in 1904 for drawing in elementary schools, one using pencil; the other, Japanese brush. This solution, however, was only temporary, and had the bad effect of clearly dividing Japanese art educators into two camps. At the same time, "art educators were tired of such arguments and became anxious to discover the true and right course of direction. Instead of arguing the relative merits of both, they tried to consider drawing from the real standpoint of education. The conclusion of this discussion was a compromise between these two ways, that art education should be based on Western Realism, within which the Japanese way should be applied as much as possible" (Shimoda, 1959b, p. 230).

The demand to mediate between the Japanese and Western ways in developing a modernized curriculum of art at the the elementary level resulted in the publication of the *New Textbooks of Drawing* in 1910.

This orientation to an eclectic way of developing an art curriculum affected Shirahama's editorial policy about the writing of the textbooks, and limited his translation of American ideas in art education into Japanese. Shirahama was not able to deal with the expressive approach in the process of developing a new art curriculum for elementary schools; rather, he took the instructional approach of teaching art in three contexts. The first context we shall consider is that of design methodology. Shirahama's attention to design methodology is evidenced by his pointing out three categories of drawing education (representation, decoration, and construction), and three elements of representative drawing (space relation, outline, and light and shade) (1907, pp. 44-45). In addition, he emphasized that systematic teaching of color theory should be contained in the elementary art curriculum (Shirahama, 1916, pp. 111-130). Those who have read Dow's *Composition* (1899) will perceive the reflection of Dow's design methodology in Shirahama's ideas. These new American concepts of space relation, outline, light and shade, color theory, and so forth were translated and introduced in the *New Textbooks of Drawing*.

The second context is children's developmental psychology. Shirahama was impressed by the increasing interest in child study movement in the field of American art education at that time. He write:

> For children's nature, various matters that one regards as "appropriate for children in the context of simplicity and easiness do not interest children." On the contrary, matters of complexity that one regards as inappropriate for children interest them greatly. For example, children tend to like more a bird than a rectangular figure, more a bird flying that sitting in a branch, more a horse running, and more a train moving. [In American elementary schools] children are, first, motivated by something significant in "children's own interest and their pleasure," then, they are introduced to drawing and painting. In other word, it is the principle of instruction that education be practiced in the context of children's essential nature. (Shirahama, 1909, pp. 8-9)

Shirahama had a sensitive eye to the developing field of educational psychology and the beginning of the child-study movement in American art education at the opening decade of the 20th century.

The third context is the special method of teaching art that Shirahama observed in several American elementary schools during his stay in Massachusetts. These methods were creating forms of silhouette, time-sketch, working drawing, pose drawing, and free-arm drawing (Shirahama, 1909, pp. 9-10).

The above three contexts were employed in the *New Textbooks of Drawing* because they were less concerned with whether to follow Western art education philosophy or Japanese. These three new contexts provided a compromise for Japanese art educators in both camps of Westernization and traditionalization, and were very acceptable to Japanese art educators.

Shirahama's policy of compromise between the Western and Japanese ways for art education was clearly indicated in his 1909 article, which summarized twelve characteristics of American art education in the elementary schools:

1. Children are not used to copying something from books, but to representing what they see daily.
2. Children are provided many opportunities for free expression painting in the first grade.
3. Children in every grade are provided lessons in time-sketch.
4. Children observe movements of an animal or figure carefully and represent its movement in time-sketch drawing.
5. Teachers do not use plaster models, but geometrical forms, animals, and plants as object for representation. (At the secondary level, plaster models are used, but not in the elementary grades.)
6. After the lesson in representing a plant form, children are taught to transform their work into a creative design pattern.
7. Children are permitted to use rulers and compasses, particularly for industrial drawing and similar design work.
8. Children are continually provided lesson in color theory from grades one through six of elementary school.
9. Children are taught the basic principles of painting and how to compose a painting.
10. Children use various media, such as pencil, colored pencil, brush and colored chalk in every grade in elementary school.
11. Children use both drawing paper and colored paper.
12. Children are made familiar with many reproductions of great masters' work of art. (The aim is not to have children copy the work, but to improve their taste.) (pp. 10-11)

Shirahama's article indicates that he was able to perceive such movements in American art eduation as "nature study," "child study," and "picture study," all of which occurred around the turn of the 20th century (Logan, 1955; Dobbs, 1972; Stankiewicz, 1985).

In short, the *New Textbooks of Drawing* which served as the only national textbooks from 1910 to 1931, reflect the instructional, or practical means of teaching art in the contexts of design methodology, children's developmental psychology, and special teaching methods. This way did little to reconcile Western art education and Japanese. The overemphasis on a strict instructional approach to teaching art, the ignoring of the expressive aspect of art, and the retention of copy or imitative drawing in the new textbooks reflect the social and educational necessity of balancing Western ideas in art education and Japanese traditional thought.

Conclusion: A Two-Way Street

Shirahama was criticized by certain art educators such as Kanae Yamamoto (1921), the leading advocate of "free drawing movement" in painting in schools during the Taisho Era (1912-1926) of Japan. He claimed Shirahama was responsible for the remains of copy work and the lack of expressive value in the new textbooks. Although this kind of criticism of the new textbooks can be found even now in various historical researches on Japanese art education, it is, I believe, not entirely correct. All criticism of the new textbooks tend to ignore one of Shirahama's most important learning from America: "Children tend to have some aesthetic quality so that we should encourage them to develop their mental and aesthetic growth. ... It is the purpose of drawing as a regular subject within school curriculum to make creative imagination available to children's mind" (Shirahama, 1907, p. 44). Shirahama certainly had an idea of expressive value ("creative imagination") in his mind, but unfortunately had no success getting the expressive value of art included in the curriculum of the *New Textbooks of Drawing*.

The case of Akira Shirahama is interesting because it illustrates the gap between what was learned from American art education and what was realized in modern Japanese art education. His case is also typical of the push-and-pull between traditionalism and modernism, nationalism and cosmopolitanism, liberalism and conservatism in the changing attitudes of the Japanese art educator toward the modernization of his nation. His limitations must be seen within the context where "modernists may be liberal or conservative; traditionalists may be for or against the policy, depending upon the dominant consensus it represents" (Passin, 1965b, p. 487).

The story of modern art education in Japan begins with Shirahama and continues into the present, but it is more than ever a two-way street as suggested by Beittel (1983):

> Somewhere between Japan and America lies a great truth—a Great Tradition where inspiration and mastery can co-exist, a disciplined spontaneity of hand, eye, mind and spirit responsive to life-world, medium, and place simultaneously. ... I know, as Cox (1977) pointed out in *Turning East,* that things Oriental pass through a prism that all but transforms them into their opposite. An irony abounds here. It is as though I have gone a Japanese way, but without the hierarchy; and Japan has gone the American way, but without the free spirit. (p. 13)

An American art educator's turning East, exactly parallels Shirahama's turning West. There is no doubt that both ways will make us richer and give us "food for thought as we make a choice for the future" in art education (Carson, 1981, p. 46). Surely, a two-way street is needed between the American and Japanese art education to enrich each of us achieve cross-cultural understanding in art education. As Beittel (1983) says, "Dialogue, love, and art" remain "a spiritual country, planetary but nonlocalized" (p. 13).

Chapter 6

Originally published in Patricia M. Amburgy, Donald Soucy, Mary A. Stankiewicz, Brent Wilson, and Marjorie Wilson, eds., *The History of Art Education: Proceedings from the Second Penn State Conference, 1989*, (pp. 59-66), Reston VA: National Art Education Association, 1992. Reprinted with permission by the National Art Education Association (NAEA),

American Influence on the History of Japanese Art Education: The Case of Seishi Shimoda

Fig. 6.1 *Feeding Her Birds* by Millet (Carpenter, 1918, p. 1).

Fig. 6.2 Japanese elementary students representing the scene of *Feeding Her Birds* by Millet (Shimoda, 1927).

Fig. 6.3 *The Principals of Art Education* (Münsterberg, 1904, p. 1).

Fig. 6.4 Japanese Edition of *The Principals of Art Education*, Shimoda Trans., (1915, p.1).

* Figures are not included in the originally published paper.

In 1984 the author presented a broad overview of the American influence on modern Japanese art education over more than one hundred years (Okazaki, 1984). In 1985 more detailed instances of the American influence on Japanese art education during the opening decade of the 20th century were presented (Okazaki, 1985a). This chapter examines the American influence found in Japanese art education in the following decade of the 1920s.

Arthur W. Dow in America turned to the Japanese to find something not in American art education. Seishi Shimoda (1890-1973) in Japan turned to America to find those elements missing from Japanese art education. This chapter examines

Shimoda's studies on American ideas in art education. The chapter concludes that Shimod's effort opened a few windows on the territory of Japanese art education in the 1920s in Japan. The author believes Shimoda's educational imagination is praised for having kept a "third eye" beyond the difference of the Western and Eastern cultures.

Shimoda's Curriculum Development

The second decade of the 20th century in Japan is referred to as "the Liberal Twenties" (Beasley, 1982). In his article "Liberalism in Japan," Dewey (1919) reported: "America had come out with fine words and had surprisingly made its words good in deeds. Autocracy out of fashion, democratic styles were in" (p. 283). There was a growing interest in democratic education among Japanese educators. The Free Drawing Movement also began in response to the liberalizing tendencies in education at the time. Kanae Yamamoto (1882-1946) started and advocated this revolutionary movement in 1918 (Kaneko, 1980). Yamamoto, after coming back to Japan from Europe, "advocated the idea that the teaching of 'Drawing' should develop the creative, aesthetic ability of each individual child. For this purpose he suggested that the child should be released from copying textbooks and be placed in nature, which he should be encouraged to draw as he felt" (Yukawa, 1965, p. 10). Such methodology has continued to the present and gained some popularity. Carson (1981) reports: "At the zoo and in the parks in Japan one can see swarms of children with their teachers, painting and drawing" (p. 43).

This movement also provided art teachers an alternative approach for curriculum development in art education—the "internal mode of curriculum development" Eisner later proposed, where "art teachers have a professional responsibility to develop programs for the students they teach" (Eisner, 1984, p. 263). It was in the 1920s that Japanese non-governmental art educators who did not approve of the government guidelines began to develop art curricula for their students. Shimoda was one of the internal mode curriculum developers. He believed that drawing education aimed not only at developing children's creativity, but also at cultivating their social and cultural awareness. The teaching of art appreciation is an important aspect of supporting and promoting children's fine and applied art activities (Shimoda, 1920, pp. 53-56).

Shimoda's art program appears in his book of 1926. In the frontispiece of the book, Shimoda quoted a notion by Pedro J. Lemos, the second editor of *The School Arts Magazine* (Logan, 1955, p. 134) and the director of the Stanford University Museum of Fine Arts (Lemos, 1939), from Lemos' *Applied Art* (1920): "The best teaching is that which results in fitting the student to study intelligently without a teacher." This notion became the aim of Shimoda's art program.

Shimoda's art program, appearing in the second part of his book, consisted of five major domains: painting, sculpture, design, crafts, and art appreciation. On the productive areas of the first four domains, Shimoda developed about thirty three lessons in each grade. Among them, on average fifteen lessons were devoted to drawing, painting, and color mixing; eight lessons concerned designing; five lessons dealt with making crafts; and five lessons had to do with sculpture. In developing sequential lessons on productive domains, he referred to seven instructional resources of art program. Five of them were from the United States. The American resources were the course of study of Los Angeles City (Farnum, 1914, pp.172-174), the program of manual arts of Horace Mann School, Teachers College, (n. d.), *Industrial Art Text Books* (1915) by Snow and Froehlich, *Theory and Practice of Teaching Art* (1912) by Dow, and *Applied Art* (1920) by Lemos.

The sequential lessons on art appreciation Shimoda developed also appear in the third part of his book. Students in each grade received three or four lessons on appreciation of works of art through black and white reproductions of masterpieces by European painters such as Leonardo da Vinci and, Whistler and Cézanne, and by Japanese painters such as Sesshu and Hiroshige. Each masterpiece Shimoda listed had a brief description about its character and the artist's life, but did not have a description of a lesson plan. However, Shimoda provided one lesson plan in the first grade on Millet's *Feeding Her Birds* as an example of how to teach art appreciation. The description consists of question/answer activity, story of the picture, the artist's biography, looking at the picture, and teaching notes. Shimoda's lesson plan was based on Carpenter's description of *Feeding Her Birds* (Carpenter, 1918, pp. 1-9). In developing instructional curriculum materials in Shimoda's appreciation program, he listed three main references from American art education literature at that time. They were *How to Show Pictures to Children* (1914) by Hurll, *Stories Pictures Tell* (1918) by Carpenter, and *Art in the Schools* (1924) by Boas. The Picture Study Movement in the United States affected Shimoda's development of art curriculum.

Shimoda's Studies of Theory and Practice in American Art Education

The internal mode of curriculum development in art education, described earlier, emerged in the 1920's in Japan. Shimoda was one of the internal mode curriculum developers. He had accomplished his duty to develop an art program for his student. There were two reasons for his success. One was that he had good information on how to develop art curriculum. He acquired the methodology of curriculum development from American art program models. He studied American art education literature appearing between 1900 and 1920, and incorporated this research into his program.

The other reason was more fundamental. Shimoda's study of American art education helped him see his own mission of art education more clearly. He had done three Japanese translations of American sources during his twenties. One of these was *The Principles of Art Education* by Münsterberg (1904). Münsterberg was a professor of psychology at Harvard University. Saunders (1966) says that his book was "the most popular and continuously reprinted" of Prang's books of art education. "Münsterberg's book discusses art from the philosophical, aesthetical and psychological points of view. His aesthetic principles emphasize form and content as they are joined in design to give unity to the art product" (Saunders, 1966, p. 3). The first part of the book which represented Münsterberg's philosophical idea of art education especially impressed Shimoda. Shimoda (1915) says that he was completely concerned this notion of Münsterberg:

Art instruction in the school is the great social scheme which the community

82

has at its disposal to train this power; that is, to open the mind for that truth which is more complete in itself than the truth of scientific knowledge, for that truth which understands the immediate reality of the objects. (Münsterberg, 1904, pp. 33-34).

Münsterberg further says that scientific knowledge provides us connections of objects while "artistic rendering of reality" grasps objects in their "complete isolation." He believes that the function of art is to "bring about this isolation and to show us the object in its immediate truth" (p. 34). Shimoda understood the importance of art education, perceived his own mission as art educator, and decided to devote his life to being an art educator. He began his research on arts and aesthetic education, and the translation of Münsterberg's book into Japanese, published in September 1915, was his first effort (Shimoda, 1915, p. 45).

Another source was *Art Education* (1914) by Bailey. "Bailey saw the purpose of art education not as mere copying or object-making." Rather he regarded it "as the development of ability to perceive beauty and order and to make things beautiful so as to reveal beauty to others" (Dobbs, 1972, pp. 52-53). Indeed, Bailey says in the opening sentence of his book (1914), "The purpose of art education is the development of appreciation for the beautiful and power to produce beautiful things" (p. 1). The book contains a comprehensive description of art education. Bailey illustrates such factors as the school estate, the schoolroom, school housekeeping, school costume, school work, specific instruction, and the teacher. These factors are important to make the practice of art education successful. Shimoda got many ideas for his art appreciation program through his translation of Bailey's book. Shimoda's Japanese translation was available in 1917. The back page of the title cover shows a picture of Bailey with his signature that was not in Bailey's original text.

The last source was *The Stranger: A Modern Miracle Play* by James Parton Haney. The Japanese translation of the play was not available as a separate volume. It was included as the Appendix to the Japanese edition of Bailey's *Art Education*. Shimoda (1917) says that Haney published the play as a pamphlet in February, 1915

(p. 154). Tall and Davidson (1921, p. 625) point that Haney wrote it for the magazine *Good Housekeeping* . The play interested Shimoda because it provided problems of art education for readers, such as "Is American art teaching functioning in the tastes and the homes of the people?" and "Are American art educators setting up artistic ideals in the community?" (Tall & Davidson, 1921, p. 625). The play consists of the author's remarks, four scenes, and an epilogue.

Shimoda translated the whole text of the play into Japanese with Haney's permission. Shimoda sent a letter July 19, 1916 to Haney, and asked Haney for permission to reprint the play. He soon replied to this asking, and gave Shimoda his permission in a letter dated August 10, 1916. Shimoda reprinted Haney's letter in the Appendix (Shimoda, 1917, p. 149). Haney says to Shimoda in his reply:

> Thank you for your kind letter of July 19. I am pleased to hear that the little play "The Stranger" has appealed to you. You have my permission to publish it in the Japanese translation—and I shall be pleased to receive copies of the play in Japanese.

The Course of Study of Baltimore County Schools in Maryland includes some parts of the play. It reprints the author's remark, third and fourth scenes, and epilogue (Tall and Davidson, 1921, pp. 625-631). Haney says in his remarks, "it is seen how Everyboy and Every girl bring a STRANGER to school" and "how the STRANGER causes much Mystery and is at last discovered by Them" (Tall & Davidson, p. 625). In the end of the epilogue, they say to the Stranger; "Why, you must be Art." All say, "Why, of course you're Art!" He replays smilingly, "Did I not say that when I was no longer a stranger to you you would know my name without the telling?" A parent says with conviction; "Why, I thought so, long ago, but your lessons were so full of common sense and useful I couldn't believe it was you" (pp. 630-31). Thus, all recognized the Stranger was the art underlying daily life. Shimoda found the meaning of art in Haney's play. It was the contribution of art to the quality of daily life that was invisible to the eye but pervading the human mind.

Shimoda had researched many other useful materials on American art education as well. Shimoda's first book (1922) on the theory of drawing education reviewed American materials. His book consists of six chapters. The second chapter describes an overview of Japanese art education history. The last chapter deals with modes of two-dimensional expression, theory of color, and theory of art. These two chapters did not refer to American sources.

The first chapter of Shimoda's book deals with an overview of historical development of Western art education (pp. 9-57). To review the outline of the American art education history, he used two secondary sources. One was *Cyclopedia of Education* (1911) edited by Monroe. The other was *Art Education in the Public Schools of the United States* (1908b) edited by Haney. He traces three tendencies in American art education history. The first was Smith's industrial drawing, the second Hall's child study movement, and the last appreciation through art. Shimoda also shows the two distinct forces in art education practice in American public schools based on Haney's description of art education history. These forces were the economic pressure as a reflection of industrial spirit and the desire for beauty as an expression of idealism. Haney (1908a) points out these forces in his article (p. 76). Shimoda said that *Industrial Art Text Books* (Snow & Froehlich, 1915) reflected the economic pressure while Münsterberg (1904), Dow (1912), and Bailey (1914) support the desire for beauty. McKibbin (1960) describes American art education in the early years of the 20th century: "in the early decades of the century the industrial arts movement was strong. *The Industrial Art Textbooks* [sic] by Bonnie Snow and Hugo Froe[h]lich had sections on design and drawing with emphasis on Art in Dress, Art in Home, and Art in Handwork. Unfortunately under these impressive titles, pattern work and tracing were advocated" (p. 64). Katter (1985) declares the primary aim of the *Industrial Art Text Books* to be the "study of art and its relation to industry" (p. 296).

Snow and Froehlich described a new theory of art: "These 'Industrial Art Text Books' are based upon a new theory and significant theory of art—the theory that 'representation' is not a basic or fundamental art principle. Ability to draw is important as a means to an end; it should not be considered as an end in itself." They also stated the instrumental rationale of industrial art education: "The average man needs to know how to furnish his house, how to choose his clothing, how to arrange his business advertisement. Through these choices he constantly cultivates his taste, and develops a general appreciation of the most suitable, the most useful and therefore the most beautiful." They regarded drawing as "the instrument and the language of art" (1915, frontispiece of each part).

Although the influence of economic pressure still continued, the desire for beauty emerged in the field. McKibbin (1960) also points out Bailey's contribution to the development of beauty and art: "Bailey was an incongruous combination of the practical and the idealistic. BEAUTY and ART were always capitalized in his thinking. His emotional eloquence swayed many highly intelligent art teachers" (p. 64).

Through the first two decades of the 20th century "practical drawing for the development of manual skill and graphic expression continued" (Katter, 1987, p. 296). However, Winslow (1928) says "A good picture has a refining influence which increases in proportion to the intelligence with which it is studied" (p. 65). As in the United States, Japanese art education faced the two forces of industrial spirit and idealism of beauty in the 1920s. Shimoda incorporated both approaches into his consideration.

The third chapter of Shimoda's book illustrates the value of art in education (1922, pp. 76-139). First, Shimoda explained the meaning of artistic activity itself in the context of Münsterberg's philosophical discussion. "Yes, connection is science, but the work of art is isolation." The "isolation is beauty whether nature or the imagination of the artist offers it" (Münsterberg, 1904, p. 21). Secondly, Shimoda points out the significance of design and craft activities for industrial use. Thirdly, he presents Kerchensteiner's studies on children's drawing to evidence the contribution of drawing to the development of children's cognition. His description about Kerchensteiner's studies was dependent on Hall's review in "Pedagogy of Drawing" (Hall, 1911, pp. 510-512).

The fourth chapter of Shimoda's book refers to aims of drawing education (1922, pp. 140-160). Shimoda presented two major types of justifications for the teaching of drawing. One was the intrinsic rationale of art itself, and the other was the instrumental rationale of art for use in other fields. Shimoda said that recent American art educators such as Dow (1912) and Bailey (1914) all were emphasizing the intrinsic consequences of art. Shimoda regarded the intrinsic justification for art as first in importance. He did not reject the instrumental role of industrial drawing, but he regarded it as secondary in art education. This belief derived from de Garmo's discussion of 1909. Logan (1965) reviews de Garmo's idea of *Principles of Secondary Education* (Macmillan, 1907, 1909). De Garmo "went on ... to develop the skills and appreciation derived from drawing and singing and restated the case for industrial drawing as it made artisans out of labors" (Logan, 1965, p. 50).

Art in school relates to aesthetic appreciation while industrial arts in school deals with industrial drawing. Today, these two approaches have different place in schools. Logan (1965) states that the separation became clear by the setting up of "industrial arts classes unrelated to art classes" after World War One in America (p. 49). In Japan, Shimoda takes the aesthetic appreciation to be more appropriate for drawing education. He considered industrial drawing to be appropriate for school art programs if students received it as general education, not as vocational education. To support his view, Shimoda referred to Farnum's report (1914). Shimoda quoted Farnum's discussion:

Two broad aims have come to be universally recognized in public school drawing work, the professional or industrial, and the cultural. ... In general there are two broad classes into which modern civilization may roughly be divided. They are the consumers and the producers. All people may be classed under the first ... . It were folly to therefore to educate all pupils in drawing or art purely from the standpoint of profession, the training of producers. (Farnum, 1914, p. 30)

Thus, the cultural aim was most suited for children. The aim of drawing in schools was to train "the senses, mind, and hand to work together" (Farnum, 1914, p. 30). In 1941 Farnum reviewed his own report of 1914: "Recognition of two broad aims in drawing, cultural and industrial, soon pointed the way to a wider understanding of art values" (p. 447).

The fifth chapter of Shimoda's book reviews various research on children's drawing (1922, pp. 161-180). He described findings by European and American researchers. Among European scholars were Claparède, Perez, and Binet (French), Ricci (Italian), Parpenheim, Göze, Levinstein, and Kerschensteiner (German), and Cooke and Partridge (British). Shimoda also traces several researches by American scholars such as Barnes, Lukens, O'Shea, Maitland, and Shinn. Shimoda's primary reference was Hall's "Pedagogy of Drawing" (1911) in which Western researchers were featured. Shimoda noted Hall's belief in the creativity of children's drawing: free-hand drawings by children "has so impressed me with the native spontaneity and creative originality of human nature as these. The naïve errors themselves, often uniquely mirth provoking, spring out of the very heart of hearts of childhood. Many effects that art deems impossible are not only boldly attempted, but accomplished" (Hall, 1911, pp. 515-516). Shimoda further quoted another of Hall's discussion: "Teaching should be to encourage and not to repress the tendency to exaggerate each new trait, and should have regard not to the finished product" (p. 518). Hall's conception of children's drawing began "to shift the emphasis in art education from the product to the child" (Efland, 1976, p. 70). Shimoda recognized the psychological point of view on the nature of children's drawing.

The sixth chapter of Shimoda's book has no direct American references (1922, pp. 181-248). However, we can find reflections on certain American concepts in his descriptions of this chapter. Shimoda tries to divide drawing curriculum into five major activities—free drawing, design, color theory, working drawing, and beauty and arts. Free drawing consists of story drawing and illustrative drawing. The design activity includes not only making ornament but also three-dimensional constructions such as household art, industrial art, and architecture. Reputation, rhythm, space, balance, symmetry, and color become elements and principles of design. The description of color theory consists of the color wheel, properties of color (hue, value, and chroma), and color harmonies. Working drawing was defined these not as mere mechanical drawing but as a useful tool for industrial art. Beauty and arts emphasized appreciation of art.

The bibliography of Simoda's book lists many American sources, some of which have been mentioned. Other American resources included Flectcher (1918), Sargent & Miller (1916), Luckiesh (1915), Munsell (1917), Rhead (1905), Izor (1916), and Hayward (1925).

The book *How Children Learn to Draw* by Sargent and Miller (1916) reflects "an experiment to discover how children learn most readily to use drawing as a common means of self-expression" (Sargent & Miller, 1916, p. 1). Belshe (1946) summarizes Sargent and Miller's idea: "Since having something to tell is the basis of good drawing, technique may actually stifle expression" (1946, p. 111). What Shimoda learned from Sargent and Miller was to psychologize the teaching of drawing.

Munsell published his first edition of the book in 1905 when he was lecturer in color composition and artistic anatomy at the Normal Art School in Boston (Munsell, Spry, & Bellamy, 1946, p. 4). Farnum stresses Munsell's contribution to modern color theory. The world "might still continue to carry on ... to a practice and analysis of color through some kind of color notation, which must have a basis built upon such work as Munsell has accomplished" (Farnum, 1947, p. 9).

Shimoda attempted a basic study of color theory in 1922. He wrote a series of four articles for a Japanese magazine *Asuno Kyoiku* (Future Education) between 1922 and 1923. The first and second articles (November and October issues, 1922) deal with a historical review of color research based on Hall's description in "Pedagogy of Drawing." The third article (December issue, 1922) introduces Munsell's theory in *A Color Notation* to Japanese readers. The last article (March issue, 1923) shows some results of his own research on elementary children's color preference in using Munsell's color system. He finds that most children did not prefer Munsell's "Middle

Color" found in or adjacent to the middle third of the value scale (Shimoda, 1923).

Frank Herbert Hayward was a supervisor in London. His book *The Lessons in Appreciation* was available from Macmillan Company in the United States in 1915. It was reprinted in 1917, 1922, and 1925. Shimoda (1924) summarizes Hayward's idea that emphasizes children's "first impression" (Hayward, 1925, pp.1-8) of aesthetic objects or phenomena in lessons on art appreciation.

Thus Shimoda's studies on the theory of American art education concentrated on his first book in 1922. He used numerous American materials of art education to clarify his philosophy of art education. Putting these pieces together, he tried to solve what Eisner (1972) later called the "intellectual puzzle" (v) of art education. Shimoda desired to place free drawing on a true pedagogic basis, but he did not achieve the solution, and no one else has done it since then either. However, his effort was worth while doing. His studies supported his further effort to develop his own curriculum for students he taught in 1926.

We can see the American art education scene between 1900-1920 in the materials Shimoda referenced. It was the transitional period of American art education because the materials Shimoda chose reflected the changing theory and practice in art education. Smith (1933) found evidence of changing American art education during two decades, 1881-1900 and 1921-30. Significant tendencies were enhanced in the second decade. American art education aimed at such developments as "taste and discrimination," "appreciation of beauty," "originality and free expression," "graphic vocabulary," and "observation and visual judgement." Practice of art education concentrated on "fundamentals of art," "household art," "drawing and painting," "art appreciation," and "industrial art." Smith says that the "most logical program ... in art incorporates five major art experiences or activities: drawing and painting, design, color, construction, and appreciation" (Smith, 1933, pp. 276-277).

Shimoda followed such tendencies of American art education because American materials he referred to emphasized them. Like American art educators, he was experiencing the transitional climate of American art education between 1900 and 1920 in Japan. The transition in art education was not limited to the United States.

It also spread to Japan through Shimoda's effort to reach beyond Japanese national border. Clark (1985) points out our unawareness of solving similar problems of art education throughout the world. In this sense, Shimoda had the awareness of global art education, or at least between the two nations, the United States and Japan.

Conclusion: A Third Eye

In teaching our students "modernism of art education" (Wilson, 1989) in Japan we always begin with the historic event of the free drawing movement. The free drawing movement of the 1920s can be praised as the first "counterbalance" (Dobbs, 1983) to state-controlled policy of art education. Since then, Japanese art education has been carried on with "a balance of power between governmental and non-governmental effort" (Okazaki, 1985b).

This movement made Japanese art educators perceive the necessity of using their energies and inventiveness for future art education through the internal mode of curriculum development in art education. Shimoda is one of those who had such energy and inventiveness. In discarding old theories of drawing education he introduced new theories of art education. It is clear that American ideas on art education supported Shimoda's energies and inventiveness for the future Japanese art education.

In his preface to the Japanese edition of *Educating Artistic Vision* (1986) Eisner describes the contribution of one culture as a source for the development of art education in another:

I recognize that no culture can simply imitate the programs or aims of education in another culture. The Japanese version of *Educating Artistic Vision* is not intended to become a recipe for Japanese art educators. It is intended to be a source of stimulation and insight. I hope it provides some intellectual tools through which Japanese art educators can reflect on their own goals and methods. If it opens up a few windows on the territory of art education, if it helps Japanese art educators see their own mission more clearly, if only by way of contrast, the translated version of *Educating Artistic Vision* will have served a useful purpose. (pp. 2-3)

Contrasting American ideas with Japanese brought Shimoda binocular vision. Shimoda presented a paper at the Tenth Congress of the International Federation for Education through Art in 1958. In his presentation of "Internationalism and Nationalism in art education from the standpoint of Japan" Shimoda concluded: "Drawing is a universal language. This naturally means that all countries must have something in common in their art education, and that art education should be based on internationalism. We are cultivating nationality in art education based on internationalism" (1959b, p. 231).

Surely, we need "a two-way street" (Okazaki, 1985a, p. 64) between America and Japan, not only in education in general but also in art education. A report, *Japanese Education Today* (1987), by the U. S. Department of Education helps American educators "to understand more clearly some of the risks and opportunities facing American education" (iv). A two-way street can "enrich each of our modes of art education and help each of us achieve cross-cultural understanding in art education" (Okazaki, 1985a, p. 64). The cross-cultural understanding by the Japanese art educator supports his or her inventiveness for future art education and counterbalances state-controlled art education.

Yet, a two-way street of art education is not enough. Shimoda used American art education literature as sources of stimulation and insight. Through American intellectual tools, Shimoda could reflect on his own goals and methods of art education. American sources helped Shimoda see his own mission more clearly. Beittel (1986) points out the limitation of "a two-way vision" in his special article for Japanese readers because "knowledge itself has material, mental and spiritual forms, each valid, each not to be replaced by another" (p. 25). He further says:

Thus for Japanese art educators to turn unthinkingly toward America now is mistake, just as it would be were I to turn unthinkingly toward Japan. ... So it is that there is a need to transcend the binocular vision of cross-cultural influence as I discussed it with my Japanese visitor. For a two-way vision is still limited to one plane. What is needed for a global, three-dimensional vision is both literally and figuratively a "third eye" —the eye capable of Divine Vision, of transformed consciousness, the eye that grasps the diversity in unity of a layered universe. (pp. 25-28)

How should we go beyond "a two-way street," or "two-way vision" in Beittel's terms? Beittel sees the "need for what the Western mystic Jacob Boehme called 'contrarieties'" (p. 28). In his review of Beittel's article, Ishikawa (1986) illustrates Boehme's concept of contrarieties in using a metaphor of the fire. The fire could become both the good and the evil for human beings. Fire with people sitting around it is the good while fire in a wooden house becomes evil. Boehme's theology desires to bridge these contrarieties only by God. Beittel expects to transcend these by the Divine Vision of Blake's mysticism (Ishikawa, 1986, p. 31).

The Divine Vision consists of such "primary words" of Buber as art, love, and religion. These "hint at the basic unity underlying art, love, and religion under the power of open dialogue," says Beittel. He suggests a justification: "our relationship to things becomes art, our relationship to persons becomes love, and our relationship to the mystery of being becomes religion" (Beittel, 1986, p. 27). The imagination is praised for having kept the Divine Vision in time of trouble in Blake's Jerusalem.

Beittel's discussion of 1986 is compatible with his earlier belief. "Dialogue, love, and art remain of a spiritual country, planetary but nonlocalized" (Beittel, 1983, p. 13). His vision of a planetary tradition could be applied to "the influences passing between cultures and the clash which sets the stage for the transcendence of difference" (Beittel, 1983, p. 7). Beittel's preface to Japanese edition of *Alternatives for Art Education Research* (1987) still emphasizes a third eye or Divine Vision in cross-cultural research.

I believe that Shimoda was successful in getting "a third eye" beyond "a two-way street" in the 1920s. He achieved it through his cross-cultural studies between the United States and Japan. Shimoda imagined the integration of the two separate subjects within elementary and secondary school curriculum, drawing and manual arts, into a single subject, art. His intention was to create an alternative to the strict standardized national drawing and manual arts curricula. He devoted himself to the development of new art curriculum in the 1920s to place children's free expression on an educational basis. Painting, sculpture, design, crafts, and art appreciation were five major art experiences or activities in Shimoda's art program of 1926.

Shimoda's effort opened a few windows on the territory of Japanese art education in the 1920s, but it was not appropriate for the time. The realization of Shimoda's inventiveness needed time. Drawing and manual arts within school curricula joined each other, and "drawing and handicraft" as a single subject was established in the national guidelines (elementary and secondary level) in 1947. The Ministry of Education replaced "drawing and handicraft" with "fine arts" in secondary schools in 1961. Shimoda (1959) described the climate of Japanese art education: "In post-war Japan great emphasis has been placed on art education for the restoration of the degenerated conditions." That is "typically represented by so-called 'Creative Art Education Movement'" in 1950s, which "advocates letting pupils develop their creative power by releasing them from repressions and also by fostering [sic] their free expression" (Shimoda, 1959, p. 230).

Shimoda had kept a "third eye" of art, love, and dialogue throughout his life. He was truly concerned with things, child and adult, and "education as dialogue" (Buber, 1971). Shimoda closed his life in 1973. It was only five-years after the 1968 revision of Japanese national guideline of art education (grades one through nine) reflecting Shimoda's inventiveness of 1926. The guideline indicated that art programs should consist of five major areas: painting, sculpture, design, craft, and art appreciation. The realization of his inventiveness will require far more than forty years. Indeed, his educational imagination is praised for having kept a "third eye" beyond the difference of the Western and the Eastern cultures.

Chapter 7

Originally published in the *Journal of Multicultural and Cross-cultural Research in Art Education*, Vol. 12, No. 1, pp. 50-65, 1994.
Reprinted with permission by the United States Society for Education through Art.

Japanese Art Education: The Contribution of Western Modernism and American Art Program during the 1920s

Fig. 7.1 Outdoor drawing by 6th grade student (Yamamoto, 1921).

Fig. 7.2 Cardboard construction (Lemos, 1920. p. 210).

Fig. 7.3 Thin wood construction (Lemos, 1920. p. 211).

Fig. 7.4 Cardboard and wood construction (Shimoda, 1926, Fig. 51).

* Figures are not included in the originally published paper.

This chapter provides information about the development of Japanese art education during the 1920s, focusing on influence from Europe and the United States. The West's influence on Kanae Yamamoto and Seishi Shimoda in the second decade of the 20th century is examined. These two Japanese art educators used the modernism of Western art and the American school art program in providing counterbalances to state-controlled centralization of art education in Japan during the 1920s. They tried to replace the old view of art education which emphasized industrial drawing with the newer approaches used to understand modern art. The regulation of using only national art education textbooks and the imported concepts of Western art effectively counterbalanced one another in dynamic tension (Thistlewood, 1991). The legacies of both Yamamoto and Shimoda can still be found in current Japanese art education practice.

In Japan, visual art is a required subject in grades one through nine. Two class periods are devoted each week to artistic activity in elementary schools. Some American art educators are interested in adopting Japanese practices (Foster, 1975, 1990; Wachowiak, 1984). Others, however, perceive that Japanese educational systems "proceed vertically from a central power base" (Ott & Hurwitz, 1984). This characterization refers to the centralized system of school curriculum, national guidelines, textbook distribution, and educational policy-making that Monbusho (the Ministry of Education, Science, & Culture) has institutionalized and controlled over a long period of time.

The Japanese style of centralization and control might worry American art educators because "there exists no ministry of education in the United States to prescribe what shall be taught, to whom, and for what ends" (Eisner, 1984, p. 259). There has been no national curricula in the United States. For American art educators, it seems that various aspects of Japanese art education, such as government control, a centralized school system, and standardized curriculum, are likely to be a kind of unimaginable educational enterprise.

Governmental and Non-governmental Educational Efforts

Aside from the Ministry of Education, Dobbs (1983) describes the non-governmental educational effort made by the variety of professional groups and societies in the following way: "Japanese art educators have through their many affiliations endeavoured to provide a counterbalance to centralization by developing different points of emphasis" (p. 8) and Japanese organizations of art education "discuss the national guide lines, review ideas at conferences and in the journals, and try to influence the textbook publishers who write the material which is finally furnished to teachers" (p. 9). The balance of power between governmental and non-governmental educational efforts is obvious. In the elementary school (grades 1-6),

Curriculum content and the sequence of instruction for each subject and grade level are specified in considerable detail by Monbusho. Teachers are free to incorporate supplementary teaching materials if they believe they enhance coverage of prescribed course content. (U. S. Office of Education, 1987, p. 28)

Thistlewood, the former president of the National Society for Art and Design in Education in Britain, also perceives how imported ideas have served to the counterbalance to centralization. In responding to Hickman's oceanic analogy (1991) that cultures are composed of "the benthonic" and "the planktonic" in Singapore, Thistlewood (1991) says:

The former is endemic and pervasive, and is the basis of a healthy culture. The latter comes and goes and serves the needs of immediacy. A balancing of founding and fashionable principles is the identified objective of a state that understands its dependency on giving raw materials aesthetic signification. This is also true of Japan, ... the importation of exotic, western modernism has been a deliberate tactic of educationalists ... , aimed at counterbalancing a normal tendency to didacticism. The national respect for regulation, and imported concepts of individual creativity, in effect counterbalance one another in dynamic tension. (p. 128)

Perhaps Thistlewood acknowledges the balancing of governmental and non-governmental educational efforts in Japanese art education.

External and Internal Modes of Curriculum Development
In Japan, the Japanese principle (uniformity/standardization) and the Western principle (individuality/divergency) have become like "a two-way street" (Okazaki, 1985a). In 1871, the Japanese Ministry of Education was established with "a mandate to create a nationwide school system under its authority" (Rubinger, 1989,

p. 228). Since then, the Ministry has adopted the Japanese principle of uniformity/ standardization. It is akin to what Eisner (1984) has called the "external mode" of curriculum development. This mode "occurs in locations outside of the context in which the materials are to be used," and "takes form most often in textbooks" (p. 264). The Japanese governmental system reinforced a normal tendency to didacticism in education in general and art education in particular. Thus, Carson (1981) believes that one "reason art is taught so carefully in Japan may be to produce a standard quality" (p. 46) that the Ministry of Education has prescribed.

Japanese art educators and professional groups, however, have used the Western principle of individuality/divergence. They have imported the Western modernist view of art as individual expression and used it as a deliberate tactic aimed at counterbalancing the didacticism of official art education policy. It is an alternative approach—the "internal mode of curriculum development" as Eisner (1984) called it—where "art teachers have a professional responsibility to develop programs for the students they teach" (p. 263).

The "internal mode" of art education curriculum development emerged in Japan in the 1920s. There were two art educators who held state-controlled art education in check. One was Kanae Yamamoto (1882-1946) who was the leading advocate of the Free Drawing Movement. He incorporated notions of individual creativity associated with European modernist art into Japanese school art. The other was Seishi Shimoda (1890-1972) who provided leadership in developing the more modernized content of art over the limited one of drawing for industrial use. He incorporated ideas from American school art programs into the Japanese school art program.

Liberalism, Individualism, and the Free Drawing Movement
Recognizing Dewey's reputation in 1919, the Tokyo Imperial University invited him to lecture (Anderson, 1959). His eight lectures were published in New York in 1920 as *Reconstruction in Philosophy*. He also spoke to about five hundred elementary school teachers on March 1 in Tokyo (Kobayashi, 1964). In his 1919

article "Liberalism in Japan", Dewey reported on the climate of Japan: "America had come out with fine words and had surprisingly made its words good in deeds. Autocracy [was] out of fashion, democratic styles were in" (p. 283).

The second decade of the 20th century in Japan is often called "the Liberal Twenties" (Beasley, 1983). There were three movements of education all of which related to one another. The first of them was *Shin Kyoiku Undo* (the new education movement) which came from a growing interest in democratic education among some Japanese educators. This movement emphasized "the individuality and initiative of the student in opposition to the standardized education of the State-controlled school system" (Sugiyama, 1981, p. 121). The new education movement devoted its entire effort to developing modern concepts of liberalism and individualism in the field of education while the Imperial Rescript of Education of 1890 stressed the objectives for education in terms of nationalist-Confucianist values (Kobayashi, 1976). Dewey's educational philosophy was most influential on the theory of this movement because his proposals could clearly be seen as modern and Western (Kobayashi, 1964; White, 1987).

The second movement, *Geijutsu Kyoiku Undo* (the arts education movement), began in response to the liberalizing tendencies in the new education movement. It aimed at promoting children's free expression in school subjects related to arts. Emphasis on free expression spread to children's literary composition, music, art and school drama (National Institute for Educational Research, 1978).

The third movement was *Jiyuga Kyoiku Undo* (the free drawing movement) in the field of art education. It was one of movements composing the arts education movement. Yamamoto, who had lived in Europe for 1912-1916, was its organizer. Yukawa (1965) summarized Yamamoto's great contribution to the innovation of theory and practice of Japanese art education:

After his return to Japan he advocated the idea that the teaching of "Drawing" should develop the creative, aesthetic ability of each individual child. For this purpose he suggested that the child should be released from copying [national] textbooks and be placed in nature, which he should be encouraged to draw as he felt. ... Copying [national] textbooks was rejected by many teachers, and children were seen everywhere—in field[s], forests and towns—drawing directly from nature. (p. 10)

Yamamoto was successful in persuading Japanese art educators to believe that any copied drawing was harmful to children. He used the Japanese term, *Jiyu* (free), to advocate children's freedom and the individualism of artists (Yamamoto, 1921). His philosophy also became popular to Japanese art educators in the 1920s.

The free drawing movement, by providing a counterbalance to the state-controlled centralization of art education, had the effect of depressing the influence of reactionary bureaucrats, and increasing the prestige of liberals. This movement contributed to the decline of me "external mode," and it provided art teachers with an alternative approach for curriculum development in art education, the "internal mode." Thus, it was in the 1920s that Japanese elementary school classroom teachers and art specialists began to develop art curricula for their students (Okazaki, 1991).

Toward a Single Subject of Modernist Art
Teachers often encouraged students to paint out-of-doors. Influenced by their environment, students were to produce their drawings and paintings spontaneously; the teacher only needed to encourage them with a little instruction. Carleton Washburne visited a Japanese elementary school in 1930, and reported: "There was an outdoor sketching class, each child choosing his own subject and sketching it with remarkable skill" (1932, p. 38).

Critics indicated that this kind of the open-ended approach was most effective for children painting in the style of French Impressionism. It was less effective for other modes of expression such as two-dimensional design. Japanese art educators were not sure how to apply this approach to teaching of design, a subject that apparently required more teacher's instruction.

Shimoda was one of those who pointed out the negative aspects of the free drawing movement in its early stage. Shimoda (1920) recognized the importance of development of the children's own creativity as proposed by Yamamoto. He also agreed with Yamamoto's view that copy work in formal drawing education was harmful to pupils. However, he had two objections to Yamamoto's approach. One was that Yamamoto limited the content of a drawing curriculum to painting only as a fine art. The other was Yamamoto's indifference to the teacher's role in helping students learn to make art. Shimoda insisted that the content of drawing curriculum should include such areas as applied arts and the appreciation of beauty. He also stated that the teacher's own invention was important in all forms of education.

Thus, Shimoda's rationale for an art curriculum was broader than Yamamoto's. His orientation to drawing education was eclectic. He believed that drawing education ought to aim not only at developing children's creativity, but also at cultivating their social and cultural awareness. According to Shimoda, the content of fine arts was especially suitable for the development of children's creativity. The content of applied arts such as two-dimensional design was most appropriate for developing pupils' visual perceptions. The teaching of art appreciation was an important aspect of the art curriculum, supporting and promoting children's fine and applied art activities. Children's expression, socialization, and appreciation of beauty would be developed through their understanding of art (Shimoda, 1920).

Shimoda took the broad approach to curriculum development while Yamamoto's approach was narrow and more in depth. The difference between Shimoda and Yamamoto may have come from their individual backgrounds in higher education. Both graduated from the Tokyo Fine Arts School, but their majors were not the same. Yamamoto received training as an artist while Shimoda received pre-service training as a secondary school art teacher.

Yamamoto spent ten-years as an apprentice of Western-style wood engraving in his teens, and entered the European Painting Program of the Tokyo Fine Arts School in 1902. The program required four years and consisted of several subjects, including the practice of drawing and oil painting (30 hours per week), anatomy, perspective, aesthetics and history of fine arts, archeology, and English or French

(Ministry of Education, 1910a). Yamamoto graduated in 1906 when he had already became a famous woodblock printer in Japan.

Shimoda, after graduating from secondary school, entered the Normal Program of Drawing of the Tokyo Fine Arts School in 1909. The Government set up the normal program in 1907 "for the special purpose of training teachers for secondary schools" (Kikuchi, 1909, p. 300). Requiring three years of study, the curriculum consisted of pedagogy and the method of teaching, aesthetics and the history of fine arts, anatomy, designing, freehand drawing, mechanical drawing, handicrafts, handwriting, English, and student-teaching practices.

The directives of the Ministry of Education at that time stated that the "normal course [program] of drawing has for its object the training of teachers of drawing for ... general education," and that the "students of this course [program] should be possessed not only of artistic powers, but of the knowledge and character essential to educators" (Ministry of Education, 1910a, p. 18). After his graduation from the school in 1912, Shimoda became an art teacher at a high school for women in Kumamoto Prefecture, in the most south-western area of Japan.

Shimoda came back to Tokyo in 1913 because of his becoming tuberculosis. He had done two Japanese translations of American sources. One was *The Principles of Art Education* by Münsterberg (1904) and the other *Art Education* by Bailey (1914). In 1918 he became an art teacher in Saitama Prefectural Normal School for Women in Saitama, twenty miles north of Tokyo.

In spite of differences in their training in higher education, Yamamoto and Shimoda's intentions were similar. They both tried to integrate the two separate subjects, drawing and manual arts, into a single subject, art within the elementary school curriculum. They intended to change attitudes of Japanese art educators from the limited view of industrial drawing toward the more modernized concept of art.

In the opening decade of the 20th century, the Ministry of Education stated that students in grades one through four should receive lessons in drawing (one hour per week). The amount of lesson time increased to two hours per week in grades five and six. Students in grades one through three could receive lessons in manual arts (one hour per week) if their school included it as an elective subject. The lesson time increased to two hours per week in grades four through six (Keenleyside and Thomas, 1937).

The Ministry of Education stated the purposes of drawing and manual arts in the elementary educational ordinance of the early opening decade of the 20th century. Drawing aimed "to cultivate in children the faculty of perceiving clearly and drawing correctly ordinary objects, and to foster the sense of beautiful" (Kikuchi, 1909, p. 186). In contrast, the manual arts aimed at training children in "habits of accurate observation, attention to detail, method and order, economy and utilization [sic], perseverance, industry, and self-control" (Kikuchi, 1909, p. 190).

The Ministry of Education (1910b) issued *Shintei Gacho* (*New Textbooks of Drawing*), and required that they serve as the only national textbook until 1931, but no national textbook for manual arts was issued. The content of this set of drawing textbooks included drawing, painting, color theory, composition, decoration, and design. Although these books were the first modernized series in the history of Japanese art education, the old view of drawing for industrial use remained. Yamamoto and Shimoda both had good support for developing their own art programs.

Yamamoto became a part-time art specialist at Jiyu Gakuen (School) in 1921. Shimoda became the full-time art specialist at Myojo Gakuen (School) in 1925. These two schools were elementary private schools, and were set up for implementing the theory of the new education movement into actual practice. Yamamoto and Shimoda individually began to make efforts to develop their own art programs in the middle of the 1920s.

Yamamoto's Art Program

Yamamoto did not define the aims and content of an art program until 1923. He stated that the three aims of his program were creating contemporary art, understanding art through various resources from daily life for creating works, and cultivating visual perception. The content of his program consisted of three main domains. The first was drawing and painting human figures, animals, still-life, landscapes, and building. The second was making ornaments and crafts for table cloths, window curtains, and cushions. The last domain was art appreciation and art criticism through critical discussion, visiting museums, and teaching the history and theory of art (Kaneko, 1980, 1992).

Yamamoto's program did not exclude other two-dimensional modes of expressions such as printmaking and graphic design. He gave no consideration to the three-dimensional modes of constructions (sculpture, pottery, and product design with various materials) in his art program. Thus, the two separate subjects, drawing and manual arts, were integrated into a single subject—art within the elementary school curriculum (Hashimoto, 1980). However, he did not develop a sequential art curriculum. Perhaps, if Yamamoto had received training as an art educator, he might have produced sequential, grade-by-grade art lesson plans.

Shimoda's Art Program
In contrast, Shimoda was successful in building a comprehensive art program. He made the first step in 1923, when he left Saitama Prefectural Normal School for Women, and took a post as a full-time art teacher in Seijo Secondary School in Tokyo. This school was connected to the Seijo Primary School, which had been set up for implementing the theory of the new education movement into practice.

In his 1923 article Shimoda expressed his idea of integrating the two subjects of drawing and manual arts into art as a single subject. In the context of visual arts, drawing education dealt with two-dimensional expression while manual arts was concerned with three-dimensional expression. He stated that an art program should consist of five major domains: painting, design, working drawing and handicrafts, sculpture, and art appreciation.

Shimoda used the ideals of the British "arts-and-craft movement" to justify the design domain of his art program. According to Efland (1990), the writings of John Ruskin and William Morris spurred the arts-and-craft movement in the 1880s in England. "The four principles of the movement were *regard for the material, regard for the use, regard for construction*, and finally, *regard for the tool*" (p. 152). The impact of the movement in the United States was seen in the publication of the *Applied Arts Books* (now *School Arts*) in 1901.

Shimoda's idea of art appreciation came from America. "American children are learning to perceive and respond to masterpieces of painting. They are exchanging their own views with other students and with their teacher. American art educators call such lessons Picture Study" (Shimoda, 1923, p. 61). Indeed, Stankiewicz (1984) describes the movement known as Picture Study. In the United States, "Lasting from 1895 through the 1920s, picture study sought to develop appreciation of fine art among school children" (p. 86). Advocates of such study "favored using these photomechanically produced halftone reproductions" (p. 86) of works of art. Shimoda's approach to art appreciation was similar to the American idea: "Appreciation of the aesthetic qualities of art was the avowed goal of picture study" (Stankiewicz, 1984, p. 86).

At the end of one of Shimoda's articles (1923) he cited an approach embraced by Pedro J. Lemos, "The best teaching is that which results in fitting the student to study intelligently without a teacher."[1] This goal became the aim of Shimoda's art program.

Shimoda made the next step in developing his art program in 1925. He developed sequential lessons of art for grades one to six within each of the five domains, created instructional materials, and experimented with them in his classroom at the Myojo Gakuen (School). His art program appears in the second part of his book (1926), *Shin Kyoiku ni Rikyaku Seru Zuga Syukou Kyoju no Jissai* (*Teaching Drawing and Manual Arts in New Education*). This book has three parts: Theory of Art Education, Practice of Art Education, and Art Appreciation. In the frontispiece of the book, Shimoda again quoted Lemos. Shimoda noted that Lemos' book (1920) was most useful in defining the scope and sequence of his art curriculum.

The aims of his art curriculum were as follows. First grade students learn to create art imaginatively and to express their ideas through their own work. Second grade students learn to create art with aesthetic unity and to perceive the qualities of their work. Third grade students study to create representative work and to understand their work as art. Fourth grade students continue to create works through the representative mode and learn to work in their own way. Fifth grade students learn the skill for representing various objects and perceive the aesthetic qualities of art work. Sixth grade students learn to create their original work through their artistic imagination and to appreciate the meaning of art.

Shimoda's art program consisted of five major domains: painting, sculpture, design, crafts, and art appreciation. The two domains of working drawing and handicrafts in Shimoda's earlier plan of 1923 were joined under the crafts domain. On the productive areas of the first four domains, Shimoda developed about thirty-three lessons in each grade. Among them, on average, fifteen lessons were devoted to drawing, painting, and color mixing, eight lessons concerned designing, five lessons dealt with making crafts, and five lessons had to do with sculpture.

Every lesson had a topic or theme. For example, the painting domain in first grade included various themes of expression. These included my pets, our teacher, our family, our school, airplanes, automobiles, trains, nursery tales, and naming colors of crayons. The themes in the sixth grade included landscape, flowers, still-life, human figures, geometrical cubes, glassware, plaster models, and color hues.

Art supplies were also listed in each domain of all grades. The painting domain in first grade required such materials as pencils, crayons, and white drawing paper. Sixth grade students needed pencils, watercolor paints, and white drawing paper. Unfortunately, descriptions of such areas as preparation, goals, teachers' activities, students' activities, and evaluation procedures were not included in the lesson plans in his book.

In developing sequential lessons on productive domains, Shimoda referred to seven instructional resources. Five of them were from the United States, and two from Japan. The content and sequence of art curriculum in each of the five American models appear in the first part of his book. The first American resource mentioned was the course of study of Los Angeles City included in Farnum's report (1914, pp. 172-174). Illustrative drawings, drawing from a posed model, landscape painting, still life drawing, nature study drawings, design, color study, and picture study were the main content areas.

The second American resource was the program of manual arts of Horace Mann School, Teachers College, New York (n.d.). The content included work in clay, fabric work, wood work, paper work, and graphics. Third was *The Industrial Art Text Books* (1915) by Snow and Froehlich, including design and color, commercial design (lettering design), costume design, interior decoration, domestic art, constructive design, object drawing, and nature drawing. Fourth was *Theory and Practice of Teaching Art* (1912) by Dow. Contents included line, dark-and-light, and color. The fifth American resource was *Applied Art* (1920) by Lemos, which included coloring, painting, design, and manual arts.

One of the two Japanese resources was the art program of the Laboratory Elementary School of Tokyo Higher Normal School in the 1920s. The other was one produced at Seijo Primary School. These two Japanese programs divided the content of art into painting, design, and manual arts as did Lemos' program.

The sequential lessons of art appreciation Shimoda developed also appear in the third part of his book. Students in each grade received three or four lessons on appreciation of works of art through black and white reproductions of masterpieces by European painters such as Leonard da Vinci, Raphael, Michelangelo, Turner, Millet, Whistler, and Cézanne, and by Japanese painters such as Sesshu and Hirosige. Each masterpiece Shimoda listed had a brief description about its character and artist's life, but did not have a lesson plan. He only provided general methodology for teaching art appreciation, such as comparison and explanation of works of art.

However, Shimoda provided one lesson plan in the first grade on Millet's *Feeding Her Birds* as an example of how to teach art appreciation. The description consists of question/answer activity, a story of the picture, the artist's life, looking at the picture, and teaching notes. The lesson plan by Shimoda was based on Carpenter's description of *Feeding Her Birds* (1918, pp. 1-9). Hurll showed the plate of *Feeding Her Birds* on her article appearing in the April 1916 issue of *School Arts Book*. She describes the picture: "The peasant mother has to work in the fields and no time to make pretty clothing for children, no time to spread a dainty table for their noonday meal. But the children seem to be equally fond of each other" (p. 480).

In developing instructional curriculum materials in Shimoda's appreciation program, he listed three main references from American art education literature. They were *How to Show Pictures to Children* (1914) by Hurll, *Stories Picture Tell* (1919) by Carpenter, and *Art in the School* (1924) by Boas.

The Legacies of Yamamoto and Shimoda

Yamamoto's leadership only lasted for the decade of the 1920s. He devoted his remaining life to being an artist. He was an outstanding contributor to the development of the Japanese modernist print. One of his landmark works of art, *Breton Girl* (1918), is included in the Honolulu Academy of Arts collection. According to Sullivan (1965), Yamamoto's early woodcuts, notably *Breton Girl*, "set the printmakers free from their bondage to tradition and pointed the way to new naturalism" (p. 292). In the Volume 5 of *the McGraw-Hill Dictionary of Art* (1969) it says that:

he was one of the leaders of the movement to revolutionize the traditional method of making Japanese wood-block prints so that the entire process would be conducted by the designer himself. (p. 545)

Munsterberg (1982) points out that:

Yamamoto ... had made his first creative print as early as 1904. After a very promising beginning, during which he made prints under the influence of European artists like Gauguin, he turned to other pursuits. (p. 163)

Shimoda's influence on the innovation of art curriculum also only lasted for the decade of the 1920s. He devoted the latter half of his life to being both a scholar of psychoanalysis and a practitioner of self-analysis techniques. He published more than seventy books, including translations, during his life time. Most of these books dealt with psychoanalysis while works on art education were rather few. More than twenty of his original works and translations are still in print. They include *Jiko Bunseki* (Self- Analysis), *Jido no Seisin Bunseki Nyumon* (*Introduction to Psychoanalysis of Children*), and *Jido-ga no Sinri to Kyoiku* (*Psychology of Children's Painting and Education*). The Japanese can also read A. S. Neill's *Summerhill* (1960) and ten other of Neill's works through Shimoda's translations. In 1968 he was awarded the Japanese Translator Prize for his translations of Neill's works.

Yamamoto and Shimoda opened a few windows on the territory of Japanese art education in the 1920s. The realization of their inventiveness needed time. Drawing and manual arts within school curricula were combined, and "art and handicraft" became a single subject and established in the national guidelines for elementary and secondary schools in 1947. The Ministry of Education replaced "art and handicraft" with "fine arts" in secondary schools in the late 1950s.

Shimoda died in 1973. In his letter to Mrs. Shimoda, Neill expressed his deep regrets for her husband's loss: "I shall send you all my sympathies and sorrow. I am sure that in the history of education his name will be high up in the list of reformers. A bright light has gone out in the dark world, but his work will live long after him" (1973, p. 1).

The 1968 revision of Japanese national guidelines of art education (grades 1-6) reflected Shimoda's 1926 inventiveness. The guidelines indicated that art programs should consist of five major areas: painting, sculpture, design, craft, and art appreciation. The realization of his inventiveness took more than forty years (Okazaki, 1992).

Yamamoto passed away in 1946. With Yamamoto, Japanese art educators recognized that art teachers should encourage their students to create their own style or mode of artistic expression. Indeed, he was the first modernist in Japanese art education. His ideas were extended in the 1950s by those he had helped towards an understanding of modernism thirty years earlier. They began the Creative Art Education Movement, of which Shimoda (1959b) has written that it "advocates letting pupils develop their creative power by releasing them from repressions and also by ... [featuring] their free expression" (p. 230).

His methodology of painting out-of-doors like the French Impressionists continues to the present and gains in popularity. Carson (1981) reports: "At zoo[s] and in the parks in Japan one can see swarms of children with their teachers, painting and drawing. Children's art work is everywhere in public places, even in the underground walkways under the main thoroughfares in Kobe, a large city of a million people" (p. 43).

In Closing

The legacies of both Yamamoto and Shimoda can still be found in current Japanese art education practice. It is true that "the national respect for regulation, and imported concepts of individual creativity, in effect counterbalance one another in dynamic tension" (Thistlewood, 1991, p. 128). Yamamoto and Shimoda can be praised for providing the early counterbalance to state-controlled policy of art education in the history of modern Japanese art education.

Both Yamamoto and Shimoda gave elementary school classroom teachers the freedom to develop their own curricula for the students they teach. They made Japanese art educators perceive the necessity of using their energies and inventiveness for the future of art education through the "internal mode" of curriculum development in art education.

There have since been many such counterbalances, including accounts which offer an alternative to the official history developed by the Ministry of Education. If there are teachers who are satisfied with the national guidelines but cannot follow them as "a score or script as a musician or an actor follows scores or scripts" (Eisner, 1981, p. 121), they attempt to create new subject matter for a curricula and new methods for teaching without ready-made content given in textbooks they employ (Okazaki, 1985b). Western ideas on art and art education will support their energies and inventiveness for the future Japanese art education (Okazaki, 1984).

In closing, Stanly-Baker (1984) sums up Japanese art best with an oceanic analogy:

> Japanese culture in general may be likened to an oyster, opening itself up to repeated onslaughts from the ocean and transforming grains of continental grit into pearls. ... In the absence of indigenous traditions and without artistic importations from abroad, throughout Japanese history, there would have been no idea to work on, and no Japanese art at all. (pp. 7-8).

Without diverse influences as grains of grit, no country has its inherent cultural values in art as pearls. MacGregor (1994) explains this oceanic analogy more clearly: "Wherever we teach, we can be sure that our programs reflect an amalgam of traditional and imported ideas" (p. 5). Diverse influences from other cultures provide a prime field of multicultural art education (Okazaki, 1995b; Kaneda, 1994; Mason, 1994).

Notes

1. I can find the notion in the back endpaper of its book (1920). Lemos is a forgotten man in the history of American art education. Efland (1990) does not mention Lemos' work. However, Winslow (1928) suggested Lemos' book as a reference book for an elementary course of study. Logan (1955) said that Lemos had succeeded Bailey as the second editor of the *School Arts Books* in 1919, but actually he was the third editor of the magazine. Lemos was also the director of the Stanford University Museum of Fine Arts (Lemos, 1939).

Chapter 8 Originally published in the *Proceedings from the 30th InSEA World Congress*, 1999. Reprinted with permission by Art Education Australia (formerly known as Australian Institute of Art Education). Reprinted from ERIC database (ED 451 089).

Dow's Conception of Teaching Art: "Harmonious Composition" and "Notan"

Fig. 8.1 Japanese ink painting by Sesshu (Dow, 1913, p. 97).

Fig. 8.2 *An Ipswich Hill*, ink painting by Arthur Wesley Dow (Dow, 1913, p. 98).

* Figures are not included in the originally published paper.

"Bi-Cultural Education/Cross-Cultural Research" has become one of the central multicultural education conceptions in the field of art education (Tomhave, 1992). Japan and the United States are separated by a vast ocean, though this ocean is also a bridge by which Eastern and Western worlds encounter each other and become integrated into one (Okazaki, 1984, 1985b, 1991, 1995b). Japanese art educators, such as Shirahama (Okazaki, 1985a) and Shimoda (Okazaki, 1992, 1994b), compared American and Japanese ideas in the earlier decades of the 20th century. An American art educator, Arthur Wesley Dow (1899/1913), similarly synthesized Japanese and American culture in his philosophy of art education. He turned toward the Japanese way of thinking, and found something that American art education lacked.

This chapter portrays the process of cross-cultural interpretation as a way of making sense of one's world in relation to those of others. While American researchers (deLemos, 1946; Mock-Morgan, 1976; Moffatt, 1977; Hook, 1987) provide their own interpretations of Dow's legacy, I attempt to explain his legacy in terms of the Oriental cultural tradition of art. It is because his ideas were "derived from his views regarding the nature of art rather than from a particular conception of children's artistic development" (Efland, 1976, pp. 68-69), that a multicultural heritage of art education is exemplified in Dow's interest in Oriental art (Smith, 1994).

Dow's Contribution to American Art Education

Researchers concerned with American art education history cannot help but deal with Arthur Wesley Dow's significant contribution to the field, if they want to provide a general perspective on historical development in the field. Many writers, in fact, pointed out Dow's great contribution in the earlier decades of the 20th century in the United States. In assessing Dow's historical role in the development of American art education, there are at least two alternative ways of looking at his enormous influence on art education.

Should he be regarded as a pioneer of aesthetic appreciation or as a pioneer of modern design education? Although both ways of interpreting Dow's work are possible (Efland, 1990), it is certain that the first way was more emphasized at the heart of his doctrine. "Dow felt that this appreciation motivated some people to create works of art and most people to desire more beauty in their environment," whereas "he advanced practice in design or composition as a means of developing this appreciation" (Lanier, 1964, pp. 31-32).

Hurwitz and Madeja (1977) pointed out Dow's intention in the context of art appreciation. Differentiating Dow's conception of art appreciation from that of the so-called "Picture Study Movement" at the turn of the 20th century, they say:

Dow lent a different tone to the movement. Dow gave teachers a set of principles of composition (developed from his study of Japanese art) that provided a readily grasped vocabulary of form that could be applied to any picture and that could thus serve as the criterion for the success or failure of a work. His basic principles of pictorial structure were line; notan, or value; and a regard for the full spectrum of color. (pp. 22-24)

What they called "basic principles" are actually what Dow termed the three elements. Eisner and Ecker (1966) illustrated that these elements were indispensable for constructing "an art product that displayed harmony and beauty": line which referred to "the contour of drawing objects, value to light and dark, and color to the hues incorporated in the picture" (p. 6). For creating harmony in composition the following five principles were to be employed: opposition, transition, subordination, repetition, and symmetry.

Dow is one of the American art educators whose work in the field of art education was influenced by Japanese traditional works of art. He got information on Japanese art through Fenollosa. Munsterberg (1957) describes that Fenollosa came to Tokyo in 1878 as a professor of political philosophy at Tokyo Imperial University, and that he stimulated "interest in the ancient art of Japan at a time when Japanese intelligentsia were rejecting the art of their country as unfit for the modern age" (p. 174).

Marry Fenollosa (1913) indicated the interaction between Dow and Fenollosa in brief preface to her husband's book, *Epochs of Chinese and Japanese Art*. She mentioned that "the classes which had graduated at the Pratt Institute under the Fenollosa-Dow system, as it is often called, were applying its principles in smaller towns all over the Union" (p. xxi). In fact, there can be found a surprising similarity between Fenollosa and Dow. "Qualities of line, notan, and colour, and the use of these in expressing great ideas," noted Fenollosa (1913), "are made the basis of classification and of appreciation" (pp. xxv-xxvi) of art. This notion corresponds closely to the first chapter titled "Line-Notan-Color" of Dow's book (1913).

Chinese Foundation of Dow's Composition

It is possible to interpret Dow's idea of harmonious composition in both Maritain and Okakura's views of the Oriental art. Chinese "Art," says Maritain (1954/1974), "is a contemplative effort to discover in Things and bring out from Things their own enlarged soul and inner principle of dynamic harmony" (p. 13). He also regards the spirit of Things as "a kind of ghost." It comes down from "the spirit of the universe" and gives Things "their typical form of life and movement" (p. 13). In this view of Chinese art work, Nature and Things are perceived not as hostile to people but as a pantheistic continuum that people might become an integral part of, through artistic and poetic intuition.

Okakura (1903/1970), a Japanese scholar of art, also finds "The Life-movement of Spirit through the Rhythm of Things" in Eastern art. He says that Oriental art can be conceived of as "the great Mood of the Universe, moving hither and thither amidst those harmonic laws of matter which are Rhythm" (p. 52). Both describe the first of six canons or principles of old Chinese painting theory, which was first set forth by Hsieh Ho at the end of the fifth century in China in his book entitled the *Ku-hua p'in-lu* (*Koga Hinroku* in Japanese) [Old Records of Classification of Paintings]. Let us examine his first canon called "ch'i-yun sheng-tung" ("ki-in sei-do" in Japanese), the most important of the six, which is necessary for understanding Dow's idea of harmonious composition.

There are generally three materials available in English dealing with Hsieh Ho's canon of painting. The first one is Chinese scholar, Chan's article (1946/1965). In his description of "ch'i yun sheng tung," Chan renders the four Chinese words as follows: "ch'i" as force, spirit, breath, or soul; "yun" as resonance, rhythm, charm, feeling, or verbalization; "sheng" as life, or the will to live; and "tung" as movement. Although these four words may be, according to Chan, "taken in pairs as ch'i yun or spiritual resonance and sheng tung or life movement" (p. 183), the phrase "ch'in-yun sheng-tung" means the nature of things, the principle according to which things possess, strong power, style and charm, the soul and mystery of things, sprit, life force, and so forth.

The second material is by Young (1969). He sums up Hsieh Ho's six canons as follows: (1) animate through spirit consonance; (2) follow the "bone method" in the use of the brush; (3) be truthful to the objects in depicting forms; (4) conform to kind in setting forth colors; (5) divide and plan in positioning and arranging; and (6) convey the past by copying and transcribing. Following this description, Young (1969) writes about the first canon: "sheng-tung is usually rendered literally as something like 'life movement,' while chi'i yun has the more mystical ring of 'spirit consonance'" (p. 191). Thus "Paintings that have the capacity to move the observer, to come alive with that special rhythmic vitality or resonance, were said to process ch'i-yun" (p. 191).The whole "range of intangible aesthetic qualities associated with the spirit and life of a great work of art is evoked in ch'i-yun sheng-tung" (p. 191). It implies "a qualitative measure or standard, something desirable but not always present in a given painting" (p. 191).

Although Hsieh Ho's first canon can be translated into English by various ways, it is conceived in any case as a qualitative measure that is concerned with spiritual essence and rhythmic vitality. Among the four words of "ch'i-yun sheng-tung," "ch'i" is a more key concept than the others. The meaning of "ch'i" is thirdly explored by Sullivan, a British scholar of Chinese art history. Sullivan (1965) summarizes Hsieh Ho's canon as follows: (1) spirit consonance and life-motion; (2) the bone method in the use of brush; (3) conformity to the object to give likeness; (4) correct color; (5) care in composition; and (6) transmission of tradition by making copies. He interprets "ch'i" as "an energy or spirit" that "gives life to all things" such as human figures, animals, birds, flowers, mountains, water, trees, rocks, and so on, and to which the painters must attune themselves so as to be able to impart this life to their paintings. As a result, "all painters and critics throughout Chinese history have held that this mysterious energy, whether external or internal, or both, is the essential quality" (p. 13).

The word "ch'i" expresses the essential quality, mysterious energy, or spirit. It has also been a significant concept in both China and Japan. For Chinese painters to express "the ch'i of a tree," for instance, they "must express the tree-nature, its structure, its peacefulness, and above all, the rhythmic vital force which gives it spirit and form" (Chan, 1946/1965, p. 183). The fact that one could find the rhythmic vitality of "ch'i" in such various things as nature, movement, force, creative power, and so on, is the same as with the Japanese traditional-style painter whose canons, as well as methods of painting, have been borrowed mostly from Chinese painting.

One example is Yasunobu Kano (1613-1685). He was president of *Edokoro* (Academy of Painting) of the Tokugawa Shogunate, succeeded to the main stock of the Kano family, and founded the Kano school. He wrote a book about the theory of painting entitled, *Gado Yoketsu* (*A Key to the Way of Painting*) in 1680. The first section of his book suggests that the basic purpose of painting is "the grasp of mysterious energy of ki-in [ch'i-yun]" (Kano, cited in Sakazaki, 1942, p. 8).

Another example is Mitsuoki Tosa (1617-1691). He was the chief of the office of painters in the Imperial Court. He created a new style of painting that added the brushwork technique to the style of the Tosa School. He also produced a book about theory and practice of painting entitled *Honcho Gaho Taiden* (*A Comprehensive History of Japanese Painting*) in 1690. The first section of the book provides a description of Hsieh Ho's six canons. He said that "ki" (ch'i) was regarded as "a reflection of living-creature's mind" (Tosa, cited in Sakazaki, 1942, pp. 31-32). Kano and Tosa both emphasized "ki" (ch'i) as a basic key to painting. Evidently Japanese traditional painters were not only influenced by the Chinese theory of painting, but also more than a thousand of years later, they had still echoes of Hsieh Ho's basic key to painting.

Together with the "ch'i-yun sheng-tung," Hsieh Ho's second canon is valued more than the remaining four in order to accomplish the transmission of this mysterious and spiritual energy to paper or silk. The first two words of his second canon are "ku-fa" (ko-po in Japanese). Although it can be directly translated as "bone method" in English, its meaning is actually "structural strength of the brushstroke, common to painting and calligraphy" (Sullivan, 1965, p. 13). Young (1969) regards the "ku-fa" as "strength and vigor in the handling of the brush" (p. 191). The individual brushstroke becomes the measure of the painting. The third, fourth, fifth, and sixth of Hsieh Ho's canons are not different from, but close to the Western criteria of painting. These four canons, however, are less valued than the first and second ones.

Maritain (1974) describes the primary intent of Chinese art as follows:

> What does the first of the famous six canons of Hsieh Ho prescribe? —To have life-motion manifest the unique spiritual resonance that artist catches in Things, inspired as he is by his communion with the spirit of the cosmos. The second canon is no less significant. If the brush strokes which render bone structure have primacy among all means of execution, to the point of making painting, so to speak, a branch of calligraphy, it is because the very vigor and alertness of these touches (together with the quality of the ink tones) express the movement of life perceived in things and its structural harmony (and they are, at the same time, a token of value of the artist's inspiration). (pp. 13-14)

For this reason, Hsieh Ho's first and second canons reveal what Maritain (1974) called "the creative subjectivity of the artist" in which the "more the poetic perception which animates art catches and manifests the inner side of Things, the more it involves at the same time a disclosure and manifestation of the human Self" (p. 17). He further says that the creative subjectivity can be found in Greek art: "Man," privileged figure though he may be, "remains an object in Nature and a Thing in the cosmos, subordinate to the perfection and divinity of the universality of Things" (p. 19).

Meeson (1981), based on Maritain's assumption above, points out the commonality of Greek and Oriental art with contemporary art. Both Minimal and Conceptual art reflect on "a shift of artistic alignment towards the characteristics of Greek and oriental art, such as Maritain describes, pointing towards change in the artist's relationship with the world around him" (p. 30). He also suggests that contemporary art might be understood by returning to the idea of intuition in art. There are at least two intuitional aspects in art. One is art as Things, and the other is the artistic process as imagination, where "the free play of ideas has yet to find a definitive form" (p. 30). Thus, we have a spiritual or intuitive approach to regenerating the characteristics of Things and Nature. This approach is essentially different from the representative and symbolic way of art, particularly in the instrumental view of art in both social and religious function (Binyon, 1911).

Instead of the representative and symbolic function of art, Dow took the spiritual approach to art in education even if he could not have used such terms as spirit consonance and spiritual resonance in his time. Dow's term "Composition" means not so much as Hsieh Ho's fifth canon, "divide and plan in positioning and arranging," as his first one, "ch'i-yun sheng-tung," particularly "ch'i" as "inner principles of dynamic harmony" or "mysterious energy."

Dow (1913) proposes that principle of composition is a "Way of creating harmony." Dow also suggests, "first cultivate the mind of students and next utilize the power" they have, such as the "power to appreciate," the "power to do something worthwhile" (p. 120). This indicates that he learned the spiritual way of art from Chinese painting through his research on Japanese art. Chang wrote a book about Chinese painters, *Li-tai Ming-hua Chi (Record of Famous Painters of all Dynasties)* in 847. In discussing the six canons of Hsieh Ho, Chang (847/1977) sees the task of Chinese painting as achieving "something more than representation" as indicated by Hsieh Ho's third and fourth canons. He says, moreover, that if a painter focused on "ch'i-yun as an essential element" in working at his art then the representation prescribed in the third and fourth canons would be naturally inherent in his/her work.

Dow's contribution lay not in altering teaching method, but in broadening the concept of art by substituting "composition" for mechanical imitation (Macdonald, 1970). Logan (1955) writes that at the time of Dow's working, the "academic mind did not recognize any value in individual use of design or color; those qualities were only incidental to a work of art. Opposed to this view, Fenollosa believed that beauty, not realism, was the true aim of art, and Dow's philosophy started with composition as the essence of beauty" (p. 110).

We should not emphasize both the modern design element and the formality of beauty in Dow's idea of composition. The underlying intention in his book, *Composition*, is to reveal the "source of power" and to show "the student how to look within for the greatest help." It also is to teach him "not to depend on externals, not to lean too much on anything or anybody" (Dow, 1913, p. 128). We should reinterpret Dow's intention in revealing the source of power as the Chinese term "ch'i." Its power discloses the qualitative wholeness in art through which the "inner world of feeling is given substance and form" (Meeson, 1982, p. 21).

Japanese Foundation of Dow's *Notan*

I have pointed out how Dow's philosophical transition from representation to spiritualism was rooted in Hsieh Ho's first canon of "ch'i," whether he knew the old root of Chinese painting or not. A problem still remains among the proposals including his book, *Composition*. Are there any reasons why Dow emphasized the concept of notan (dark-and-light), the second element in his synthetic method of teaching art? He devoted half a page of his book to identifying and defining its conception. It is easy to understand why Dow defined the concept of line as the first element of teaching art. Chinese traditional ink-painting has emphasized lines.

Okakura (1903/1970) describes the lack of dark and light in old Chinese paintings at the time of Hsieh Ho. Line takes "the place of nerves and arteries, and the whole is covered with the skin of colour" so that Hsieh Ho "ignores the question of dark and light" (p. 52). He also says that all paintings at that time were made by "covering the ground with white line and laying upon this the rock-pigments, which were accentuated and marked off from each other with strong black lines" (p. 53).

The concept of *notan* did not come from Chinese traditional painting, but has been borrowed from Japanese art. The first edition of Dow's *Composition* includes illustrations, all of which were from Japanese traditional brush drawing. Three American and British researchers refer to the concept of notan. First, Logan (1955) defines its meaning as describing "value, or dark and light" (p. 110). Second, Wilson (1974) regards it as "describing the contrast of light and dark" (p. 258). Lastly, Macdonald (1970) says much the same thing. "Notan, so dominant in Japanese art, is the balance of light and dark areas, a different concept from representation of natural light and shades as understood by nineteenth-century teachers" (p. 348).

Their interpretations of the Japanese term *notan* are worried about the use of this strange Japanese word for Westerner. I think Macdonald's definition is closer to Dow's intention in adopting the Japanese word *notan*. The original Japanese word *notan* actually consists of two Chinese words: "*no*" and "*tan*." The former means degrees such as depth, darkness, thickness, concentration, strength, or density. The latter has the meanings of light, faint, pale, fleeting, or transitory. Thus, *notan* means the degree or gradation of subtle tone, excluding pure white and black, by which subjective feelings are represented and fused together.

What *notan* expresses is aesthetic awareness of tone sensibility. It is not mechanically or systematically structured but subjectively organized in a state of composing or fusing light and dark on the surface of a drawing. Saunders (1966) provides a closer description to the real meaning of the word *notan* than Macdonald does. In citing Dow's revised 13th edition of *Composition* (1929), Saunders (1966) writes:

By NOTAN, he [Dow] meant the light and dark balance of the object, whether it was a building, a picture, or nature. He distinguished between light and dark here and light and shadow that he considered a single fact of external nature. Notan is not just black and light and white (a two value system) but includes gray in a three-value system or degree of gray in a more than three-value system. (p. 9)

In the 1913 version of Dow's *Composition*, Dow makes a careful distinction between *notan* as "an element of universal beauty" and light and shadow as "a single fact of external nature" (p. 8). He puts forth justifications for his belief: "Notan, a Japanese word meaning 'dark, light,' refers to the quantity of light reflected, or the massing of tones of different values"; and "Notan-beauty means the harmony resulting from the combination of dark and light space—whether colored or not—

whether in building, in picture, or in nature" (p. 7). It is clear that Dow used the term *notan* in the broadest sense possible. The term *notan* means much more than the term "value" as an element of modern design in the German Bauhaus system of design education. He carefully added two hyphens to translate *notan*: "Dark-and-Light."

Dow (1913) regards painting as visual music. The quality of making the natural scene a good subject for a picture is "the 'visual music' that the Japanese so love in [the] rough ink painting of their masters where there is but a hint of facts" (p. 54). He also suggests that to recognize *notan* as an individual element will simplify "the difficulty of tone-composition and open the way for growth in power" (p. 54).

The idea of visual music was borrowed from Fenollosa. He contributed to the regeneration of fourteenth century Japanese ink-painting style during his stay in Japan (Munsterberg, 1957). His major influence on Dow is the teaching of Chinese and Japanese ink painting style, "sumi-e." It is a typical art form of painting various subjects (figures, flowers-birds, and landscape) using "sumi" (black Indian ink) with *notan* by means of special brush strokes. First developed in China during the middle of T'ang Dynasty (618-906) and expanded in the Northern and Southern Schools in the Sung Dynasty (906-1279), "sumi-e" was incorporated into Japanese art during the Kamakura Period (1192-1333).

As a result, the Chinese ink-painting style was modified. It became more fashionably sophisticated during the Muromachi Period (1338-1573). Sesshu (1420-1506), a priest-artist, went to Ming China (1368-1644), where he studied the technique of Chinese painting. He finally established his unique style of ink-painting after coming back to Japan. Thus "sumi-e" is not a Japanese style of painting but a modification of a Chinese style. Color was added to "sumi-e" in the latter half of the sixteenth century in Japan. This became the official painting style of Tokugawa Shogunate, Kano School, in the Edo Period (1603-1867).

Such a story of Chinese and Japanese interactive development in the history of painting explains why Dow placed the three element of line, *notan*, and color in his synthetic method of teaching art. The Meiji Period (1867-1912) of Japan was the time of modernizing Japanese society and culture. Okakura, a Japanese philosopher of art, contributed to the regeneration of the traditional style of Japanese art, with support from Fenollosa. He (1903/1970) refers to the line-notan-color mode of Chinese and Japanese painting:

> European [art] work ... has lost greatly ... structural composition and line expression, though it has added to the facility of realistic representation. The idea of line and line-composition has always been the great strength of Chinese and Japanese art, though the Sung and Ashikaga [Muromachi] artists have added the beauty of dark and light [notan]—without forgetting that the artistic, and not the scientific, was their goal—and the Toyotomi epoch [the late sixteenth century of Japan] has contributed the notion of composing in colour. (p. 54)

Okakura's description confirms an assumption that Dow's line-notan-color context of synthetic art instruction was fully justified not by European art but by Chinese and Japanese art. His notion also includes another important point. The characteristics of dark and light (*notan*) are artistic, not scientific. The artistic character of *notan* has come from the interaction of ink, paper, and water through brush strokes. Yashiro (1969) called it "a sense of stained quality," which contributes to various aspects of Japanese art. He concludes that an artist engaging in the work of ink-painting would experience a complete transformation of his/her attitudes towards art from representatism to spiritualism.

In an effort to philosophically generalize the specific term *notan*, Dow (1913) termed it an essential quality. It needs to integrate "dark and light space," to construct "tone-composition," and to build up "harmony." He valued the importance of "Notan-beauty" much more than line and color because half of his book *Composition* is devoted to an explanation of the term *notan*. Dow says the fundamental fact that synthetically related masses of dark and light convey an impression of beauty, which is entirely independent of the categorical meaning, but dependent on the aesthetic and qualitative response to a hint of facts. He describes it as "a grove of dark trees on a light hillside or a pile of buildings against the morning sky" (p. 54).

Thus, "we," says Dow, "at once feel the charm and call the effect 'picturesque'" (p. 54). When one looks unfocused at the surface of a thing, one could find something like chaos of dark and light. Dow calls it "tone-composition." Whether before or after one recognizes it as something like a patch of damp, a tea mark, or an ink stain, its subtle quality of dark and light reminds him/her of an imaginative object or associative event. Both are enlarged by "the power and mystery" (Dow, 1913, p. 53) into an organic whole of association. Dow (1913) writes:

> As there is no one word in English to express the idea contained in the phrase "dark-and-light," I have adopted the Japanese word "notan" (dark, light). It seems fitting that we should borrow this art-term from a people who have revealed to us so much of this kind of beauty. ... The Orientals rarely represent shadows ... . They prefer to model by line rather than by shading. They recognize Notan as a visual and distinct element of the art of painting. (p. 53)

Dow's finding in the dark-light surface of a thing takes us back to the art form of "sumi-e" in which a cosmic world of dark-and-light goes all over the place after being put on the paper. Complex tones of dark-and-light in ink-painting are more valued than coloring in oil painting. Dow recognized such pervasive quality not through European but through Oriental art, especially Japanese traditional painting prior to the modem Japanese period. He believed that the term *notan* was suitable for representing the essential quality in teaching aesthetic appreciation.

The term *notan* becomes one property. Dow (1911) used the term to talk about a structural method of art teaching. Thus, "art," says Dow, "is studied in this way in Japan" and "designers for the great Japanese industries of lacquer, metal, and textile, are trained by the pure Japanese (synthetic) method" (p. 232). *Notan* becomes a center of the effort to synthesize "the action of the human mind in harmony building" (Dow, 1911, p. 231). A report of 1929 showed that "'dark-light,' a term closely associated with Dow's theory, was used 528 times in the 36 art books studied; 'notan' was used 157 times" (Stankiewicz, 1990, p. 97). The term "value" smelled too much of the traditional scientific scheme in the Western world. It was too mechanical to specify the quality of harmony as visual music.

Conclusion: Mind and Quality

The present chapter finds that Dow's idea of harmonious composition has its basic roots in the Chinese theory of painting. Especially, Hsieh Ho's first canon might have caused Dow's philosophical transition from a representative approach to teaching art in terms of Western art tradition to a spiritual one in the context of the Oriental art tradition. In an effort to re-interpret Dow's transformation of Oriental art for Americans, this chapter proposes that the Chinese character "ch'i" is a key word to Chinese as well as Japanese traditional art.

Another finding of the chapter is that the meaning of *notan* is close to something like what is qualitatively felt. Viewing a phenomenon of *notan*, such as an ink-stain, can disclose the quality of harmony as visual music. Saunders (1966) sees the word *notan* to have "only historical meaning" (p. 9). *Notan*, however, makes us see an exploratory model for the vividness of quality in the work of art. Dow's extensive work becomes one bridge in the two-way street of Eastern and Western cultures, and is well worth considering in today's efforts in attempting to understand the "other" in art education from diverse cultures (Okazaki, 1997).

Chapter 9

Originally published in the *Journal of Aesthetic Education*, Vol. 37, No. 4, pp. 84-93, 2003.
Reprinted with permission by University of Illinois Press.

Arthur Wesley Dow's Address in Kyoto, Japan (1903)

Fig. 9.1 "The Speech of Mr. Dow," *Hinode Simbun* [Hinode Daily News], December 16, 1903. p. 3.

Fig. 9.2 "Professor Dow's View on Japanese Art," *Osaka Mainichi Simbun* [Osaka Mainichi Daily News], December 17, 1903, p. 7.

Fig. 9.3 "Professor Dow's Lecture on Art," *Osaka Asahi Simbun, Kyoto Furoku* [Osaka Asahi Daily News, Appendix to Kyoto Area], December 17, 1903, p. 1.

* Figures are not included in the originally published paper.

Researchers concerned with the historical development of American art education cannot help but acknowledge Arthur Wesley Dow's significant contribution to the field. Although many writers have recognized him as one of greatest figures in art education (Read, 1945; Logan, 1955; Efland, 1990; Wygant, 1993; Smith, 1996), it was not until the end of the twentieth century that art historians discovered his impact on the early development of modernist American art.

Several exhibitions of Dow's work have been shown, most notably: "Arthur Wesley Dow and American Art and Crafts" (Green & Poesch, 1999), in Stanford, Chicago, and Fort Dodge, Iowa (1999 and 2000) and "Harmony of Reflected Light:

The Photographs of Arthur Wesley Dow" (Enyeart, 2001), at the New Mexico Museum of Fine Arts (2001). In addition, two galleries in New York showed exhibitions of Dow's work in 1999 and 2000, respectively. These exhibitions indicate a rediscovery of Dow's work and his role, as well as a wider interest in the integral aspects of modernism in American artworks.

Joseph Masheck (1997) recognized Dow's post-impressionistic aesthetic of flat surface design as influential on modernism in painting and the graphic arts (p. 48). Nancy Green (1999b) sees Dow as "one of the first Western artists who did not simply imitate Japanese art, but who actually used the traditional Japanese woodcut techniques to create modernist prints" (p. 65). Leah Ollman (2000) writes, "Those who credit Dow as a conduit to American modernism see his traces everywhere" because "Dow is revealed at the end of the rainbow, as the common ancestor" (p. 67) who spread his theory and practice of art and art education. James Enyeart (2001) states that "Dow can now receive appropriate critical assessment of his work as a photographer and his impact on pictorial and modernist photography" (p. 9).

Dow is one of the few Americans whose work in the field of art and art education was influenced by Japanese traditional art. He came to Japan in October 1903 and spent three months in Japan, including six weeks in Tokyo and a month in Kyoto. His address in Kyoto in mid-December of that year has been mentioned in biographical studies (Moffatt, 1977; Mock-Morgan, 1976). However, a detailed account of what Dow said to the Japanese public has previously been unknown due to lack of a historical source.

Contemporary Japanese newspaper articles are the primary source for the contents of this address. The purpose of this chapter is to translate these source materials into English, providing a definitive description to encourage further research on Dow as an outstanding artist and educator. This chapter describes his activity in Japan, provides useful primary sources about his address, and discusses the content of the address. Implications for a cross-cultural interpretation are discussed in the concluding remarks.

128

Dow in Japan

Dow was born in Ipswich, Massachusetts on April 6, 1857. He studied art in Boston and Paris, and exhibited his paintings at Salon, in Paris from 1886-1887. He established his summer school of art in Ipswich (1891-1907) and became the curator of Japanese art at the Boston Museum of Fine Arts in 1897. He was an instructor of art at the Pratt Institute in Brooklyn from 1895-1904; taught composition at the Art Student's League in New York from 1897-1903; and served as a professor and the director of fine arts at Teachers College, Columbia University from 1904-1922 (*Who's Who in America*, 1920, p. 803). Dow first studied Japanese art at the Boston Museum of Fine Arts under the direction of Ernest Fenollosa, and then during his residence in Japan.

Arthur Johnson's 1934 biography provides the most detailed description of Dow's life and works. In fact, "every subsequent publication about Dow has relied on this biographical information, and in some cases Dow's aesthetic sources, contained in Johnson's short text of about one hundred pages" (Enyeart, 2001, p.10). According to Johnson (1934), Dow

> kept a careful day-by-day record during these months, and to read these notebooks, some six in number, is to see the world through the eyes of a sensitive spirit for whom all about him was form and colour. If, at any later time, some adequate survey of his life is written, it ought to include much of these notebooks for in them is hidden in many a beautiful phrase about that larger beauty of the world as it spread itself out before him. (p. 72)

Unfortunately, only the first notebook survives; the other five were lost after Johnson's death in 1949. Johnson was able to use all six notebooks of the Dow Travel Diary in making his accurate description of Dow's round-the-world journey.

The first notebook (1903) is now part of the Arthur and Dana Dow Papers at the Smithsonian Institution; "Arthur Dow Travel Diary (1st Note Book, Ipswich to Daitokuji, Kyoto, Trip around the world, Westward)," in Arthur and Dana Dow

Papers, Archives of American Art, Reel No. 1209 (Washington D.C., Smithsonian Institution, n.d.). Dow's brother's diary is also included in the collection, "Dana Dow Travel Diary" (1903).

According to the first notebook, his brother Dana's diary, and Johnson's biography, Dow, his wife Minnie, Dana, and two friends departed from San Francisco on September 19, 1903, and arrived in Yokohama, Japan on October 7. His three-month trip included visits to Tokyo (October 19 to November 21) and Kyoto (November 28 to December 22). Johnson (1934) provides a detailed description of Dow's address, attributed to the second notebook.

> On the evening of December the fourteenth Dow was asked to speak before the Chamber of Commerce of Kyoto... . It was a gathering of all the businessmen and the educators of the city and men who were interested in art. This group listened for more than an hour while Dow told them of [his] interest in their art and what it meant and should mean to the Western world. He took this opportunity to state very frankly his opinions relative to the error he felt many Japanese artists were making in giving up their own tradition and accepting without question those of Europe. ... In honor of the occasion a group of the best *No[h]* players had been assembled and they gave a play in the strictest academic manner. (p. 77)

Although Johnson provides the only detailed account of Dow's address, there is almost no description of the content. What did Dow say to his Japanese audience for more than an hour?

Dow's Address to the Public in Kyoto

A summary of his address, which he may have written in the second notebook, has been lost along with the notebook. However we may find this information in contemporary news stories, as, "the Japanese press was very much interested in Dow's visit and kept the public informed of his movements, what he was saying and his opinions of Japanese artists and craftsmen" (Johnson, 1934, pp. 77-78). In fact, more than twenty newspaper articles on Dow in both Kyoto and Osaka appeared in three local publications. These articles verify his previously unknown day-by-day itinerary. Local articles published simultaneously in three papers directly concerned Dow's address of December 14th.

A Kyoto edition of *Osaka Asahi Shimbun* (Osaka Asahi Daily News) provides a rather short report on Dow's address. It appeared on December 17th and was entitled "Professor Dow's Lecture on Art" (p. 1). The article began by saying that Professor Dow spoke in the *Noh* (a Japanese traditional drama) theatre on Kawaramachi Avenue in Kyoto. More than 60 persons attended. Mr. Nishimura, who had arranged the meeting, introduced Professor Dow to the Japanese audience as a great contributor to the development of American art. Dow's lecture was interpreted by Mr. Chiba, the vice-president of Doshisha Girls' School.

Dow introduced himself and explained his first impression of Japanese traditional painting. He came to this country in order to study fine arts, having studied Japanese art for years. His desire to study Japanese fine arts began when he saw the paintings of Eisen, and the old paintings of Shubun at the Boston Museum of Fine Arts. He appreciated the present opportunity to look at the many treasures in Japan's temples.

Dow discussed the difficulty of art in his speech. The weakness of contemporary artists, he said, was the poor quality of their designs. At that time, the fact that the designer and the maker were dissociated from each other brought about many difficulties in the process of creating artworks. He was making an effort to solve this problem and to improve society with fine arts.

In order to preserve the natural environment, he mentioned burying electric wires, discouraging advertising signs, and forbidding reckless deforestation. During his stay in Japan, he was studying the melding of interior design with landscapes. In this connection, the Japanese artist who impressed him most was Sesshu, whose brush-touches made Dow feel they were done by the Goddess of Art.

In his concluding remarks, he hoped that the Japanese would preserve the works of their traditional art. Throughout the world, those who studied the fine arts of other countries often tended to overlook the fine arts of their own country. He hoped that Japanese would overcome this neglect. Professor Dow's lecture ended at 8:20 pm. As a token of appreciation to Mr. and Mrs. Dow, two programs of *Kyogen* (*Noh* comedy) were performed. The audience adjourned at 9:00 pm.

Another newspaper (*Osaka Mainichi Shimbun* [Osaka Mainichi Daily News], 17 December 1903) provided a longer report on Dow's address, entitled "Professor Dow's View on Japanese Art" (p. 7). This article is reprinted in *Bijutsu Shinpo* (Art News), 20 December 1903 (p. 5). Julia Meech (1990) summarizes:

> As reported by the Japanese press, he [Dow] claimed to have been influenced most by the early ink painters Sesshu and Noami. American art education, he said, had suffered from the habit of learning by rote, copying rather than learning art as a craft or skill; Americans could learn from Japanese art, especially as regards the integration of painting and architecture in the interiors of the temples of Kyoto. He hoped that his own aesthetic theories might improve the general level of American society. "If I could give you a word of advice," he concluded, "then it is that you should maintain and study your own remarkable indigenous art forms. It is of no benefit to the Japanese to be intoxicated with Western art and to forget what is good about Japanese art." (p. 177)

The following version of Dow's address in the *Osaka Mainichi Shimbun* reports precisely what he said to the Japanese. The article stated Dow said that he began to study Japanese art at least 20 years before. The paintings from which he received the first deep impressions were the works of such masters as Shubun, Sesshu, and Noami. After that, he studied the paintings of other Japanese masters systematically. Then he invented a method of art education appropriate for his country.

At that time, the method of art education in the United States, France, and elsewhere was copying objects based on exact observation. It bound students to external objects and they missed the refinement of designs. Dow believed that it was impossible for them to freely express themselves. Therefore, he changed the methods of art education completely, based on art forms and color that were found in many works of Japanese masters. For example, for elementary schools in the United States, he recommended that students use a brush, *sumi* (or Indian ink), and Japanese paper. In addition, he proposed using Japanese color woodcut prints for teaching color theory. He believed that this could increase students' appreciation of art.

Japanese potters such as Kenzan designed their own works, constructed them with clay, and baked them in kilns. In the same way, Dow hoped that American potters would be able to make their own valuable works. However, U.S. designers and the manufacturers had become dissociated and many products were now manufactured with machines. Dow encouraged Americans to produce handicrafts. He thought that human hands should produce objects for human use and so he attempted to build a studio for textiles and casting.

Dow mentioned that although great buildings were constantly being constructed in the United States, Americans did not know how to design the interior of these buildings. Unlike great Japanese masters who had designed the landscaped paper sliding doors and ceilings in royal palaces and temples, American students had not developed this ability to design. Both the landscape drawings with Indian ink by Tanyu in Daitokuji Temple, and the wall paintings of Masanobu in Myoshinji Temple made a deep impression on him. Therefore, he considered designing the interiors of United States buildings with landscapes

Through encouraging refined taste and concepts of art Dow hoped to create a better aesthetic environment. For example, he wanted to bury all electric wires; he hoped to stop the desecration of the natural environment by billboards; and he was eager to discontinue the use of paper in newspapers produced from the trees cut down in lush forests. The traditional arts and crafts of Japan taught him the importance of protecting the natural environment.

Finally, if asked for advice, he would tell them to preserve Japanese works of art for the world. He would encourage them to study the distinctive characteristics of their own art and ask them not to become so fascinated with foreign art that they forgot their own distinctive works. Upon returning to the United States, he intended to use his many wonderful impressions and experiences in Japan to improve American art education.

The third article, simply titled "The Speech of Mr. Dow" (*Hinode Shimbun* [Hinode Daily News], 16 December 1903, p. 3), provides longest account of Dow's address. The article summarized both the opening and closing of Dow's speech. Mr. Nishimura, President of the Chamber of Commerce of Kyoto, asked Mr. Dow to give a speech, which 50 people attended. Dow began by saying that he began to study Japanese art about 15 to 20 years ago. Most drawing material used in Japanese painting was not available in the United States at that time. His systematic study of Japanese art showed him how problems in art education could be overcome. Dow pointed out that conventional art education was practiced from outside to inside. For example, art students in France or the United States were encouraged only to imitate art. However, copying the external world was inadequate to develop the artistic abilities of students. In addition, the method of developing a consciousness of art in the internal worlds of students was also developed at this time. Dow suggested that in the history of art, artistic design was applied to various things when art prospered. He felt that research in Japanese aesthetics could help overcome these defects in Western art education.

In this era of scientific and engineering advancements, increasing use of machines had hastened the decline of handicraft. He hoped to revive as much handicraft as possible. In America, those who designed goods and those who manufactured them had become dissociated from each other. However, he believed that to create a true work of art, one should take responsibility for all the processes, from its initial design to its manufacture as a final product.

Dow recognized that the Japanese pottery production system in which only one person designed the object, constructed it with clay, and baked it in a kiln was ideal for creating a work of art. Based on this system, he constructed a small textile factory and a pottery studio, which changed the method of art education completely. He was working hard to develop a close relationship between arts and crafts, proposing that students should create various handmade products in elementary schools. He also developed a new method of art education that could help to improve society. He intended to have people acquire a profound awareness of art. The reason he had reformed the method of elementary art instruction was to provide children with a real taste of art.

Dow concluded by encouraging the Japanese to always preserve the characteristics and strength of their art, warning them that when they studied the art of another country, with its different art forms and styles, people often lost interest in the art of their own country. He hoped that they would not forget the special features of Japan, especially Japanese art, even if the art of other countries might be worth studying. He wanted the entire world to overcome this tendency.

What Dow said to His Japanese Audience

English versions of Japanese primary source materials on Dow's address reveal what he said to his Japanese audience. First of all, the fact that Dow's turning to the East exactly paralleled Japanese turning to the West reflects his warning to the Japanese public of accepting Western art without question.

Dow's proposals for preserving the natural environment in his address prove that he should be regarded as a pioneer of aesthetic appreciation. Dow (1912) believed that appreciating art motivated some people to create works of art and most people to desire more beauty in their surroundings.

Dow stated that the interiors of the temples of Kyoto taught him the integration of art and architecture. This concept seems to be one of the most useful lessons from Japanese art during his stay in Japan. Dow emphasized that painters of the East were always designers because they not only painted pictures, but also designed buildings, wall paintings, ceilings, cupboards, cabinets, and books of illustrations.

The connection of decorative with pictorial art further led Dow to consider art as a method for social reconstruction. His idea of integrating art with society was evidenced by his experiences with the interiors of Buddhist temples of Kyoto, where he saw the monochromatic ink paintings by Tanyu Kano (1602-1674) and Masanobu Kano (1434-1530) decorating the sliding panels.

Dow's 1903 address showed that his own approach to teaching arts and crafts came as much from his appreciation of the decorative art in Japan and China as from the Arts and Crafts Movement of England. Dow never accepted the dissociation between designer and maker. His method suggested an extension to other media in arts and crafts.

Dow considered art as a human expression. Oriental ink paintings reflect artistic qualities which do not recreate a scene realistically, but emphasize a strong empathy with nature. In this context, Dow discussed the Japanese ink painting of artists such as Shubun, Sesshu (1420-1506), Noami (1397-1471), and Tomonobu Kano (1843-1912) who taught *haboku* (splashed-ink) techniques to Dow in mid-November of 1903. "The brush strokes of the great Sesshu," noted Dow (1917), "have more condensed power in them than Matisse ever dreamed of" (p. 116). Dow's system of teaching art provided a spontaneous and subjective approach to art education. An extreme flexibility for personal expression was permitted, as seen in the stark contrasts between two of Dow's students, Max Weber and Georgia O'Keeffe (Lancaster, 1968-1969, p. 287).

Dow discussed a wide range of issues—art, education, and society, providing much more than a mere warning to the Japanese not to give up their traditional art for the new Western form.

Concluding Remarks

Dow left Japan on December 27 from Nagasaki, the westernmost port of entry. In 1904, he traveled to China, Sumatra, India, Egypt, Greece, and France. He finally returned to Boston on June 19. Dow describes his world tour: "Part of 1903 and '04 were spent in Japan, India, and Egypt observing the native crafts and gathering illustrative material" (Dow, 1913, p. 5). In fact, Shirahama (1908), a Japanese art education researcher in America from 1904 to 1905, heard Dow lecture at Teachers College, Columbia University, comparing the use of color in Italian works of art, with Japanese color prints.

This chapter has provided the first definitive description and detailed account of Dow's address. Newly discovered primary source materials (Japanese press reports) on Dow's address could further serve as historical reference sources. In addition, the Ipswich Historical Society has preserved nearly two hundred snapshots that Dow took in Japan, which could also be a rich source of biographical information (Enyeart, 2001, p. 93).

Dow rebelled against the academicism of art, which ultimately "brought the ideals of the East to American art" (Cox, 1923, p. 89). In contrast, Japanese artists were no longer secure in the old of the East and not yet fully adapted to the new of the West. In other words, as Melanie Davenport (2000) said, "Just as artists can learn to draw more precisely by attending to the spaces between shapes, so too might art education benefit from attending to the spaces between cultures where interaction takes place" (p. 372).

The story of modernist art and art education in America begins with Dow and continues into the present. Dow's extensive work in the late nineteenth and early twentieth centuries becomes one bridge in the two-way street between Eastern and Western cultures, and is well worth considering in today's attempts to understand the "other" through art and art education. Japanese art educators have compared American and Japanese ideas for more than a century (Okazaki, 1984, 1994b). American art educators have similarly synthesized Japanese and American culture of art in their theories of art education (Beittel, 1990; Dobbs, 1983; Toku, 2001; Wilson, 1999). Cross-cultural research portrays the process of cross-cultural interpretation as a way of making sense of one's world in relation to the worlds of others (Okazaki, 1991, 1995b, 2001).

Chapter 10 Originally published in the *Proceedings of the 32nd InSEA World Congress* 2008.
Reprinted with permission by the Organizational Committee,
the 32nd InSEA World Congress.

Arthur Wesley Dow's Lecture in Kyoto, Japan (1903)

●ダオ教授の演説　同氏は昨朝同志社公會堂に於て同校男女學生を集め伊太利アッセンチー町の教會に保存せるヂヤルコー筆「フランセスの慈悲」の畫に就て一場の演説をなしたり又京都商業會議所會頭西村治兵衛氏は同氏を招待し美術上に關する談話を請ふ筈なるが日時場所は未定なりと

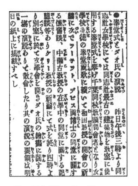

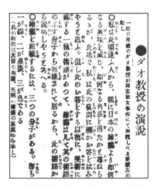

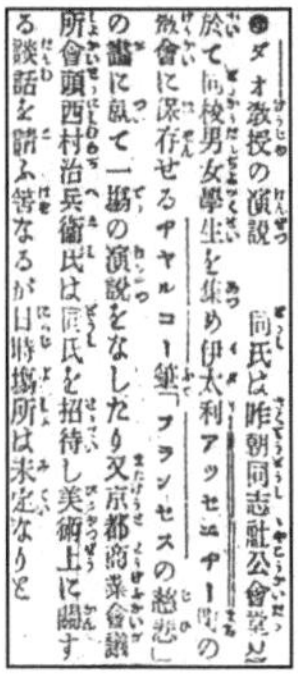

Fig. 10.1 "Professor Dow's Speech," *Hinode Simbun* [Hinode Daily News], December 10, 1903, p. 2.

●奉堂式とダオ氏の演説　昨日午後三時より同志社女學校にては同志社最古の建築物を教室に使用する奉堂式を擧げ千葉同校教頭司會者となり女學校生徒の奉堂祝歌に續いて和田教授の開會の辭に次でラーネッド、デビス兩博士の同堂に關する懐舊談、中瀬古教授の在學中の同堂に關する談話等ありケリー教授の祈禱にて式を終り四時より別室に於て文學會を開きダオ氏の繪畫に關する一場の演説ありて散會したり其の演説の要領は明日の紙上に掲載すべし

Fig. 10.2 "Opening Ceremony of Teaching Rooms and Mr. Dow's Speech," *Hinode Simbun* [Hinode Daily News], December 12, 1903, p. 2.

●ダオ教授の演説

一昨日米國のダオ教授が同志社女學校にて演説したる要領左の如し

○私は此頃逢ふ人から、頻に日本の繪畫より如何なる興味を感じ、如何なる利益を得たかと尋ねらるゝが、此席で私は此の質問に聊かお答を試みやうと思ふ。但し此のお答をする以前に、美術に關する一種の術語があつて、繪畫は凡て其の術語の示す分子から組織されて居るから、此の術語から説明しやうと考へる。

○繪畫を組織するには、三つの分子がある。即ち一が線、二が濃淡、三が色である

（此時教授は友信の偶畫、光琳の繪畫の實演等を示し）

Fig. 10.3 "Professor Dow's Speech," *Hinode Simbun* [Hinode Daily News], December 13, 1903, p. 3.

* Figures are not included in the originally published paper.

Arthur Wesley Dow (1857-1922) turned toward the Japanese way of thinking around the turn of the twentieth century, and found something that American art education lacked. A multicultural heritage of art education is exemplified in Dow's interest in Oriental art (Smith, 1994). Dow was regarded as the American teacher of Oriental art (deLemos, 1946). He obtained information on Japanese art through Ernest Fenollosa who hired Dow as a part-time assistant curator in his Department of Japanese Art at the Boston Museum of Fine Arts in the fall of 1893. Four years later, in September 1897, "he was appointed keeper of Japanese Paintings and Prints at the Museum of Fine Arts for two years" (Meech, 1990, p. 168) because no qualified successor to Fenollosa had yet been found.

Dow and Japan

The first edition of Dow's book, *Composition*, was published in 1899, and widely read. It went into seven printings, and was reissued in 1913. The revised edition of his book had also gone through thirteen editions by 1931. Most recently, it was reprinted in 1998 and in 2007. Indeed, "During the first three decades of this century, Americans attending art classes in public schools were most likely influenced by the teachings of Arthur Wesley Dow and his understanding of Japanese principles of art" (Foster, 1992, p.104).

Dow developed his synthetic method of creating art instead of the traditional method of copying nature and life. Dow believed that all kinds of art were created from the three elements as line, *notan* (dark-and-light), and color using the five principles as opposition, transition, subordination, repetition, and symmetry (Michael, 1983). Dow's method encouraged students to discover what was in their own artworks. This was the alternative to the copybook exercises in use in art classes in American public schools.

"Notan became a classroom word" (Lancaster, 1963, p.236) because Dow's synthetic method had always been very popular with art teachers. A report from 1929 showed that "'dark-light,' a term closely associated with Dow's theory, was used 528 times in the 36 art books studied; 'notan' was used 157 times" (Stankiewicz, 1990, p. 97). In addition, his book included a number of full-page plates that showed Japanese artists' application of the elements and principles of design. Art students across the nation also became familiar with the lineal and tonal fine point of Japanese painting. As a consequence, "Many Americans have become acquainted with the fundamentals of Japanese painting through Arthur Wesley Dow" (Lancaster, 1963, p. 235).

Dow is an influential figure both in the history of American art education (Logan, 1955; Mock-Morgan, 1976; Hook, 1987; Efland, 1990; Wygant, 1993; Smith, 1996) and in the history of American modernist art (Meech, 1990; Masheck, 1997; Green, 1999a, 1999b; Poesch, 1999; Ollman, 2000; Enyeart, 2001; Sanieman Gallary, 1999; Fairbrother, 2008). Dow came to Japan in early October of 1903. Of

140

his three months in Japan, he spent six weeks in Tokyo and one month in Kyoto. The fact that he gave his address to the public in Kyoto in mid-December of that year has been mentioned in biographical studies on Dow (Johnson, 1934; Moffatt, 1977). The detailed account of what Dow said to the Japanese public has been known because of a finding of a historical source (Okazaki, 2003).

Dow's Lectures to University Students

During Dow's month-long stay in Kyoto, he was not only invited to give a public address, but also to give two lectures in art at a university. The first lecture was given on December 9, and the second on December 11. These two facts had been unknown to American researchers on Dow until today because Johnson (1934) did not mention them in his description of Dow's travels in Japan.

Dow's two lectures were reported in local newspapers. His first lecture was reported in the December 10 issue of *Hinode Shimbun* (Hinode Daily News). The article made a very brief comment on Dow's speech: "At Doshisha Auditorium on yesterday morning, Mr. Dow gave students a lecture on 'St. Francis' Mercy,' a painting by Giotto, which is preserved at the Assisi Church in Italy. Then Jihei Nishimura, the president of the Chamber of Commerce of Kyoto, invited Mr. Dow to give a lecture in art, but the place and time are undecided" ("Dao Kyoju," 1903a, p. 2).

At that time, the large white, Western-style building in front of the Kyoto Palace was Doshisha, a Christian university. It was founded in 1875 under the auspices of the American Board Mission. Its success was due to Mr. Neesima (Davis, 1890), one of the most eminent of the early Japanese converts to Presbyterianism. This powerful institution included a special Theological Department, a Girls' School, a Science School, a Hospital, and a Nurses' Training School (Chamberlain & Mason, 1891) in the last decade of the nineteenth century.

Dow's speech was most appropriate for the students of the Christian institution because his topic was concerned with St. Francis' mercy. It might have been in reference to a fresco wall painting called "St. Francis Preaching to the Birds" which Giotto (1266?-1337) produced at Assisi in about 1290. His frescoes in the church illustrate the life of St. Francis (Taber, 1913). During the late Middle Ages, an revival of Christianity spread through at the Europe. The approach of having works of art to relate the Christian experience to real life is most powerfully seen in the works of Giotto, whose narrative works at Assisi are recognized as the most charming achievement of painting because he expressed human feelings with clarity and poetry (Jameson, 1899). Dow's lecture on Giotto would be interesting to the Japanese students because Dow had toured Italy in 1897 in order to study thirteenth century art at Florence, Venice, and Assisi (Hook, 1987).

The December 12 issue of *Hinode Shimbun* also reported on the second lecture, which Dow gave at the Chapel of Doshisha Girls' School, now, Doshisha Women's College where Mary Florence Denton (1857-1947), a missionary from the "Woman's Board of Missions for the Pacific," taught (Clapp, 1955). The school provided Dow, his wife and brother with guest rooms for their stay, and Denton contributed to the success of Dow's work in Kyoto. His travel diary (1903) noted that she met him at Kyoto Station, introduced him to Japanese print shops, invited him to dinners, and handled the Japanese press (Entry for November 28 to December 4). Notice of Dow's lecture was given in the December 13 issue of *Himode Shimbun*. The article provides a longer report on Dow's speech ("Dao Kyoju," 1903b) than the first one.

It begins to say that American Professor Dow had addressed at Doshisha Girls' School two days earlier. People whom Dow met frequently asked him about his interest in Japanese traditional paintings and the benefits he got from it. He promised to try to answer these such questions in his lecture. However, before that, he wanted to talk about the technical elements of the art. That was because, in his opinion, all paintings could be explained with in terms of three elements of design: line, *notan*, or "dark-light," and color. Dow showed students reproductions of art such as a drawing in Indian ink by Tomonobu Kano (1843?-1912) and the paintings of Korin Ogata (1658-1716). According to Dow, the Indian ink drawing had space that divided the whole into its parts. Each portion was associated with line. The painting had *notan* and color. He thought that if one were aware that paintings were organized

142

with these three elements, one could better appreciate the paintings.

However, Dow believed that even if these three elements could be assembled in a painting, it would not automatically result in a work of art. One could truly recognize the importance of art only if one had God-given ability to appreciate art by viewing it in terms of these three elements. Dow proved that although Japanese painting was very simple, it well reflected the ability to appreciate art. He did not regard art merely as a copy of natural appearance. That is to say, art is not limited to a realistic expression. Artists could express themselves with the three elements mentioned before of line, *notan*, and color, but works of art could be produced only when a painter had the power of aesthetic appreciation given by God. Though the paintings of Tomonobu or Korin expressed the natural objects, they had not simply copied these objects. Moreover, their paintings included significant meanings that integrated the three elements very well. Consequently, their work was considered by Dow to be aesthetic.

When asked about the Japanese painters who had the greatest influence on him, Dow's first answer was Sesshu who had created many masterpieces for the later generations. Dow believed that Sesshu had received from God the ability to appreciate these works. Sesshu's works gave the impression that Venus herself had created them.

Dow was also deeply impressed by painting of Eisen. In fact, he had gone to the Boston Museum of Fine Arts specifically to see many works of Eisen on display there. Furthermore, acting upon a recommendation, he looked at the work of a painter more famous than Eisen: Soga Shubun, Sesshu's teacher, and they had a strong impact on him. After that, he had learned that there were numerous famous masterpieces in Kyoto. He thus became very eager to visit Kyoto.

Here, Mr. Dow showed the students "Shoso Hakkei," a work of Sesshu, that consists of eight views of one landscape. Although this painting is simple, a harmonious quality can be seen in it. One could perceive it as visual music of brush strokes. Dow found the same perceptive quality in the painting "Shoso Hakkei" by Shubun at Daitokuji Temple and in the landscapes of Motonobu Kano at Myoshinji

Temple. At that time, it was the fashion in the United States to decorate the interior of a building with many works of landscapes. Dow learned that the same method of decoration had already been used in the temples of Kyoto since ancient times.

After that, Mr. Dow discussed the books of painters such as Korin and Hokusai. Such books, he said, were very useful materials for teaching American children about painting. Dow closed his lecture by saying that these books were also very useful to explain the essence of painting because they splendidly illustrated harmonious composition with the three design elements of line, *notan* and color.

What Dow said to the Students
After his world trip, Dow became Director of Fine Arts at Teachers College, Columbia University in 1904. It was there that Dow developed his method of synthetically creating art instead of the traditional method of copying nature and life. In 1913, he noted "The art courses are now arranged in progressive series of synthetic exercises in line, dark-and-light, and color. Composition is made the basis of all work in drawing, painting, designing and modeling —of house decoration and industrial arts —of normal courses and of art training for children" (p. 5).

Dow's method suggested an extension to other media in art and crafts. He believed that the true purpose of teaching art was the education for appreciation which would lead everyone to desire finer form and more harmony of tone and color in their surroundings and things for daily use. Thus he declared that a nation's ideals are revealed in its art as the expression of the spirit of the whole people (Dow, 1912).

In his lectures of 1903, Dow recalled seeing a work by Eisen which gave him his first deep impression of Japanese painting. After that, he became interested in the works of Shubun at the Boston Museum of Fine Arts. This first encounter with Japanese art Dow told in Japan should be identified. Citing Johnson (1934), historical researchers have often stated that Dow's first impression of Japanese art was the works of Hokusai (1760-1849), a Japanese painter distinguished for his Mt. Fuji prints. In fact, "Johnson and subsequent historians have characterized Dow's epiphany in discovering reproductions of Hokusai woodblocks at the Boston Public

144

Library as the catalyst for the unique contribution" to his book *Composition* (Enyeart, 2001, p. 34). However, this is in error accepted as fact and must be corrected.

It is not clear what works of Japanese art Dow looked at there because Johnson did not record them. However, it is known that Dow looked at the works of Shubun and Sesshu at the museum. Although the life of Shubun, a Zen priest-painter who lived around the mid-fifteenth century, is unknown, he was one of the great masters in the history of Japanese painting. He has been acknowledged as the father of Japanese ink-painting school because he was the teacher of the greatest master Sesshu (1420-1506), who firmly established the Japanese school of ink painting. The reproductions of works by both Subun and Sesshu were included in Dow's book (1913). He regarded Shubun as a "Chinese who founded a school in Japan in the fifteenth century," and Sesshu as "one of the greatest painters all time" (p. 53). "The works of Oriental masters," said Dow, "felt the power and mystery of Notan" (p. 53).

What *notan* expresses is aesthetic awareness of tone sensibility. It is not mechanically or systematically structured but subjectively organized in a state of composing or fusing light and dark on the surface of a drawing. The characteristics of dark and light (*notan*) are artistic, not scientific. The artistic character of *notan* has come from the interaction of ink, paper, and water through brush strokes. Yashiro (1969) called it "a sense of stained quality," which contributes to various aspects of Japanese art. He concludes that artists engaged in the work of ink painting would experience a complete transformation of their attitudes towards art from strict representation to spiritual expression. Dow (1913) briefly describes the history of Chinese and Japanese ink painting:

> Supreme excellence in the use of ink was attained by the Chinese and Japanese masters. Impressionism is by no means a modern art (except as to color-vibrations) for suggestiveness was highly prized in China a thousand years ago. ... To them we look for the truly artistic interpretation of nature; for dramatic, mysterious, elusive tone-harmony; for supreme skill in brush-

work (p. 96).

The artistic quality of the highly prized "suggestiveness" results in Dow's intentions of revealing "the sources of power," showing students "how to look within for greatest help," and "teaching them not to depend on externals, not to learn too much on anything or anybody" (Dow, 1913, p. 128).

Oriental ink paintings reflect artistic qualities, not of recreating a scene realistically in an artwork, but of discovering a strong empathy with nature. Broadly speaking, they differ from modern Western artworks in three ways: "literary appeal based on linear simplicity, symbolic expression and decorative quality" (Kurita, 1987, p. 151). In this context, Dow discussed other Japanese ink painting artists such as Noami (1397-1471) and Tomonobu Kano who taught *haboku* splashed-ink techniques to Dow in mid-November of 1903.

And Now, Some Concluding Remarks

Although Dow is already recognized as one of greatest figures in the field of art education, it was not until the end of the 20th century that art historians discovered his impact on the early development of modernist American art. Dow has long been regarded not as a creative artist but as an influential teacher. Among his students were Edna Boies Hopkins, Georgia O'Keeffe, Max Weber and Alvin Langdon Coburn. The first interest in his work and his role as an artist might be an exhibition of his works (Moffatt, 1977) at the National Collection of Fine Arts, Smithsonian Institution, in 1977. The second interest in his color woodcuts work was expressed in the exhibition, "Japonisme Comes to America" (Meech & Weisberg, 1990), held in both America and Japan in 1990. Later, in 1997 Dow's book of an "Americanized and modernized version of Japanese design" (Wilson, 1989, March), *Composition*, was reprinted (1997, 2007).

An exhibition, "Arthur Wesley Dow and American Art & Crafts" (Green & Poesch, 1999), was held in Stanford, Chicago, and Fort Dodge, Iowa in 1999 and 2000. In addition, two galleries in New York showed exhibitions of Dow's work in 1999 and 2000, respectively the most recent exhibition, "Harmony of Reflected Light: The photographs of Arthur Wesley Dow" (Enyeart, 2001), was presented at the New Mexico Museum of Fine Arts in 2001.

This chapter has provided definitive descriptions of both Dow's lectures in Kyoto in mid-December of 1903. It has given a detailed account of what Dow said to Japanese students that had hitherto been unknown. The finding of primary source materials, that is, Japanese press reports on Dow's address and other lectures could provide some new historical references sources for further biographical research on Dow.

These newly discovered Japanese sources could not only supply useful information on his lectures, but also help us understand what Dow said to the Japanese a century ago. This chapter reveals that Dow have his first encounter with the works of Eisen, and that Dow looked at the works of Shubun and Sesshu at the Boston Museum of Fine Arts. In fact, this museum has fifty-four *Ukiyo-e* works of Keisai Eisen (1790-1848).

Chapter **11**   Originally published in *Art Education*, Vol. 38, No. 4, pp. 6-10,1985.
Reprinted with permission by the National Art Education Association (NAEA).

What American Art Educators Learned from the Japanese: A Response to Carson and Dobbs

Fig. 11.1 Japanese	Fig. 11.2 Invited Address by	Fig. 11.3 Japanese	Fig. 11.4 Japanese
Edition (1998) of	Brent Wilson at the Annual	Edition (1990) of	Edition (2010) of *Art*
Teaching Drawing	Conference of Bijutsuka Kyoiku	*Cognition and*	*and Cognition* (Efland,
from Art (B. Wilson,	Gakkai in Japan (March, 1989).	*Curriculum* (Eisner,	2002). M. Fujie,
Al Hurwiz, & M.	Translator: Dr. M. Nagamachi.	1982). N. Nakase,	K. Nakamura,
Wilson. 1987), M.		K. Fukumoto,	A. Okazaki, I. Ikeuchi,
Keitoku, A. Okazaki,		M. Nagamachi, &	T. Abe, T. Ikegami, &
& T. Abe trans.		A. Okazaki trans.	Y. Iwashaki trans.

* Figures are not included in the originally published paper.

Current Trends in Japanese Art Education

I am pleased to have read two fine articles in *Art Education* dealing with trends in Japanese art education. Carson's "What American art educators can learn from the Japanese" appeared in November 1981, and Dobbs' "Japan Trail '83: American art education odyssey to the Orient" appeared two years later in November 1983.

Carson reported her visit to preschools and elementary schools in Kobe, one of the largest cities in Japan with over a million people, and gave her impressions of how Japanese teachers teach drawing and painting to children in art classrooms. Dobbs told how five American, middle school students from New York were selected for a two-week American Art Education Odyssey to Japan in July 1983. He also documented events they experienced while participating in the summer program, organized by the Asia Society with support from TDA of Japan.

Both articles, I think, help American art educators understand how Japanese art education is conducted at both elementary and secondary levels. If there are American art educators interested in Japanese art education, they would find little else on the subject except a 1957 article by Japanese art educator, Muro. Carson and Dobbs both attempt to provide useful information about theory and practice, policy-making process, textbook distribution, development and history of the education system, the art education association, and art education programs in the schools of Japan. There is little doubt that they succeeded to make brief but valuable reviews of Japanese art education available to readers in the United States and other countries where English is spoken. The point likely to interest Japanese art educators, however, is not the factual discussion of Japanese art education but American views about cultural and social background of Japanese traditions.

Criticism of Japanese Art Education

Questions both educators had during their visits in Japan are almost the same, although their goals were different. Going beyond the usual tourist viewpoint, they both wanted to learn why artworks by Japanese children are so sophisticated and why our students have such skillful hands in manipulating materials and tools. Both writers wrote about the unimaginable centralized system of school curriculum, national guidelines, textbook distribution, and educational policy-making that the Ministry of Education has institutionalized and controlled for a long time. They did not expect art education as a school subject under such a rigid system.

The Japanese system of art education is questioned because "Japanese respect conformity, whereas Americans individuality" (Carson, 1981, p. 46) and because "this highly delineated flow of school curriculum ideas in Japan is hard to imagine in the United States" (Dobbs, 1983, p. 7). Thus, Carson(1981) believes one "reason art is taught in Japan may be to produce a standard quality, whereas in America art educators ... encourage divergent responses" (p. 46) or that "It is inconceivable," says Dobbs(1983), "that American art educators would accept the Japanese style of centralization and control" (p. 7).

For each of the American art educators, it seemed that various aspects of Japanese art education, such as government control, a centralized school system, standardized curriculum, stereotyped instruction, etc., are likely to be kinds of educational enterprise fraught with potential danger. The fact that Japanese art educators do not feel this way confused them. Conformity/standardization in Carson's discussion and centralization/control in Dobbs' discussion were rejected as negative aspects of Japanese art education. Carson and Dobbs also focused upon the cultural background of Japanese art education and how the long aesthetic and artistic traditions of Japan pervade the whole land and society. Two vivid examples of inquiring into the qualities of aesthetic phenomena in Japanese culture and life styles are shown in the following:

At every level of Japanese life, aesthetic choices are evident, from the careful positioning of food on a plate, the wrapping of a gift, the arrangement of flowers, to the consistently tasteful blend of bamboo, stone, wood and clay in their utensils, tools, parks, and shrines. (Carson, 1981, p. 44)

... the Japanese youngster is exposed to a variety of Japanese arts during such cultural practices as the Tea Ceremony, which involves attention to pottery; ikebana; scroll painting and calligraphy; landscape gardening; lacquerware; as well as to such non-visual aesthetic phenomena as the taste and smell and touch of tea, the sound of running water, and so forth. Certainly these are all valuable sources for aesthetic appreciation. (Dobbs, 1983, p. 6)

Concerning negative aspects of schooling and positive aspects of Japanese culture, there is similarity between the professional views of both educators. Both share an impression of positive aspects of Japanese art education as well as negative aspects of strict institutionality and control in art education and general education within Japanese schools. Others who have visited Japan, as art educators or researchers in other fields, could provide similar opinions about Japanese modes of schooling and culture. The clear point in both articles is that positive aspects of Japanese cultural foundations is what American art educators can learn from the Japanese, whereas negative aspects of Japanese schooling is what they cannot.

Formal Schooling

Carson's and Dobbs' criticism of Japanese art education has interested me greatly. I believe Japanese art educators can learn something from their views though I have a question with their assessment of arts and aesthetic education in informal settings outside of schools. Are there clear distinctions between positive aspects of informal learning and negative aspects of formal schooling in Japanese art education?

One reason for the centralization, says Kobayashi, professor of comparative education at Kyoto University, comes from the fact that

> Japan has a long history of centralization ... Centralization thus is accepted as a natural form of government ... Proponents of centralization hold, however, that the direct equation of democracy and decentralization is false. ... centralization of Japanese educational administration should be judged from its actual implications and efforts on the realities of Japanese education. (1976, p. 84)

Even if Americans understand the long tradition of centralization of Japanese feudalism, however, I suppose that democratic centralization would be doubtful because democracy, which encourages people to go their individual ways, seems incompatible with centralization that motivates people to conformative or standardized ways.

I think democratic centralization in Japanese education means a balance of power between governmental and non-governmental efforts. In art education, the

Ministry of Education has political powers that authorize guidelines that cannot be accomplished by officers responsible for art education in the Ministry without the support of non-governmental professionals; there are only two specialists of art education in the Ministry of Education. "The political process in Japanese art education," is therefore greatly "influenced by the variety of professional groups and societies which lobby the Ministry" (Dobbs, 1983, p. 8), and those members often contribute to making and renewing guidelines for art education that indicate educational objectives grade by grade.

There are many textbooks for art education made by the Ministry and by several publishing firms. Although educational goals or objectives for art education are settled by the Ministry with support of non-governmental professionals in art education, responsibility for what content should be included in the art curriculum and for structuring learning activities from grade to grade belongs to textbook writers. These are usually university professors or elementary and secondary teachers employed by publishers of textbooks. For this reason, non-governmental Japanese art educators play an important role in decision-making about national guidelines and writing textbooks based on different views about what art education is for.

The power of non-governmental art educators provides some insightful art teachers with possibilities. National guidelines for art education in Japan include tentative guidelines, but have been revised and renewed in 1947, 1951, 1958, 1968, and 1976. If there are teachers who are satisfied with the national guidelines but cannot follow them as "a score or a script as a musician or an actor follows scores or scripts" (Eisner 1981, p. 121), they attempt to create new subject matter for art curricula and new methods for teaching without ready-made content given in textbooks they employ.

One reason that force approaches to new practices of art education come from the fact that the art world never stops in its development and what Rosenberg call *The Tradition of the New* (1959). Another reason has to do with educational situations as well as cultural, economic, and political trends. If a teacher's energy and inventiveness has to do with expansion of the contemporary art world and translating its artistic phenomenon into art curriculum, he/she may meet with little success. If this new approach to visual arts education is carried into the field through journals, magazines, conferences, and workshops, the Ministry of Education cannot help but include new approaches in the next revision of the national curriculum and authorize it as new standard subject matter for art education. In other words, the Ministry cannot determine the content of art curriculum without using non-governmental assistance.

The Japanese style of setting national standards by guidelines and counterbalances to centralization by non-governmental art educators, however, are ambivalent. We have profitable feedback systems for discarding old art education practices and introducing new ones though we also have dangerous forces that cause the Ministry to overemphasize one particular ideology. Our energies and inventiveness for future art education can be harmed, and our counterbalance can be destroyed.

Informal Schooling

I believe that our national guidelines for art education arc temporary and should not be followed strictly and that they need constantly to be revised. Merits and demerits of centralization and counterbalance and Japanese attitudes toward conformity are essentially ambivalent. Argument about merits and demerits of conformity can be linked with positive aspects of Japanese cultural traditions that Carson and Dobbs both mentioned in their articles. According to one analysis, attitudes toward conformity have come from a Japanese sense of dependence that has been given the name *amae* by Doi, a medical psychologist at International Christian University in Tokyo. He has given some thought to Japanese aesthetic sensibility:

> In this sphere ... *amae* sensibility seems to play a very large role. "Beauty" usually implies that an object is pleasing to the senses ... This has much in common with the experience of *amae*, since *amae* ... seeks to achieve identity with another. Of course, it is absolutely essential ... that the other

person should understand one's purpose and acquiesce in it ... It is for this reason ... that some people turn to Zen and other religions, and the same motivation ... also drives some people to the pursuit of beauty ... The fact that the Japanese as a whole area are more aesthetically inclined than other people may be based on the same reason: if one dwells continuously in the world of *amae* ... it would seem, they seek beauty whether they wish it or not. (Doi, 1973, p. 79)

Although Doi's view of aesthetics and beauty does not define these terms, it is useful for understanding Japanese attitudes to conformity to *amae* as a sense of dependence. If such a tendency in Japanese thinking is applied to life and art, an orientation to conformity has great merit in conducting life, making art, or responding to both life and art. For example, there is "moon viewing", which Carson says is one important national event at harvest time in Japan and which characterizes a Japanese reverence for nature and aesthetics. To Japanese people, the moon immediately evokes autumn and a whole extended semantic field including nature and human affairs. Such totality of association is called an invisible aesthetic resonator hidden under a tiny piece of nature, therefore, as the result of age-long accumulations of cultural experience. For this reason, the moon itself serves as a hint of things that can be "enlarged by dint of its power into an organic whole of association" (Izutsu & Izutsu, 1981, p. 16).

The activity of moon viewing symbolizes a total experience of the art of life or the life of art itself that makes indissolurable relationships among poetry, man, and things. Oriental art is a contemplative effort to discover and bring out encaged souls and inner principles of dynamic harmony (Maritain, 1953, p. 13). Nature and things are perceived not as hostile but as a pantheistic continuum that people can become an integral part of, through artistic and poetic intuition, as when a "baby smiles and the whole crowd is transported" (Suzuki, 1956, p. 281). Although such totality of experience is found in the typical thought of Zen, that stresses self-discipline of indivisibility, such experiences are not limited to Oriental art and life. "By extension, this orientation is the same for the one who inquires into or interprets art making and responding to art" (Beittel, 1979b, p. 53).

There is not so much distance between Japanese attitudes toward aesthetic situations and American attitudes because this is a place in which people's qualitative thinking or stream of consciousness becomes a "fusion" (Pepper, 1953) and in which their concepts and felt qualities encounter each other (Pepper, 1966).

In Conclusion

Japanese toward conformity have great merit when applied to the art or way of art in life. On the contrary, this attitude becomes related to social and political situations in which vertical organization in Japanese society is emphasized (Nakane, 1972). If this attitude lacks any axes of coordinates characteristic of Japanese thought (Maruyama, 1961), the following two dangers emerge: when people become estranged from universality and overemphasize temporal particulars, it becomes easy to adopt an opportunism that compromises with specific circumstances or situations; and when spatial particulars are overemphasized, it is easy to lapse into a narrow ethnocentrism (Nakamura, 1977). I believe, however, that conformative orientations have a positive side when they arise from a long process of opinion-sharing and desire for harmony. They can be used as "a process, not only of individuation, but also *integration*, which is the reconciliation of individual uniqueness with social unity" in arts and aesthetic education (Read, 1945, p. 5).

Japan and the United States are separated by a vast ocean, though this ocean is also a bridge by which eastern and western worlds encounter each other and become integrated into one. The long time interrelationship between Japan and the United States goes back more than one hundred and thirty years, from when Commodore Perry's squadron of ships arrived in Japan in 1853 to when the United States made Japan open up to the modern world. Since then, even in Japanese art education, serving "as food for thought as we make choices for the future" in art education (Carson, 1981, p. 46).

There isn't space to describe all these impacts here, though I would like to talk about what Japanese art educators learned from Americans in other opportunities. As a final word in this chapter, I offer the following notion of what a Japanese art educator has learned:

> In religion the Future is behind us. In art the Present is the central. The tea-master held that real appreciation of art is only possible to those who make of it a living influence ... Thus the tea-master strove to be something more than the artist—art itself. It was the Zen of aestheticism. Perfection is everywhere if we only choose to recognize it. Rikiu loved to quote an old poem which says: "To those who long only for flowers, fain would I show the full-blown spring which abides in the toiling buds of snow-covered hills." (Okakura, 1906, pp. 151-152)

Chapter **12** Originally published in Albert A. Anderson & Paul E. Bolin eds., *History of Art Education: Proceedings of the Third Penn State International Symposium* (pp. 41-51), University Park, PA: The Pennsylvania State University, 1997. Reprinted with permission by Albert A. Anderson & Paul E. Bolin.

Understanding the "Other" in Art Education: A Biographical Interpretation of Beittel's Writing

Fig. 12.1 Japanese Edition (1987) of *Alternatives for Art Education Research* (Beittel, 1973). M. Nagamchi trans.

Fig. 12.2 Vase, stoneware by Kenneth R. Beittel, H. 7 cm. W. 12 cm, D. 12 cm. Coll: Akio Okazaki.

Fig. 12.3 Kenneth R. Beittel in his studio. Photo: Akio Okazaki (1984).

* Figures are not included in the originally published paper.

Japan and the United States are separated by a vast ocean, though this ocean is also a bridge by which Eastern and Western worlds encounter each other and become integrated into one (Okazaki, 1984, 1985b). Japanese art educators, such as Shirahama (Okazaki, 1985a; Foster, 1992) and Shimoda (Okazaki, 1992, 1994b), compared American and Japanese ideas in the earlier decades of the 20th century. American art educators, Arthur Dow (1899/1913) and Kenneth Beittel, similarly synthesized Japanese and American culture in their philosophies of art education. Beittel (1968), in particular, turned toward the Japanese way of thinking, and found something that American art education lacked. His efforts reflect his ongoing Japanese way in pottery (Jordan, 1991).

But when did his transition from the American way of "creativity" to the Japanese way of "tradition" take place? Did he go to Japan, and then change his mind? Or did he change his mind, and then go to Japan? Both interpretations are plausible, but I believe the latter. I will provide justification for my belief in my following discussion.

Interpreting the Clash Between Cultures

Beittel's (1989) book, *Zen and the Art of Pottery*, provides an explanation of his long inquiry into Japanese cultural values in pottery. In the book, he probes his experiences in the Japanese pottery community for clues to the clash between progressive and traditional forces on contemporary art education.

The push-and-pull between creative expression and traditional skills was instrumental in changing the attitude of Kenneth Beittel's international philosophy of art. Beittel asks a fundamental question in the book by telling a story:

When I speak of the East and pottery, I draw from my experience with the Arita tradition, its details and its rituals. So what may be needed is immersion within one tradition simultaneous with liberation from it. In pottery, the West is high on liberation but low on tradition. On viewing clay pieces of Western art students, my Japanese teacher said, "Expression only; no depth." But we could as well say of much traditional art in the East: "Tradition only; no expression." Both traditions appear to be lacking. (p. 9)

His findings are similar to those expressed by Gardner (1989), in his book *To Open Minds: Chinese Clues to the Dilemma of Contemporary Education*. Although their respective Eastern countries were different, Japan for Beittel and China for Gardner, their conclusions were the same. Both authors discover approaches to teaching art that were far different from those in America. They also accept the influences passing between cultures and welcome the clash that sets the stage for transcending the differences. I would like to sketch how Beittel has reached this stage by referring to his past articles.

Changing the Objectives of Beittel

In the first half of his academic career, Beittel was praised for his pioneering effort to conduct sophisticated empirical-scientific researches on creativity in the visual arts (Beittel, 1953, 1956). His quantitative research methods, such as factor analysis of creativity, were strange to the majority of art educators at the time, who still were embraced by the mystery of artistic creativity (Beittel, 1960).

Although Beittel devoted himself to scientific research, he did not exclude other possibilities for research in art education. For example, he pointed out "a creative value complex" or the "found significant relationships between assessments of creativity in products, in people, and in process attitudes have been interpreted as an argument against making any one of these singly the criterion for creativity in the visual arts" (1959, p. 35). In his editorial for the Fall 1961 issue of *Studies in Art Education*, he encouraged philosophical and historical researchers to submit their works to the journal. He emphasized that emprical research need not be the only means of investigator's discourse.

He published four articles in 1963, two of which were based on scientific research using the factor analysis method (Beittel, 1963a; Beittel & Burkhart, 1963a). The other articles were phenomenological descriptions of children's art (Beittel, 1963b) and philosophical reflections on art (Beittel & Burkhart, 1963b).

The latter two essays showed evidence of his shift towards qualitative research. In his first essay, Beittel (1963b) provided narrative descriptions of his interviews with the small child David. In the interview Beittel used two methods in inquiring into David's thought processes in making stoneware: first, "a careful observation and transcription of what went on in making one piece," and, second, the "story construction" method (p. 27).

The second essay (Beittel & Burkhart, 1963b) stressed that the student's process in making crafts was to be the "departure from the known into the unknown" (p. 9), not the unknown into the known. A crafts worker's continuous concern for his or her creation gave to the craft its essential sense of reality.

The Emergence of the Two-way Street

These two essays helped me understand the beginning of Beittel's "two-way street": Western philosophical mind and Eastern art discipline (Okazaki, 1985a).

One way was to acknowledge the state of being that was primordial before the subjective and the objective. Beittel's article of 1964 confirmed the return to the human state of mind. Therefore, his interest was no longer in giving a "complex answer to a simple and static question" (p. 285). Instead he suggested an "open tracking system" (p. 285) for creative learning in and through art where both the learner and researcher were able to read the learner's state of mind at many points in time.

I think that Beittel took James' "holistic and phenomenological approach" and his introspective method as "a form of phenomenological description" (Watson & Evans, 1991, p. 375). In "the sequential drawing context in the absence of instruction," Beittel said:

> I have thus thought to protect myself from excessive generalities or an excessive catalogue of the atomistic, by seeking some vision of dynamic wholeness which still does not rely on vitalism or lapse into nominalism. Thus all experiments dealing with this context have a "naturalistic" aspect to them complementing the desire to control for individual differences and to manipulate the learning environment. (1966, pp. 205-206)

During his five-month porcelain-making apprenticeship in 1967 in Arita, Japan, he also recognized another difference among Eastern artists. He found that the American concept of creativity, the concern for originality and self-expression, was foreign to the Japanese mind. He acknowledged that the past had produced fine wares, but today's best wares were still close to the old methods and forms, the traditional nature of Japanese crafts. To his eye, it was as though the Western artist had lost his own sense of creativity on the one hand, while on the other hand young Japanese artists who turned to the West without feeling and discipline appeared to have lost their way (Beittel, 1968).

The issue of cross-cultural influences, or, the two-way street between cultures, is common among the Americans and the Japanese. Beittel has devoted the latter half of his academic career to the solution of how to transcend the differences between the two cultural values in art. His apprenticeship with the Japanese master, Manji Inoue (one of Japan's Living Intangible Cultural Treasures), contributed greatly to his search for the "lost ingredient" from the perspective of this foreign culture (Beittel, 1968, p. 27). He imagined the birth of "a world culture," and wrote, "As in the scriptural injunction, one loses oneself to find oneself" (Beittel, 1968, p. 27).

In the early 1980s, he acquired two modes of transcending the clash between cultures. One mode is what he called "a third eye," derived from the Western Medieval theology, and the other mode was the ancient strand of "body-mind integration," found in Zen philosophy.

A Symbolic Third Eye

Beittel already had the idea of "a potential 'third eye' or 'mid-wife of the preconscious'" (1974, p. 3). He makes its meaning more clear in his special article of 1986 for Japanese readers. It means "a global, three-dimensional vision" capable of "Divine Vision." According to Beittel, the third eye understands the "need for what the Western [German] mystic Jacob Boehme called 'contrarieties'" (p. 28). Beittel sees the need for these contrarieties.

Boehme's concept of contrarieties can be illustrated in using the metaphor of the fire. Fire can be both good and evil for human beings. Fire with people sitting around it is good, while fire in a wooden house becomes evil. Boehme's theology desires to bridge these contrarieties only by God. Beittel expects to transcend these by the Divine Vision of Blake's mysticism (Ishikawa, 1986).

Beittel (1986) suggests a justification for having kept the imagination of the third eye, "our relationship to things becomes art, our relationship to persons becomes love, and our relationship to the mystery of being becomes religion" (p. 27). Beittel concludes his article of 1986 in quoting the question Plotinus raised, "For how can one describe, as other than oneself, that which, when one saw it, seemed to be one with oneself?" Beittel (1986) proposes that we grasp the meaning of Divine Vision in moving into "a speechless realm" (p. 29) equally inhabited by mystic and artist. Then we can end raising the same question Plotinus raised.

Beittel's discussion of 1986 is compatible with his earlier belief (1983), "Dialogue, love, and art remain of a spiritual country, planetary but nonlocalized" (p. 13). This notion reflects "the spectrum of consciousness" of Wilber (1977) which consists of three major bands, the ego level, the existential level, and the level of mind, and four minor ones, the transpersonal, the biosocial, the philosophic, and the shadow levels. Thus Beittel (1989) goes on "the way toward a planetary consciousness" (p. 9) in art, which finally results in his latest book of 1991, *A Celebration of Art & Consciousness.*

The Self-Discipline of Body-mind Integration

Beittel wants to relate the Zen stance to art. According to him (1979a), the stance in the present allows one to organize "wholistically and qualitatively whatever is being experienced, thought, or created" (p. 53). He contends that this orientation is the same for "the one who inquires into or interprets art making and responding in art" (p. 53).

The term "moon viewing" characterizes Japanese reverence for nature and aesthetics. To Japanese people, the moon immediately evokes autumn and a whole extended semantic field including nature and human affairs. Izutsu & Izutsu (1981) called such totality of association "an invisible aesthetic resonator hidden under a tiny piece of nature," as "the result of age-long accumulations of cultural experience." For this reason, the moon itself serves as a hint of things that can be enlarged by "dint of its power into an organic whole of association" (p. 16).

The activity of moon viewing symbolizes a total experience of the art of life or the life of art. According to Maritain (1954/1974), it makes "indissoluble relationships among poetry, man, and things." Oriental art is a contemplative effort to discover and bring out "encaged souls and inner principles of dynamic harmony" (p. 13). Nature and things are perceived not as hostile but as a pantheistic continuum of which people can become an integral part through artistic and poetic intuition.

When a "baby smiles and the whole crowd is transported" (Suzuki, 1956, p. 281), such totality of experience is found in the typical thought of Zen, which stresses the self-discipline of indivisibility in order to transcend the stream of self-consciousness (Okazaki, 1985b). Beittel is right because the attitude of the artist toward his life is that of the student of Zen toward his life. The self-discipline in both art and life achieves a meditative state of body-mind integration (Beittel, 1979b).

The Japanese refer to it as "Geido" (the aesthetic-way of life). It is a kind of Taoism in which people devote themselves to the pursuit of an artistic activity or aesthetic situation. In the aesthetic way of life, artists must work out their own enlightenment through long years of training. They depend on their direct, personal experience and their meditation on the essential oneness of all things in the universe. Enlightenment emerges by seeing all arts as "one single thread string" (Basho, cited in Izutsu & Izutsu, 1981, p. 67). In this sense, a master of art who has the enlightened eye-hand-mind becomes a living tradition of art itself. By extension, "the enlightened eye" of the artist can be used to conduct research on the enhancement of educational practice (Eisner, 1991).

Beittel (1974) believed that an artist conveys something similar to "an impersonal living tradition undergirded by the surrounding culture" (p. 5). One thing became certain to him fifteen years later: "without vital tradition man has no way of transforming the everyday into the sacred" (Beittel, 1989, p. 9).

Finding "The Great Tradition"

Beittel understands the two-way street between cultures in saying that: "things Oriental pass through a prism that all but transforms them into their opposite. An irony abounds here. It is as though I have gone a Japanese way, but without the hierarchy; and Japan has gone the American way, but without the free spirit" (1983, p. 13).

We hope the prism that ideas pass through does not change things too much. Beyond the binocular vision of cross-cultural influence (Okazaki, 1991), Beittel elaborates a symbolical third eye that is still emphasized in his preface to the Japanese edition of *Alternatives for Art Education Research* (1987).

According to him (1986), the eye understands "the need for turning toward the 'forgotten truth'" (p. 28). Ultimately, his inquiry into the forgotten truth results in finding the two sides of "The Great Tradition" (Beittel, 1989). One side belongs to the planetary tradition that comes from the very idealism of Western metaphysics. It helps us to grasp the diversity in the unity of a layered universe. During his long academic career, Beittel's stance as researcher has shifted from behavioral psychologist to metaphysical philosopher.

The other side belongs to the living tradition that comes from the naturalism of Eastern art discipline. The philosophy of Japanese art can be found in the Haiku poetry of Basho, a seventeenth century Japanese "pilgrim-poet" (Britton, 1980, p. 7), "Go to the pine if you want to learn about the pine, or to the bamboo if you want to learn about the bamboo. And doing so, you must leave your subjective preoccupation with yourself" (Basho, cited in Yuasa, 1966, p. 33). Beittel (1989) comments on this notion, "we allow self to drop away so that we may return to things as they are in their own original nature. In this way we become the pine tree, we become the bamboo" (p. 23).

This attitude has served not only as a literary virtue but also as an artistic one in the tradition of Japan. The artist and the witnessed event move each other. By extension, it is the same way that the master/artist and apprentice/student(s) in a studio also move each other. Then art itself becomes the means by which this experience of shared displacement can be conveyed to others. The sense of dependence on others (Doi, 1980) in this situation can be used in "the process of pilgrimage" (Rimer, 1988) to others.

In a contemporary sense Beittel's stance as the artist of pottery has shifted from creator for his own sake to the pilgrim to others in art. This is why Beittel uses the ancient phrase "East and West of the Great Tradition" (1989, p. 26). The pilgrimage to others is needed for Beittel in order to transcend the difference between cultures. We are familiar with the process of pilgrimage when we are doing research or making art. If we make a pilgrimage to our tradition of philosophy, we use historiography, "'rational reconstructions' of the argument of great dead philosophers" (Rorty, 1984, p. 49). We hope to treat them as contemporaries with whom we can exchange views. If they are great dead artists or poets, or formless of tradition, then we use artistic or poetic reconstruction.

I think of Beittel as the poetic reconstructor of art education research. Beittel's work illustrates how well this secular pilgrim's tension fits in the following model of Turner (1974), "Go to nature; forget yourself; forget time; return to the world to share what you know with others" (cited in Rimer, 1988, p. 122).

I believe that this model is appropriate for understanding why Beittel (1972, 1973, 1984a) has asked for "alternatives to his alternatives" (Hamm, 1976, p. 305). Understanding what you are doing now where you are committed to a particular view requires understanding an alternative view (Eisner, 1989). Sharing what you know in your pilgrimage with others through writing requires a specific metaphor. This is "rhetoric deconstruction" (Trembath, 1989).

The Metaphor of the Japanese Tea-ceremony

Beittel is not a problem-solver, but a reporter on his continuous pilgrimages to others (Beittel, 1982). He has become "co-creator." He says that "infinite otherness of the artist as person is enhanced as well as the otherness of his arting" (1974, p. 5). I would like to replace the word artist with researcher: infinite otherness of the researcher as person is enhanced as well as the otherness of his researching. Surely, Beittel's focus is not on kind but on depth. He introduces us into "the circle dance which is arting-knowing[-]arting, as text, as ontological inquiry in art education" (Beittel, 1980-1981, p. 155).

The dance he invites us to can be illustrated by using the metaphor of the Japanese tea-ceremony (Cha-no-yu) in which powdered tea is served in a ceremonial yet artistic way. The host (tea-master) takes the almost care in preparing his tea room, the adjacent garden, tea utensils, a hanging scroll, a flower arrangement at an alcove, and the provision of simple dishes for the guests (students) in the tea room.

The participants in a tea ceremony may share a common atmosphere in which the same qualitative world is merged with others. It aims at developing an aesthetic situation of co-experience, an aesthetic deepening of daily life itself. Harmony, reverence, purity and tranquility (Hammitzsch, 1979) become pervasive qualities of the place. Indeed a tea room, which a tea master sets, is the topic of "pure experience" (Nishida, 1923/1973) in moving from action to seeing and from art to morality.

One at a time, the host and guests exchange the tea-bowl, which is a very important artistic creation for its rustic simplicity and refined elegance. The formal process of exchanging the tea-bowl is as follows: the host puts a small amount of tea in the tea-bowl, pours some water in the bowl, whips the tea into a bright green mixture; the bowl is placed before the first guest; he bows to the host and the other guests, then lifts the bowl with both hands and slowly, sip by sip, drinks all the tea; he returns the tea bowl to the host who cleans the bowl and prepares tea for the next guest. This process continues until each guest is served (Aesthetic Education Program, n.d., p. 26).

Suppose that Beittel is the host, we are the guests, the tea-bowl is a "pilgrimage to others," and the tea room, the field of art education. What would happen? I can only offer the following notion of what we art educators could learn from him.

> In art the Present is the eternal. The tea-master held that real appreciation of art is only possible to those who make of it a living influence. ... Thus the tea-master strove to be something more than the artist,—art itself. It was the Zen of aestheticism. (Okakura, 1906, pp. 151-152)

In using the metaphor of a tea-room, Beittel becomes "a living icon or image of the competent teacher" (Short, 1984, p. 104). I think he is far from being an "aesthetic partisan for creativity" (Beittel, 1968) or "Coonskinner" for "The Tradition of the New" (Gray, 1982). He is like a contemporary Meta-Zen-Master (Raunft, 1991). By extension, the KRB symposium, held at the University of Illinois, April, 1991, was a kind of Japanese tea-ceremony.

To Open Minds

Beittel's career reflects the internationalization of the art education field from the perspective of cross-cultural research in art education. Without his deep experience of a specific Japanese tradition of art, Beittel (1983) acknowledges that his grasp of Zen in Japanese art would be less sure and that his vision of a planetary tradition in pottery would not have arisen. His continuous pilgrimages to Japanese art have been done together with the pilgrimages to others in America.

Beittel's concern with the great tradition is similar to those in Bloom's *The Closing of the American Mind* (1987), but their positions are different from each other: Beittel as pilgrim, seriously going to another tradition, and Bloom as conservative, simply going back to extending one tradition. Beittel's intention is, I think, to open the world art educators' mind. He is the first developer of a world culture in the field of art education while Gardner is the second.

We are living in a shrinking world of technological societies. The changes in Japan have been more than matched by those in the United States. We have always been more interested in tomorrow than yesterday, whether yesterday was ten days, ten weeks, or ten decades ago. Such external changes in the world no longer match with the evolutional renewal of Beittel's versions. Rather, the changes of his world-view come from his pilgrimage to others, whether they are in the present or the past, whether in the West or the East.

In 1990 he said, "There is no identity called 'Ken Beittel' that would not better be set aside at this moment" (p. 7). I think his probe is best fitted to his remark of 1963 about the child David's stoneware. When David finished a series of his works, Beittel asked him, "What would you like to go into next?" and he answered, "I don't know. I just have to start" (1963b, p. 27). Beittel conceived that the truth for David was actually deeper. Later in 1989, he says: "the natural, the human, and the divine appear to the initiate who sees pottery as a way, as an esoteric discipline" (p. 26).

I see the feeling of David as a Zen stance. He doesn't care about the push-and-pull between his past and his future. Instead, he is only in the present, or what Pepper (1966) called the "qualitative immediate present" (cited in Beittel, 1979a, p. 53). Surely, Beittel, as David, just has to start his pilgrimage anytime, anywhere. Any of his changes reflects one of his pilgrimages to otherness because "To study oneself is to forget oneself" (Dogen, cited in Beittel, 1984b, p. 105). Thus he can secure the "beginner's mind," the "Zen of the simple act of making" (Beittel & Beittel, 1991, p. 284).

In using the metaphor of the tea-ceremony again, each of Beittel's papers is the same as the tea-ceremony which he sets. The readers of the text become his invited guests. Beittel's intention is, I believe, to open art educators' minds.

The Living Journeying Itself

I consider my discussion above as an interpretation. What I have may seem like a sketch rather than a finished picture. Yet, I have made some remarks about Beittel's work: he went to Japan because he had changed his mind; during his stay in Japan, he was faced with the dilemma of creativity and tradition; coming back to the United States, he has been making his pilgrimages to others not only in other cultures, but also in his own culture; and he is a living influence to open our minds.

Through his experiences of the living tradition of Arita pottery in Japan, Beittel has envisioned "a Great tradition neither East nor West, one of planetary scope, transcultural, transhistorical, and transpersonal" (Beittel, 1985, p. 51). His vision emerged in the early 1970s. He (1973) focused on the stream of consciousness of the artist in the making of drawing through the agency of a special participant observer.

I believe that his psychological research on drawing was done through "the Jamesian mind ... [as] artist final and last" (Barzun, 1985, p. 909). Interpreting "the mind-experience psychology" of James as "the art of human understanding," Leary

170

(1992) said, "it was perfectly legitimate—even necessary—to use analogies and metaphors, often from the realm of the arts, in the development of his [James'] psychological and philosophical doctrines" (p. 158).

Finally, Beittel's latest book (1992), entitled *A Celebration of Art & Consciousness*, confirms the return to the human state of mind in art. Its return reminds Beittel of Lowenfeld (Beittel, 1982/1983) and of his prophetic comment to Beittel in the mid-fifties, "You know, Ken, art is about sprit, what else?" (Beittel & Beittel, 1991, p. 283). In the epilogue of the book, he poetically celebrates the artist's form of the eternal present:

> Out of the depths of the Earth a faraway sound arose. It was the sound of beings preparing to do Art again. It was not new beings and a new Sprit, yet it was new beings with a new Sprit, for Sprit never manifests in the same way twice. The winged centaur knows both the summit of pure Sprit and the valley of pure Matter—and it moves toward that unity through Art. Sprit is Artist. (p. 303)

He finds himself as the winged "man as centaur" (Wilber, 1977, Chap. 9) in the eternal manifest, similar to the sky in which one poetically dwells. The manifest like the sky is "the artist's form of the eternal present," "the *now* that has no space—that has no time" (Beittel & Beittel, 1991, p. 150). By extension, it can be applied to the teacher's form of the eternal present (Nagamachi, 1988).

Whatever view one takes of Beittel's continuous pilgrimages (or silent dialogues in his term) to others (or otherness), one can not help but admire "the living journeying itself" (Beittel, 1974, p. 6) which he sets out to throughout his life. Its sprit is beautifully expressed by the Japanese 17th century pilgrim-poet Basho (1980), who states in the prologue of his *Narrow Road to a Far Province.*

> The passing days and months are eternal travelers in time. The years that come and go are travelers too. Life itself is a journey; and as for those who

spend their days upon the waters in ships and those who grow old leading horses, their very home is the open road. And some poets of old there were who died while travelling. (p. 29)

Basho's poetic pilgrimage was done in 1689. I think Beittel is the celebrated pilgrim-artist-researcher. Let's hope that the reportage of Beittel's other artistic pilgrimages will be coming to us soon. In this sense, the KRB symposium, "Still More Beittel Epilogues," held at the University of Illinois, April 1991, is called not Beittel's Epilogues, but the Prologue to the next journey in art education research.

The story of Beittel's pilgrimages to others is reminiscent of Christo's project, the huge yellow and blue umbrellas on the lands of both the United States and Japan in October 1991. As being "the winged centaur," Beittel is dwelling in the sky.

His extensive work is one bridge in the two-way street of cultures through which cross-cultural researchers in art education on each side have to pass. It also becomes one gate to "an alternate path for inquiry into art" (Beittel, 1971) through which psychological and philosophical researchers have to pass.

All new researchers are encouraged to read "Beittel's work for research alternatives as well as for personal consolation along the lonesome road of intellectual pursuit" (Stokrocki, 1992, p. 2). A pilgrimage to others makes the living journeying itself that which is invaluable (Beittel, 1995, 1997). Thus the two-way street between cultures in art and art education will be wide open.

References

Adams, J. (2006). Book review [Review of the book *Histories of art and design education: Collected essays*, by M. Romans]. *The International Journal of Art & Deign Education, 25* (2), 241-242.

Aesthetic Education Program (n.d.). *Cha-no-yu: Experimental version.* St. Louis, MO: CEMREL, Inc.

Akagi, R., & Yamaguchi, K. (2019). The evolution of drawing education in modern Japan: The impact of traditional and introduced methods on the artworks of elementary students in the Meiji era. In N.Nanobashvili, & T.Tentenberg, (Eds.), *Drawing education worldwide! Continuities-transfers-mixtures* (pp. 235-254). Heidelberg: Heidelberg University Publishing.

Anderson, R. S. (1959). *Japan: Three epochs of modern education.* Washington, D.C.: U.S. Government Printing Office.

Ando, K. (1997). A phenomenological study of art education in Japan after 1945. In A. A. Anderson & P. E. Bolin (Eds.), *History of art education: Proceedings from the third Penn State international symposium* (pp. 460-466). University Park, PA: The Pennsylvania State University.

Arai, K. (1948). Bijutsu Kyoiku no kyokasho [Textbooks of fine arts education]. In Society for the Study of Education of Tokyo Bunrika University (Ed.), *America kyokasho no kenkyu* [Studies of the American textbooks] (pp. 173-184). Tokyo: The Kaneko Syobo.

Arthur Wesley Dow. (1920/1921). *Who's who in America, 11*, 803.

Bailey, H. T. (1900). *A sketch of the history of public art instruction in Massachusetts.* Boston: Wright and Potter Printing.

Bailey, H. T. (1914). *Art education.* Boston: Houghton Mifflin. (The Japanese edition published under the title, *Futsuu kyoiku niokeru geijutsu kyoiku* [Shimoda trans.]. Tokyo: Dainihon Tosho, 1917).

Baker, K. R. (1985). J. Liberty Tadd, who are you? *Studies in Art Education, 26* (2), 75-85.

Barbosa, A. M. (1984). Walter Smith's influence in Brazil and the efforts by Brazilian liberals to overcome the concept of art as an elitist activity. *Journal of Art & Design Education, 3* (2), 233-246.

Barkan, M., Chapman, L. H., & Kern, E. J. (1970). *Guidelines: Curriculum development for aesthetic education.* St. Ann, Mo: CEMREL Inc. (ERIC: ED No. 048 274)

Barzun, J. (1985). William James: The mind as artist. In S. Koch & D. E. Leary (Eds.), *A century of psychology as science* (pp. 904-910). New York: McGraw-Hill.

Basho, M. (1980). *A Haiku journey: Basho's narrow road to a far province* (rev. ed.) (D. Britton, Trans.). Tokyo & New York: Kodansha International.

Battiata, M. L. (2014). *Elements of influence: Composition and the students of Arthur Wesley Dow* (Doctoral dissertation). Available from ProQuest Dissertations and Theses database. (UMI No. 1556685)

Beasley, W. G. (1982). *The modern history of Japan* (3rd revised ed.). Tokyo, Charles E. Tuttle.

Beittel, K. R. (1953). *Some experimental approaches to the aesthetic attitudes of college students.* (Unpublished doctoral dissertation). The Pennsylvania State University.

Beittel, K. R. (1956). Experimental studies of the aesthetic attitudes of college students. In M. Barkan (Ed.), *Research in Art Education* (7th Yearbook) (pp. 47-61). Washington, D. C.: National Art Education Association.

Beittel, K. R. (1959). Molesting or meeting the Muse: Look at the creativity complex in the visual arts. *Studies in Art Education, 1* (1), 26-37.

Beittel, K. R. (1960). Art. In C. W. Harris (Ed.), *Encyclopedia of educational research* (3rd ed.) (pp.77-87). New York: Macmillan.

Beittel, K. R. (1961). Editorial. *Studies in Art Education, 3* (1), 3.

Beittel, K. R. (1963a). Factor analysis of three dimensions of art judgment complex: Criteria, art objects and judges. *Journal of Experimental Education, 32* (2), 167-173.

Beittel, K. R. (1963b). David's stonewares. *School Arts, 63* (1), 23-27.

Beittel, K. R. (1964). On the relationships between art and general creativity: A biased history and projection of a partial conquest. *School Review, 72* (3), 272-288.

Beittel, K. R. (1966). Sketches toward a psychology of learning in art. In K. R. Beittel & E. L. Mattil (Eds.), *A seminar in art education for research and curriculum development* (pp. 173-217). University Park, PA: The Pennsylvania State University. (ERIC Document Reproduction Service No. ED 10 000)

Beittel, K. R. (1968). Teacher as student: Impression on studying ceramics in Japan. *Art Education, 21* (5), 26-27.

Beittel, K. R. (1971). An alternate path for inquiry into art. *Art Education, 24* (1), 30-33.

Beittel, K. R. (1972). *Mind and context in the art of drawing.* New York: Holt, Rinehart, and Winston.

Beittel, K. R. (1973). *Alternatives for art education research.* Dubbqus, Iowa: W. C. Brown. (The Japanese edition published under the title, *Orutanatibu* [M. Nagamachi, trans.].

Osaka: Sanko Syobo, 1987).

Beittel, K. R. (974). Formative hermeneutics in the arting processes of an other: The philetics of art education. *Art Education, 27* (9), 2-7.

Beittel, K. R. (1979a). Unity of truth, language, and method in art education research. *Studies in Art Education, 20* (1), 50-56.

Beittel, K. R. (1979b). The teaching of art in relation to body-mind integration and self-actualization in art. *Art Education, 32* (7), 18-20.

Beittel, K. R. (1979c). Toward an art education theory on qualitative responding to art. *Review of Research in Visual Arts Education, 10*, 33-40.

Beittel, K. R. (1980-81). Metaphysics, method and meaning in ontological inquiry into art making. *Canadian Review of Art Education Research, 6 & 7*, 148-156.

Beittel, K. R. (1982). Art education. In H. E. Mitzel (Ed.), *Encyclopedia of educational research* (Vol. 1) (5th ed.) (pp. 159-171). New York: Macmillan.

Beittel, K. R. (1982/1983). Rouenferudo to atarashi jidai no bijutsu [Lowenfeld and art for a new age] (M. Nagamachi & A. Okazaki, Trans.). *Kyoiku Bijutsu* [Art in Education], *44* (10), 29-32. (Original English work published 1982, *Art Education, 35* (6), 18-21).

Beittel, K. R. (1983). The empty box: The potter as first violinist. *Journal of Multi-cultural and Cross-cultural Research in Art Education, 1* (1), 7-14.

Beittel, K. R. (1984a). Still other alternatives. *Visual Arts Research, 10* (2), 15-21.

Beittel, K. R. (1984b). Great swamp fires I have known: Competence and the hermeneutics of qualitative experiencing. In E. G. Shorts (Ed.), *Competence* (pp. 105-121). New York: University of Press of America.

Beittel, K. R. (1985). Art for a new age. *Visual Arts Research, 11* (1), 45-60.

Beittel, K. R. (1986). Kunan no tokini seinaru yokenryoku chotkanryoku dosatsuryoku wo mochitudukerukoto [To keep the divine vision in time of trouble] (M. Nagamachi, trans.). *Kyoiku Bijutsu* [Art in Education], *47* (11), 25-29.

Beittel, K. R. (1987). Nihongo ban heno jobun [Preface to the Japanese edition of *Alternatives for Art Education Research*]. In K. R. Beittel, *Orutanatibu* [Alternatives for Art Education Research] (M. Nagamachi, trans.) (pp. 3-5). Osaka: Sanko Syobo.

Beittel, K. R. (1989). *Zen and the art of pottery*. Tokyo and New York: Weatherhill.

Beittel, K. R. (1990). Zen and art of pottery. *Art Education, 43* (2), 6-15.

Beittel, K. R. (1995, October). Fateful fork in the road: The 1965 red book. Paper presented at the Third Penn State Symposium on the History of Art Education. University Park: PA, The Pennsylvania State University.

Beittel, K. R. (1995). Preface. In M. Stokrocki (Ed.), *New waves of research in art education* (i-ii). Kalamazoo, MI: Western Michigan University, Dept. of Art. Reprinted from ERIC database. (ED 395 871)

Beittel, K. R. (1997). Fateful fork in the road: The 1965 red book. In A. A. Anderson & P. E. Bolin (Eds.), *History of art education: Proceedings from the third Penn State international symposium* (pp.533-539). University Park, PA: The Pennsylvania State University.

Beittel, K. R., & Beittel, J. (1991). *A celebration of art & consciousness.* University Park, PA: Happy Valley Healing Arts.

Beittel. K. R., & Burkhart, R. C. (1963a). Strategies of spontaneous, divergent, and academic art students. *Studies in Art Education, 5* (1), 20-41.

Beittel. K. R., & Burkhart, R. C. (1963b). Crafts in education: Continuity and reality in crafts. *Craft Horizons, 23* (5), 8-9.

Belshe, F. G. (1946). *A history of art education in the public schools of the United States* (Doctoral dissertation, Yale University). *Dissertation Abstracts International, 25* (7), 3956, 1965 (University of Microfilms No. 65-02019).

Binyon, L. (1911). *The flight of the dragon: An Essay on the theory and practice of art in China and Japan, based on original sources.* London: John Murray.

Bloom, A. (1987). *The closing of the American mind.* New York: Simon & Schuster.

Boas, B. (1924). *Art in the school.* Garden City, NY: Doubleday, Page.

Borgmann, C. B. (1986). As Christo wraps the art scene ... Are educators ready? *Art Education, 39* (1), 19-22.

Boyle, R. J. (2013). Arthur Wesley Dow in Japan. Art. *Archives of American Art Journal, 52* (1/2), 58-69.

Brittain, W. L. (1979). *Creativity, art and the young child.* Upper Saddle River, NJ: Prentice Hall. (The Japanese edition published under the title, *Yoji no zokeisei to sozosei* [K. Kurokawa, et. al. trans.]. Nagoya, Japan: Reimei Syobo, 1983).

Britton, D. (1980). Introduction. In M. Basho. *A haiku journey: Basho's narrow road to a far province* (rev. ed., D. Britton, Trans.) (pp. 5-23). Tokyo & New York: Kodansha International.

BT. (2000). Abstract. *Document resume* (p. 1). Reprinted from ERIC database. (ED 451 089)

Buber, M. (1971). Education as dialogue. In M. Levit (Ed), *Curriculum* (pp. 282-294). Urbana: University of Illinois Press. (Reprinted from *Between Man and Man*, New York: Macmillan, pp. 90-102).

Buckley, J. (1908). Normal art schools. In J. P. Haney (Ed.), *Art education in the public schools of the United States* (pp. 325-351). New York: American Art Annual.

Burn, R. S. (1852). *The illustrated London drawing-book*. London: Levry, Robson, and Franklyn.

Carpenter, F. L. (1918). *Stories pictures tell* (Book One). Chicago: Rand McNally.

Carson, J. (1981). What American art educators can learn from the Japanese, *Art Education, 34* (6), 42-44, 46.

Chalmers, F. G. (1985). South Kensington and the colonies: David Blair of New Zealand and Canada. *Studies in Art Education, 26* (2), 69-74.

Chalmers, F. G. (2004). Learning from histories of art education: An overview of research and issues. In E. W. Eisner & M. D. Day, (Eds.), *Handbook of research and policy in art education* (pp. 11-31), Mahwah, NJ: Lawrence Erlbaum Associates.

Chamberlain, B. H., & Mason, W. B. (1891). *Handbook for travelers in Japan* (3rd ed.). London: John Murry.

Chan, W. (1946/1965). Chinese art. In D. Runes & H. G. Schrikel (Eds.), *Encyclopedia of the arts* (rep. ed.) (p. 183). London: Peter Owen.

Chang, Y. (847/1977). *Lekidai meiga ki* [Li-tai ming-hua Chi] (T. Nagahiro, trans.). Tokyo: Heibonsha.

Chapman, J. G. (1847). *The American drawing-book*. New York: G. S. Redfield, Clinton Hall.

Chapman, J. G. (1864). *The American drawing-book*. New York: W. J. Widdleton.

Chapman, L. H. (1978). *Approaches to art in education*. New York: Harcourt Brace Jovanovich.

Civil Information and Education, (1948). *Education in the new Japan*. Vol. I, Washington, D.C.; U.S. Government Printing Office.

Clapp, F. B. (1955). *Mary Florence Denton and the Doshisha*. Kyoto, Japan: Doshisha University Press.

Clark, G. A. (1985). Art and global education. *Art Education, 38* (4), 5.

Committee for Facilitating Research (1986). *Teacher training in Japan*. Tokyo: Daiichi Hoki.

Cox, G. J. (1923, June). The horizon of A. W. Dow. *International Studio. 77*, 88-94.

Cross, A. K. (1896). *Free-Hand drawing: A manual for teachers and students*. Boston: Ginn & Company.

Cross, A. K., & Swain, A. (1898). *Outline of drawing lessons for primary grades*. Boston: Ginn & Company.

Dao kyoju no bijutsu enzetsu [Professor Dow's lecture on art]. (1903, December 17). *Osaka*

Asahi Shimbun, Kyoto Furoku [Osaka Asahi Daily News, Appendix to Kyoto Area], p. 1.

Dao kyoju no enzetsu [Professor Dow's speech]. (1903, December 10). *Hinode Shimbun* [Hinode Daily News], p. 2.

Dao kyoju no enzetsu [Professor Dow's speech]. (1903, December 13). *Hinode Shimbun* [Hinode Daily News], p. 3.

Dao kyoju no nihon bijutsukan [Professor Dow's view on Japanese art]. (1903, December 17). *Osaka Mainich Shimbun* [Osaka Mainichi Daily News], p.7. (Reprinted in *Bijutsu Shinpo* [Art News], p. 5, December 20, 1903).

Dao shi no enzetsu [The speech of Mr. Dow]. (1903, December 16). *Hinode Shimbun* [Hinode Daily News], p. 3.

Davenport, M. (2000). Culture and education: Polishing the lenses. *Studies in Art Education*, *41*(4), 361-373.

Davis, J. D. (1890). *A sketch of the life of Rev. Joseph Hardy Neesima, L. L. D. president of Doshisha, Kyoto*. Tokyo: Z. M. Maruya.

De Garmo, C. (1909). *Principles of secondary education: The studies*. New York: The Macmillan.

De Lemos, P. (1946, September). Oriental art and the American art teacher. *School Arts, 47*, 27-36.

Dewey, J. (1919, October 4). Liberalism in Japan: I The intellectual preparation. *The Dial*, *67*, 283-285.

Dewey, J. (1963). *Philosophy and civilization*. New York: Capricorn Books.

Dobbs, S. M. (1972). *Paradox and promise: Art education in the public schools* (Doctoral dissertation, Stanford University). *Dissertation Abstract International, 33* (5), 2139-A, 1973 (University Microfilms No. 72-30622).

Dobbs, S. M. (1983). Japan trail '83: American art education odyssey to the Orient. *Art Education, 36* (6), 4-11.

Doi, T. (1981). *The anatomy of dependence*. Tokyo: Kodansha International.

Dow, A. W. (1895). Some reasons for studying Japanese art. In *Arthur Wesley Dow papers,* Archives of American Art (Reel No. 1033), Washington D. C., Smithsonian Institution.

Dow, A. W. (1899/1903). *Composition* (5th ed.). Garden City, NY: The Baker and Taylor. (1st ed. published 1899).

Dow, A. W. (1903). Arthur Dow travel diary (1st note book, Ipswich to Daitokuji, Kyoto, trip around the world, westward). In *Arthur and Dana Dow papers,* Archives of American Art (Reel No.1209), Washington D. C., Smithsonian Institution.

Dow, A. W. (1908). Training in the theory and practice of teaching art. *Teachers College Record, 9* (3), 1-54.

Dow, A W. (1911). Art, method of teaching. In P. Monroe (Ed.), *A cyclopedia of education* (Vol.1) (pp. 230-232). New York: Macmillan.

Dow, A. W. (1912). *Theory and practice of teaching art.* New York: Teachers College, Columbia University.

Dow, A. W. (1913). *Composition* (rev. ed.). Garden City, New York: The Country Life Press (Originally published, 1899).

Dow, A. W. (1917, January). Modernism in art. *American Magazine of Art,* pp. 113-116.

Dow, A, W. (1998). *Composition.* Berkeley, California: University of California Press. (Reprinted from 13th ed. 1920, and added Introduction by Masheck).

Dow, A, W. (2007). *Composition.* Mineoda, NY: Dover. (Reprinted from 9th ed. 1920).

Dow, D (1903/1904). Dana Dow travel diary, 1903-1904. In *Arthur and Dana Dow papers,* Archives of American Art (Reel No.1209), Washington D. C., Smithsonian Institution.

Eckroade, G. A. (1979). *Political socialization and schooling: American views of Japanese educational politics from 1872 to 1952* (Doctoral dissertation, The University of Maryland, 1979). Dissertation Abstracts International, *40,* 6224A. (University Microfilms No.80-12656)

Efland, A. D. (1976). Changing views of children's artistic development: Their impact on curriculum and instruction. In E.W. Eisner (Ed.), *The arts, human development, and education* (pp. 65-86). Berkeley, CA: McCutchan.

Efland, A. D. (1990). *A history of art education: Intellectual and social currents in teaching the visual arts.* New York: Teachers College Press.

Efland, A. D. (2002). *Art and cognition: Integrating the visual arts in the curriculum.* New York: Teachers College Press. (The Japanese edition published under the title, *Bijutsu to chino to kansei* [M. Fujie, I. Ikeuchi, T. Ikegami, K. Nakamura, A. Okazaki, T. Abe, & Y. Iwasaki trans.]. Tokyo: Nihon Bunkyo Syuppan, 2011).

Eisner, E. W. (Ed.), (1971). *Confronting curriculum reform.* Boston: Little, Brown, & Co. (The Japanese edition published under the title, *Karikyuramu kaikaku no soten* [K. Kihara, Y. Kato, & N. Koya trans.]. Nagoya, Japan: Reimei Syobo, 1974).

Eisner, E. W. (1972). *Educating artistic vision.* New York: Macmillan. (The Japanese edition published under the title, *Bijutsu kyoiku to kodomo no chiteki hattatsu* [N. Nakase, A. Maemura, K. Yamada, Y. Minosaku, A. Okazaki, T. Miyazaki, N. Mizushima, Y. Kaga, and H. Abe trans.]. Nagoya, Japan: Reimei Syobo, 1986).

Eisner, E. W. (1979). Cross-cultural research in arts education: Problems, issues, and prospects. *Studies in Art Education, 21* (1), 27-35.

Eisner, E. W. (1981). The author responds. *Journal of Aesthetic Education, 15* (1), 120-125.

Eisner, E. W. (1982). *Cognition and curriculum: A basis for deciding what to teach and how to evaluate.* New York: Longman. (The Japanese edition published under the title, *Kyoikukatei to kyoikuhyoka* [N. Nakase, M. Nagamachi, K. Fukumoto, & A. Okazaki trans.]. Tokyo: Kenpakusha, 1990).

Eisner, E.W. (1984). Alternative approaches to curriculum development in art education. *Studies in Art Education, 25* (4), 259-264.

Eisner, E. W. (1986). Nihongo ban heno jo [Preface to the Japanese edition of *Educating artistic vision*]. In E.W. Eisner, *Bijutsu kyoiku to kodomo no chiteki hattatsu* [Educating artistic vision] (pp. 1-3). Nagoya, Japan: Reimei Syobo.

Eisner, E.W. (1989, November 21). The professional education of teachers of art: Conception and location (invited address), Daigaku Bijutsu Kyoiku Gakkai [Society of University Art Education Conference], Wakayama, Japan.

Eisner, E. W. (1991). *The enlightened eye: Qualitative inquiry and the enhancement of educational practice.* New York: Macmillan.

Eisner, E. W. (1992). The efflorescence of the history of art education: Advance into the past or return from the present? In P. Amburgy, D. Soucy, M. A. Stankiewicz, B. Wilson, & M. Wilson (Eds.), *The history of art education: Proceedings from the second Penn State conference, 1989* (pp. 37-41). Reston, VA: National Art Education Association.

Eisner, E. W., & Ecker, D. (1966). What is art education. In E. W. Eisner & D. Ecker (Eds.), *Readings in Art Education* (pp.1-13). Waltham, Mass.: Blaisdell.

Enyeart, J. L. (2001*). Harmony of reflected light: The photographs of Arthur Wesley* Dow. Santa Fe, NM: Museum of New Mexico Press.

Fairbrothers, T. (2007). *Ipswich days: Arthur Wesley Dow and his hometown.* New Haven, CT: Yale University Press.

Farnum, R. B. (1914). *Present statues of drawing and art in the elementary and secondary schools of the United States.* Washington D.C.: Government Printing Office, (U. S. Bureau of Education Bulletin 1914, No. 13, Whole No. 586).

Farnum, R. B. (1941). The early history of American art education. In G. M. Whipple (Ed.), *Art in American life and education* (pp. 445-447). Bloomington, Ill.: Public School Publishing. (The 40th yearbook of the National Society for the Study of Education).

Farnum, R. B. (1947). Introduction. In A. H. Munsell, *Color notation* (tenth ed.) (pp. 6-9).

Baltimore, MD: Munsell Color.

Faulkner, R., Ziegfeld, E., & Gerald, H. (1941). *Art today: An introduction to the fine and functional art.* New York: Henry Holt.

Fenollosa, E. (1913/1963). *Epochs of Chinese and Japanese art* (Vol.1) (rep. ed.). New York: Dover.

Fenollosa, M. (1913/1963). Preface to *Epochs of Chinese and Japanese Art.* In E. Fenollosa, *Epochs of Chinese and Japanese art* (Vol.1) (rep. ed.) (pp. i-xxvi). New York: Dover.

Fisher, R. M., & Bickel, B. (2006). The mystery of Dr. who? On a road less traveled in art education. *Journal of Social Theory in Art Education, 26,* 28-57.

Flectcher, F. M. (1918). *A memorandum on the Aims and Methods of Art Teaching in Day Schools.* London: John Hogg.

Foster, M. S. (1975). Materials for teaching art in Japan: Textbooks and posters for the elementary grades. *Art Teacher, 5* (2), 23-26.

Foster, M. S. (1990). Art education in Japan. *School Arts, 89* (9), 12-15.

Foster, M. S. (1992). Exchanges between American and Japanese art educators: What did they learned from each other? In P. Amburgy, D. Soucy, M. Stankiewicz, B. Wilson & M. Wilson (Eds.), *The history of art education: Proceedings from the second Penn State conference, 1989* (pp. 104-108). Reston, VA: National Art Education Association.

Froehlich, H. B., & Snow, B. E. (1904-1905). *Text books of art education* (Bks. I-VI). New York: Prang.

Fujie, M. (2003). A comparative study of artistic play and Zokei-Asobi. *Journal of Aesthetic Education, 37* (4), 107-114.

Fukumoto, K. (2003). Does art education dream of Disneyland? *Journal of Aesthetic Education, 37* (4), 32-41.

Gardner, H. E. (1982). *Artful scribbles: The significance of children's drawings.* New York: Basic Books. (The Japanese edition published under the title, *Kodomono byoga,* [M. Hoshi trans.]. Tokyo: Seishin Syobo, 1996).

Gardner, H. E. (1984). Art, mind, and brain. New York: Basic Books. (The Japanese edition published under the title, *Geijutsu, seishin,* soshite zuno. [N. Nakase & K. Morishima trans.]. Nagoya, Japan: Reimei Syobo, 1991).

Gardner, H. E. (1989). *To open minds: Chinese clues to the dilemma of contemporary education.* New York: Basic Books.

Garoian, C., Quan, R., & Collins, D. (1977). Christo: On art, education, and the running fence. *Art Education, 30* (2), 16-19.

Grauer, K. (1994). Editorial. *InSEA News, 1* (3), 3.

Gray, J. U. (1982). Redcoatism and cookskinism revised as research in art education. *Studies in Art Education, 23* (2), 36-44.

Green, N. E. (1999a). Arthur Wesley Dow and American arts & crafts. *American Art Review, 11*(6), 214-221.

Green, N. E. (1999b). Arthur Wesley Dow: Artist and educator. In N. E. Green & J. Poesch (Eds.), *Arthur Wesley Dow and American arts & crafts* (pp. 55-86). New York: The American Federation of the Arts.

Green, N. E. & Poesch, J. (1999). *Arthur Wesley Dow and American arts & crafts.* New York: The American Federation of the Arts.

Haga, T. (1971). The formation of realism in Meiji painting: The artistic career of Takahashi Yuichi. In D.H. Shiverly (Ed.), *Tradition and modernization in Japanese culture* (pp. 221-256). Princeton, N.J. Princeton University Press.

Hall, G. S. (1911). *Educational problems* (Volume II). New York: D. Appleton.

Hamm, G. B. (1976). Kenneth Beittel on art education research. *Leonardo, 9* (4), 303-305.

Hammitzsch, H. (1979). *Zen in the art of the tea ceremony.* (P. Lemesurier, Trans.). Great Britain: Element Books Ltd.

Haney, J. P. (1908a). The development of art education in the public schools. In J. P. Haney (Ed.), *Art education in the public schools of the United States* (pp. 21-78). New York: American Art Annual.

Haney J. P. (Ed.) (1908b). *Art education in the public schools of the United States.* New York: American Art Annual.

Haney, J. P. (1916). Letter to Seishi Shimoda. August 10, 1916. In H. T. Bailey, *Futsuu kyoiku niokeru geijutsu kyoiku* [Arts education in general education] (S. Shimoda, trans.) (Appendix, p.149). Tokyo: Dainihon Tosho.

Hashimoto, H. (1980). Yamamoto Kane no kyoikujissen nimiru sidoho nituiteno kosatsu [Reappraisal of Kane Yamamoto's method in art education]. *Kagoshima Daigaku Kyoiku Gakubu Kenkyu Kiyo* [Bulletin of the Faculty of Education, Kagoshima University], *32,* 99-124.

Hayward, F. H. (1915/1925). *The lessons in appreciation.* New York: The Macmillan.

Hickman, R. (1991). Art education in a newly industrialized country. *Journal of Art & Design Education, 10* (2), 179-188.

Hino, Y. (1997). Art "for living's sake" and education: The work of individual life "in the historical world". In A. A. Anderson & P. E. Bolin (Eds.), *History of art education:*

Proceedings from the third Penn State international symposium (pp.193-199). University Park, PA: The Pennsylvania State University.

Hino, Y. (2003). Restriction and individual expression in the "play activity/zokei asobi." *Journal of Aesthetic Education, 37* (4), 19-26.

Hook, D, J. (1987). *Fenollosa and Dow: The effect of an Eastern and Western dialogue on American art education.* (Doctoral Dissertation, The Pennsylvania State University, 1987). (University Microfilms No. 88-07,793).

Hurll, E. M. (1914). *How to show pictures to children.* Boston: Houghton Mifflin.

Hurll, E. M. (1916). Beautiful pictures to enjoy. *School Arts Book, 15* (8), 476-481.

Hurwitz, A. & Madeja, S. S. (1977). *The joyous vision.* Englewood Cliffs, N.J.: Prentice Hall.

Ishikawa, T. (1986). Baiteru no "Divine Vision" tositeno geijutsu kyoiku [The "Divine Vision" proposed by Beittel and its implication for arts education: A review]. *Kyoiku Bijutsu* [Art in Education], *47* (11), 30-31.

Ishizaki, K., & Wang, W. (2003). Postmodern approach to art appreciation for integrated study in Japan, *Journal of Aesthetic Education, 37* (4), 64-73.

Iwano, M. (2003). Art as part of daily life: A cross-cultural dialogue between art and people. *Journal of Aesthetic Education, 37* (4), 114-121.

Izor, E. P. (1916). *Costume design and home planning.* Boston: Atkinson, Mentzer.

Izutsu T., and Izutsu, T. (1981). *The theory of beauty in the classical aesthetics of Japan.* Holland: Martinus Nijhoff.

James, W. (1918). *The principles of psychology.* New York: Henry Holt.

Jameson, M. (1890). *Legends of the monastic orders as represented in the fine arts.* London: Longmans.

Japanese National Commission for UNESCO. (1958). *The making of compulsory education in Japan.* Tokyo: Ministry of Education.

Japanese National Institute for Educational Research. (1978). Modernization of education in Japan [Special issue], *Research Bulletin of the National Institute for Educational Research, 7.*

Johnson, A. W. (1934). *Arthur Wesley Dow: Historian-artist-teacher.* Ipswich, MA.: Ipswich Historical Society.

Jordan, L. (1991). A master potter. *T & G* (A free magazine in & near State College & Penn State), *26* (1), 12-23.

Kaneda, T. (1994). Children's art activities in non/less-industrialized societies: A case study in Nepal. *Art Education, 47* (1), 20-24.

Kaneda, T. (2003). The concept of freedom in art education in Japan. *Journal of Aesthetic Education, 37* (4), 12-19.

Kaneko, K. (1978a). Zoku nihon no kindai bijutsu kyoiku shi (9) [A history of modern Japanese art education, Part 9]. *Biiku Bunka* [Magazine for Art Education], *28* (7), 42-45.

Kaneko, K. (1978b). Zoku nihon no kimlai bijutsu kyoiku shi (10) [A history of Japanese modern art education, part 10.] *Biiku Bunka* (Magazine for Art Education), *28* (8), 46-49.

Kaneko, K. (1978c). Zoku nihon no kindai bijutsu kyoiku shi (12) [A history of Japanese modern art education part 12]. *Biiku Bunka* [Magazine for Art Education], *28* (12), 44-49.

Kaneko, K. (1979). Zoku nihon no kindai bijutsu kyoiku shi (13) [A history of modern Japanese art education, Part 13]. *Biiku Bunka* [Magazine for Art Education], *29* (1), 42-45.

Kaneko, K. (1980). Zoku nihon no kindai bijutsu kyoiku shi (27) [A history of modern Japanese art education, part 27]. *Biiku Bunka* [Magazine for Art Education], *30* (9), 60-65.

Kaneko, K. (1981). Meiji shoki no honyaku zuga kyokasho to sono genpon no kenkyu [On the translations of drawing books in the early Meiji era]. *Ibaragi Daigaku Kyoiku Gakubu Kenkyu Kiyo* [Bulletin of the Faculty of Education, Ibaragi University], *30*, 19-34.

Kaneko, K. (1985). Meiji syoki zuga kyokasho to sono genpon no kenkyu [On the citations from Chapman's and Coe's books to Japanese drawing books in the early Meiji Era]. *Ibaragi Daigaku Kyoiku Gakubu Kiyo* [Bulletin of the Faculty of Education, Ibaragi University], *34*, 55-69.

Kaneko, K. (1992). *Kindai nihon bijutsu kyoiku no kenkyu: Meiji jidai* [A study of modern Japanese art education: The Meiji era]. Tokyo: Chuokoron Bijutu Syuppan.

Kaneko, Y. (2003). Japanese painting and Johannes Itten's art education. *Journal of Aesthetic Education, 37* (4), 93-101.

Katter, E. (1985). Hands-on instructional resources for the teaching art: A historical perspective. In B. Wilson & H. Hoffa (Eds.), *The history of art education: Proceedings from the Penn State conference* (pp. 295-314). Reston, VA.: National Art Education Association.

Kauppinen, H., & Diket, D. (1995). Multi-cultural and cross-cultural issues. In H. Kauppinen & R. Diket (Eds.), *Trends in art education from diverse cultures* (pp. 133-139). Reston, VA: National Art Education Association.

Kawakami, T. (1871). *Seiga Sinan* [Guide to Western pictures], Part 1. Tokyo: Ministry of

Education.

Kawakita, M. (1974). *Modern currents in Japanese art* (C. S. Terry, trans.). New York: John Weatherhill.

Keenleyside, H. L. L., & Thomas, A. F. (1937). *History of Japanese education and present educational system*. Tokyo: The Hokuseido Press.

Keitoku, M. (1980). Bijutsu kyoiku no tenkai [Development of art education]. In M. Keitoku (Ed.), *Zuga kosaku bijutsuka kyoiku no riron to tehkai* [Theory and development of art and crafts education in the public schools]. Tokyo: Daiichi Hoki.

Kikuchi, B. D. (1909). *Japanese education*. London: John Murray.

Kobayashi, T. (1976). *Society, schools and progress in Japan*. Oxford: Pergamon Press.

Kodansha Encyclopedia of Japan (1983). vol.4, Herts: International Book Distributors Ltd.

Kumamoto, T. (1973). Bijutsu kyoiku to kenkyu 1 [Studies in art education part 1]. *Biiku Bunka* [Magazine for Art Education], *23* (3), 3-7.

Kumamoto, T. (1982). Jidoga no rekishi 1 [A history of children's painting part 1]. *Biiku Bunka* [Magazine for Art Education], *32* (6), 54-57.

Kurata, K., Hayashi, K., & Saikoji, T. (1980/1983/1986/1989). *Zugakosaku* [Art and handicrafts] (6 vols.). Osaka: Nihon Bunkyo Syuppan.

Kurisuto no anburera keikaku [Christo's umbrellas project]. (1991, October 22). *Asahi Shimbun* [Asahi Daily News], p. 9.

Kurisutoten [The Exhibition of Christo]. (1991, October 28). *Asahi Shimbun* [Asahi Daily News], p.31.

Kurita, I. (1987). *Japanese identity*. Tokyo: Syodensha.

Lancaster, C. (1968-69). Synthesis: The artistic theory of Fenollosa and Dow. *Art Journal*, *28* (3), 286-287.

Lanier, V. (1964). *Teaching secondary art*. Scranton, PA: International Textbook.

Leary, D. E. (1992). William James and the art of human understanding. *American Psychologist*, *47* (2), 152-160.

Lemos, P. J. (1920/1933). *Applied art*. Mountain View, CA: Pacific Press.

Lemos, P. J. (1939). *The art teacher*. Worcester, Mass.: The Davis Press.

Logan, F. M. (1955). *Growth of art in American schools*. New York: Happer & Brothers.

Logan, F. M. (1965). Development of art education in the twentieth century U.S.A. In J. J. Hausman (Ed.), *Report of the commission on art education* (pp. 49-67). Washington D.C.: National Art Education Association.

Lowenfeld, V. (1939). *The nature of creative activity*. New York: Harcourt Brace. (The

Japanese edition published under the title, *Jido bijutsu to sozosei*. [K. Mizusawa trans.].
Tokyo: Bijutsu Syuppan Sha, 1960).

Lowenfeld, V. (1954). *Your child and his art*. New York: Macmillan. (The Japanese edition
published under the title, *Kodomo no e* [M. Katsumi trans.]. Tokyo: Japan: Hakuyosha,
1956).

Lowenfeld, V. (1957). *Creative and mental growth* (3rd. ed.). New York: Macmillan. (The
Japanese edition published under the title, *Bijutsu niyoru ningenkeisei*, [K. Takeuchi, T.
Horiuchi, & K. Katsui trans.]. Nagoya, Japan: Reimei Syobo, 1963).

Luckiesh, M. (1915). *Color and its appreciations*. New York: D. Van Nostrand.

Macdonald, S. (1970). *The history and philosophy of art education*. London: University of
London Press.

MacGregor, R. N. (1994). Editorial: International assets. *Art Education, 47* (1), 4-5.

Madeja, S. (1977). *Through the arts to the aesthetics: The CEMREL aesthetic education
program*. St Louis, MO: CEMREL Inc. (ERIC ED 160 492)

Maritain, J. (1954). *Creative intuition in art and poetry*. Cleveland: World Publishing.

Maritain, J. (1954/1974). *Creative intuition in art and poetry*. New York: New American
Library. (Originally published 1954).

Martin, M. W. (1980). Some American contributions to early twentieth-century abstraction.
Art Magazine, 54 (10), 158-165.

Maruyama, M. (1961). *Nippon no shiso* [Japanese thought], Tokyo, Iwanami Shoten.

Masheck, J. (1997). Introduction: Dow's "way" to modernity for everybody. In A. W. Dow,
Composition (pp. 1-61), Berkeley, CA: University of California Press.

Mason, R. (1994). Artistic achievement in Japanese junior high schools. *Art Education, 47*
(1), 8-19.

Mason, R., Nakase, N., & Naoe, T. (1998). Craft education at the cross road in Britain and
Japan. *Journal of Multi-cultural and Cross-cultural Research in Art Education, 16* (1),
7-25.

Massachusetts Normal Art School. (1904). *Circular and catalogue for the thirty-second year
1904-1905*. Boston: Wright & Potter Printing.

Masuda, K. (1992). The transition of teaching methods in Japanese art textbooks. In P.
Amburgy, D. Soucy, M. A. Stankiewicz, B. Wilson, & M. Wilson (Eds.), *The history of
art education: Proceedings from the second Penn State conference, 1989* (pp. 98-103).
Reston, VA: National Art Education Association.

Masuda, K. (2003). A historical overview of art education in Japan. *Journal of Aesthetic*

Education, 37 (4), 3-11.

McKibbin, M. A. (1960). Fifty years of theory and practice. In R. Ebken (Ed.), *Prospect and retrospect: 1910-1960* (pp. 62-79). Kutztown, PA: Eastern Arts Association.

Meech, J. (1990). Reinventing the exotic Orient. In J. Meech & G. P. Weisberg (Eds.), *Japonisme comes to America: The Japanese impact on the graphic arts, 1876-1925* (pp. 95-234). New York: Harry N. Abrams.

Meech, J., & Weisberg, G. P. (Eds.). (1990). *Japonisme comes to America: The Japanese impact on the graphic arts, 1876-1925.* New York: Harry N. Abrams.

Meeson, P. (1981). Art as symbol or thing. *British Journal of Aesthetics, 21* (1), 22-31.

Michael, J. A. (1983). *Art and adolescence: Teaching art at the secondary level.* New York: Teachers College Press.

Ministry of Education. (1871). *Seiga shinan* [Guide to Western pictures] (T. Kawakami, trans. and ed.). Tokyo: The author.

Ministry of Education. (1910a). *Education in Japan* (Part 8, Art education). Tokyo: Ministry of Education.

Ministry of Education. (1910b). *Sintei gacho* [New textbooks of drawing]. Tokyo: The Author.

Ministry of Education. (1910c). *Teachers edition of Shitei gacho* (Bks. I). Tokyo: The Author.

Ministry of Education (1983). *Course of study for elementary schools in Japan.* Tokyo: The Author. (Japanese edition published 1977).

Ministry of Education (1989). *Education in Japan.* Tokyo: Gyosei.

Ministry of Education, Science and Culture (1990). *Japanese government politics in education, science and culture, 1990.* Tokyo: Ministry of Finance.

Ministry of Education, Science and Culture (1994). *Education in Japan: A graphic presentation.* Tokyo: Gyosei.

Miyamoto, S. (1878). *Shogaku hutsu gagakubon* [Drawing for use in elementary schools]. Tokyo, Ministry of Education.

Mock-Morgan, M. E. (1976). *A historical study of the theories and methodology of Arthur Wesley Dow and their contribution to teacher training in art education.* (Doctoral Dissertation, University of Maryland, 1976). (University Microfilms No. 77-9514).

Moffatt, F. C. (1977). *Arthur Wesley Dow (1857-1922).* Washington D. C.: The Smithsonian Institution Press.

Monroe, P. (1911). *A cyclopedia of education.* New York: Mscmillan.

Motomura, K. (2003). Media literacy education in art: Motion expression and the new vision of art education. *Journal of Aesthetic Education, 37* (4), 58-64.

Munsell, A. E. O., Spry, W., & Bellamy. B. S. (1946). Preface. In A. H. Munsell, *A color notation* (tenth ed.)(pp. 3-5). Baltimore, Md.: Munsell Color.

Munsell, A. H. (1917). *A color notation.* Boston: Geo. H. Ellis.

Munsterberg, H. (1957). *The arts of Japan: An illustrated history.* Tokyo: Charles E. Tuttle.

Munsterberg, H. (1982). *The Japanese print.* Tokyo & New York: Weatherhill.

Münsterberg, H. (1904). *The principles of art education.* New York: The Prang . (The Japanese edition published under the title, *Geijutsu kyoiku no genri* [S. Shimoda, trans.], Tokyo: Zuga Kyoiku Tushinsha, 1915).

Muro, O. (1957). Adventure in a secondary school. *Art Education, 10* (1), 8-10.

Nagamachi, M. (1988). *Teaching in the eternal present: Art education as radical support of art-making.* (Doctoral dissertation, The Pennsylvania State University). (UMI ADD 88-26796).

Nagamachi, M. (1997). History of art education and Zen—From the "Zen" (non-dual) point of view. In A. A. Anderson & P. E. Bolin (Eds.), *History of art education: Proceedings from the third Penn State international symposium* (pp. 52-57). University Park, PA: The Pennsylvania State University.

Nagamori, M. (2003). Encounter between hyper-media art education: A retrospection of Jean-Jacques Rousseau of memories of art education. *Journal of Aesthetic Education, 37* (4), 41-50.

Nakamura, H. (1977). The way of thinking of Japanese people. In H. Murakami, & E. G. Seidensticker (Eds.). *Guides to Japanese culture* (pp. 61-65). New York: Japan Publications Trading.

Nakamura, K. (2009). The significance of Dewey's aesthetics in art education in the age of globalization. *Educational Theory, 59* (4), 427-440.

Nakamura, K., & Okazaki, A. (2003). Symposium: Aesthetic education in Japan today. *Journal of Aesthetic Education, 37* (4), 1-3.

Nakamura, T. (1979). *Nihon bijutsu kyoiku no hensen* [Development of Japanese art education]. Tokyo: Nihon Bunkyo Syuppan.

Nakane, C. (1972). *Japanese society.* Berkeley: University of California Press.

Nakase, N., & Murakami, A. (1994).The Japanese national curriculum. *INSEA News, 1* (1) 14.

Naoe, T. (2003). Art education in lower secondary schools in Japan and the United Kingdom. *Journal of Aesthetic Education, 37* (4), 101-107.

National Institute of Educational Research. (1978). Modernization of education in Japan

(Special issue). *Research Bulletin of the National Institute for Educational Research*, No. 17.

Neill, A. S. (1973, January 28). Letter to Mrs. Shimoda.

Nishida, K. (1923/1973). *Art and morality* (D. A. Dilworth & V. H. Viglielmo, Trans.). Honolulu: The University Press of Hawaii. (Original Japanese work published 1923).

Okada, H. (1997). Journey for inquiring into the truth of the art expression of children: Changes in the interpretation of children's paintings in Japan since 1945. In A. A. Anderson & P. E. Bolin (Eds.), *History of art education: Proceedings from the third Penn State international symposium* (pp. 467-475). University Park, PA: The Pennsylvania State University.

Okada, M. (2003). Music-picture: One form of synthetic art education. *Journal of Aesthetic Education, 37* (4), 73-84.

Okakura, K. (1906). *The book of tea*. New York: Duffield.

Okakura, K. (1903/1970). *The ideal of the East* (rep. ed.). Tokyo: Charles E. Tuttle.

Okamoto, Y. (2003). A sense of reality. *Journal of Aesthetic Education, 37* (4), 26-32.

Okazaki, A. (1984). An overview of the influence of American art education literature on the development of Japanese art education. *Journal of Multi-cultural and Cross-cultural Research in Art Education, 2* (1), 82-95.

Okazaki, A. (1985a). American influence on the history of Japanese art education: The case of Akira Shirahama. In B. Wilson & H. Hoffa (Eds.), *The history of art education: Proceedings from the Penn State conference* (pp. 59-66), Reston, VA: National Art Education Association.

Okazaki, A. (1985b). What American art educators learned from the Japanese: A response to Carson and Dobbs. *Art Education, 38* (4), 6-10.

Okazaki, A. (1991). European modernist art into Japanese school art: The free drawing movement in the 1920s. *Journal of Art & Design Education. 10* (2), 189-198.

Okazaki, A. (1992). American influence on the history of Japanese education: The case of Seishi Shimoda. In P. Amburgy, D. Soucy, M. A. Stankiewicz, B. Wilson, & M. Wilson (Eds.), *The history of art education: Proceedings from the second Penn State conference, 1989* (pp. 109-117). Reston, VA: National Art Education Association.

Okazaki, A. (1994a). Art teacher training in Japan. *INSEA News, 1* (3), 13-16. Reprinted from ERIC database. (ED 385 477)

Okazaki, A. (1994b). Japanese art education: The contributions of European modernism and American art programs during the 1920s. *Journal of Multicultural and Cross-cultural*

Research in Art Education, 12 (1), 50-65.

Okazaki, A. (1995a). Art education research: Beittel's cross-cultural interpretation in pilgrimages to others. In M. Stokrocki (Ed.), *New waves of research in art education* (pp. 1-7). Kalamazoo, MI: Western Michigan University, Dept. of Art. Reprinted from ERIC database. (ED 395 871)

Okazaki, A. (1995b). American contemporary art into Japanese school art: Play activities in the 1980s. In H. Kauppinen & R. Diket (Eds.), *Trends in art education from diverse cultures* (pp. 175-180). Reston, VA: National Art Education Association.

Okazaki, A. (1997). Understanding the "other" in art education: A biographical interpretation of Beittel's writing. In A. A. Anderson & P. E. Bolin (Eds.), *History of art education: Proceedings from the third Penn State international symposium* (pp. 41-51). University Park, PA: The Pennsylvania State University.

Okazaki, A. (1999). Dow's conception of teaching art: "Harmonious composition" and "Notan." *InSEA 30th world congress proceedings* (CD), Australian Institute of Art Education. Reprinted from ERIC database. (ED 451 089)

Okazaki, A. (2001). The two-way street in the history of American and Japanese art education. In *Proceedings of APSEC 2000 Asia-Pacific art education conference* (pp. 49-61). Hong Kong, China: The Hong Kong Institute of Education.

Okazaki, A. (2003). Arthur Wesley Dow's address in Kyoto, Japan (1903). *Journal of Aesthetic Education, 37* (4), 84-91.

Okazaki, A. (2005). European modernist art into Japanese school art: The free drawing movement in the 1920s. In M. Romans (Ed.), *Histories of art and design education: Collected essays* (pp. 229-238). Bristol, UK: Intellect Books.

Okazaki, A. (2008). Arthur Wesley Dow's lecture in Kyoto, Japan (1903). *Proceedings* of the *32nd InSEA world congress 2008 in Osaka, Japan* (CD, PJ035), The Organizational Committee.

Ollman, L. (2000). Arthur Wesley Dow: Democratizing art. *Art in America, 88* (11), 63-67.

Ott, R. W., & Hurwitz, A. (1984). Introduction: International art education. In R. W. Ott, & A. Hurwitz, (Eds.), *Art education: An international perspective* (pp.1-8), University Park, PA: The Pennsylvania State University Press.

Passin, H. (1965a). *Society and education in Japan.* New York: Teachers College, Columbia University.

Passin, H. (1965b). Modernization and Japanese intellectual: Some comparative observations. In M. B. Jansen (Ed.), *Changing Japanese attitudes toward modernization* (pp. 447-

487). Princeton, N. J.: Princeton University Press.

Pepper, S. C. (1953). The concept of fusion in Dewey's aesthetic theory. *Journal of Aesthetics and Art Criticism, 12* (2) 169-176.

Pepper, S. C. (1966). *Concept and quality.* La-Salle, Illinois: Open Court.

Poesch, J. (1999). Arthur Wesley Dow: The beauty of simplicity. In N. E. Green & J. Poesch (Eds.), *Arthur Wesley Dow and American arts & crafts* (pp.109-126). New York: The American Federation of the Arts.

Raunft, R. (1991, April). *Meditative thinking, empowerment and caring: The liberating pedagogy of Dr. Kenneth R. Beittel.* Paper presented at the KRB Symposium, The University of Illinois, Urbana/Champain, IL.

Read, H. (1945) *Education through art* (2nd ed.). London: Faber and Faber. (The Japanese edition published under the title, *Geijutsu niyoru kyoiku* [T. Uemura & K. Mizusawa trans.], Tokyo: Bijutsu Syuppan Sha, 1953).

Read, H. (1974). *A Concise history of modern painting* (New edition). London: Thames and Hudson.

Reischauer, E. O. (1964). *Japan: past and present* (revised 3rd ed.). Tokyo: Charles E. Tuttle.

Reischauer, E. O. (1981). *Japan: The story of a nation* (3rd ed.). Tokyo: Charles E. Tuttle.

Rhead, G. W. (1905). *Principle of design.* London: B. T. Batsford.

Rimer, J. T. (1988). *Pilgrimages: Aspect of Japanese literature and culture.* Honolulu: The University of Hawaii Press.

Romans, M. (2005). Introduction: Rethinking art design education histories. In M. Romans (Ed.), *Histories of art and design education: Collected essays* (pp. 11-18). Bristol, UK: Intellect Books.

Rorty, R. (1984). The historiography of philosophy: Four genres. In R. Rorty, J. B. Schneewind, & Q. Skinner (Eds.), *Philosophy in history* (pp. 49-75). Cambridge: Cambridge University Press.

Rosenberg, H. (1959/1994). The tradition of the new. Boston: Da Capo Press.

Rosenfield, J. M. (1971). Western-style painting in the early Meiji period and its crisis. In D. H. Shiverly, (Ed.), *Tradition and modernization in Japanese culture* (pp. 181-219). Princeton, N.J.: Princeton University Press.

Rubinger, R. (1989). Continuity and change in mid-nineteenth-century Japanese education. In J. J. Shields (Ed.), *Japanese schooling: Patterns of socialization, equality, and political control* (pp. 224-233). University Park, PA: The Pennsylvania State University Press.

Sakazaki, S. (1942). *Nihonga no seishin* [The spirit of Japanese-style painting]. Tokyo:

Tokyodo.

Sargent, W., & Miller, E. E. (1916). *How children learn to draw*. Boston: Ginn.

Saunders, R. J. (1966). A history of the teaching of art appreciation in the public schools. In D.W. Ecker (Ed.), *Improving the teaching of art appreciation* (pp. 1-48). Columbus, Ohio: The Ohio State University Research Foundation. (ERIC Document Reproduction Service No. 011 063).

Seki, M. (1925). *Geijutsu kyoiku shiso shi* [A history of art education, philosophy]. Tokyo: Koseikaku.

Seki, M. (1928). *Zuga kyoju no kihon mondai* [Basic problems of drawing instruction]. Tokyo: Monas.

Seki, M. (1931). *Zuga gakushu genron* [Principles of learning in drawing]. Tokyo: Bunka Shobo.

Shields, J. J. (Ed.) (1990). *Japanese schooling*. University Park, PA: The Pennsylvania State University Press.

Shimoda, S. (1915). *Setsu yaku geijutsu kyoiku no genri nituite* [My translation of the Principles of Art Education into Japanese]. *Kinko*, No. 5, pp. 42-45.

Shimoda, S. (1917). Yakusya iwaku [Translator's note]. In H. T. Bailey, *Futsuu kyoiku niokeru geijutsu kyoiku* [Art education in general education] (Shimoda trans.) (Appendix, pp. 153-154). Tokyo: Dainihon Tosho.

Shimoda, S. (1920). Jiyu-ga mondai no hihan [Problems of the free drawing: A critical discussion]. *Teikoku Kyoiku* [Education in Imperial Japan], No. 458, 51-56.

Shimoda, S. (1922). *Shin zuga kyoiku no kensetsu* [Building a theory of new drawing education]. Tokyo: Tokyo Kyoiku Sha.

Shimoda, S. (1923, Murch). Shikisai kyoiku no kisoteki kenkyu [A basic study of color theory in education]. *Asuno Kyoiku* [Future Education], 47-51.

Shimoda, S. (1924). Geijutsu kansho no kyoiku [Teaching appreciation of arts]. In *Geijutsu kyoiku no saishin kenkyu* [Contemporary research in arts education] (pp. 311-343). Tokyo: Bunka Shobo Shuppan.

Shimoda, S. (1926). *Shin kyoiku ni rikyaku seru zuga shukou kyoju no jissai* [Teaching drawing and manual arts in the new education movement]. Tokyo: Zyuhokaku.

Shimoda, S. (1927). *Geijutsu kyoiku wo kichotoseru teigakunen no kyoiku kiroku* [Teaching in the lower grades through arts]. Tokyo: Heibonsha.

Shimoda, S. (1959a). *E ni miru kodomo no shinri* [Psychology of children's painting]. Tokyo: Toto Syobo.

Shimoda, S. (1959b). Internationalism and nationalism in art education from the standpoint of Japan, In *FEA congress report: Xth congress of the International Federation for Education through Art* (pp. 229-231). Ravernsburg, Otto Maier.

Shimoda, S. (1972). *Kaigai shicho no eikyo* [Forein countries' influence on Japanese art education]. In N. Ide (Ed.), *Bijutsu kyoiku genri* [Principles of art education] (pp. 36-42). Tokyo: Gakugei Shorin.

Shirahama, A. (1904). *Zuga kyoju ho* [Methods in drawing instruction]. Tokyo: Dai Nipphon Tosho.

Shirahama, A. (1907). Zuga kyoju ho [Methods in drawing instruction]. *Zuga Kyoiku* [Drawing Education], No.11, 43-45.

Shirahama, A. (1908). Zuga kyoiku ni tsukite [On the drawing education]. *Shinano Kyoiku* [Education in Shinano District], No. 265, 2-5.

Shirahama, A. (1909). Kaigai zuga kyoiku no jissai [Drawing education in foreign countries]. *Kyoiku Jiron* [Educational Critique], No. 859, 7-11.

Shirahama, A. (1911). *Zuga kyoju no riron to jissai* [Theory and practice of drawing education]. Tokyo: Dai Nippon Tosho.

Shirahama, A. (1916). *Shintei gacho no seishin oyobi sono riyo ho* [The editorial policy of the New Textbooks of Drawing and how to use it]. Tokyo: Kyoiku Shicho Kenkyu Kai.

Shively, D. H. (1971). The Japanization of the middle Meiji. In D. H. Shively (Ed.), *Tradition and modernization in Japanese culture* (pp.77-119). Princeton, N. J.: Princeton University Press.

Shorts, E. G. (1984). *Competence.* New York: University of Press of America.

Silverman, R. H. (1982). *Learning about art: A practical approach.* Newport, CA: Romar Arts.

Smith, J. B. (1933). Trends of thought in art education. *The School Review, 41,* 266-277.

Smith, M. (1924). *History of the Massachusetts normal art school 1873 to 1923-24.* Boston, MT: Massachusetts Normal Art School.

Smith, P. J. (1982). Germanic foundations: A look at what we are standing on. *Studies in Art Education, 23* (3), 23-30.

Smith, P. J. (1994). Multicultural issues: Dilemmas and hopes, *Art Education, 47* (4), 13-17.

Smith, P. J. (1996). *The history of American art education: Learning about art in American schools.* Westport, CT: Greenwood Press.

Smith, W. S. (1873/1876). *Teacher's manual of free-hand drawing and designing and guide to self-instruction* (rep. ed.). Boston: L. Prang. (Original work published 1873)

Snow, B. E., & Froehlich, H. B. (1915). *Industrial art text books* (Parts 1-6). New York: The Prang.

Sodoshiki to daoshi no enzetsu [Opening ceremony of teaching rooms and Mr. Dow's speech]. (1903, December 12). *Hinode Shimbun* [Hinode Daily News], p. 3.

Stankiewicz, M. A. (1985). A picture age: Reproductions in picture study. *Studies in Art Education, 26* (2), 86-92.

Stankiewicz, M. A. (1990). Rules and inventions: From ornament to design in art education. In D. Soucy & M. A. Stankiewicz (Eds.), *Fraiming the past: Essays on art education* (pp. 89-101). Reston, VA: National Art Education Association.

Stankiewicz, M. A. (2007a). Capitalizing art education: Mapping international histories. In L. Bresler (Ed.), *International handbook of research in arts education, part 1* (pp. 7-30). Dordrecht, The Netherland: Springer.

Stankiewicz, M. A. (2007b). Book review [Review of the book *Histories of art and design education: Collected essays,* by M. Romans]. *Studies in Art Education, 49* (1), 73-76.

Stankiewicz, M. A. (2009). Constructing an international history of art education: Period, patterns, and principles. *The International Journal of Arts Education, 7* (1), 1-20.

Stankiewicz, M. A. (2016). *Developing visual arts education in the United States: Massachusetts Normal Art School and the normalization of creativity.* New York: Palgrave Macmillan.

Stanley-Baker, J. (1984). *Japanese art.* New York: Thames and Hudson.

Stokrocki, M. (1992). Introduction. In M. Stokrocki (Ed.), *New waves of research in art education* (Machine-readable computer disk) (pp. 1-5). The Seminar for Research in Art Education [Producer and Distributor].

Stokrocki, M. (1995). Introduction. In M. Stokrocki (Ed.), *New waves of research in art education* (iii-vi). Kalamazoo, MI: Western Michigan University, Dept. of Art. Reprinted from ERIC database. (ED 395 871)

Sugiyama, A. (1983). Shin kyoiku undo [New education movement]. In *Kodansha encyclopeida of Japan* (vol. 7) (p. 121). Hemel Hempstead, UK: International Book Distributors.

Sullivan, M. (1965). *Chinese and Japanese art* (The book of art, vol. 9). New York: Grolier.

Suzuki, D. T. (1956). *Zen Buddhism: Selected writings of D. T. Suzuki.* (W. Barrett, ed.). New York: Doubleday & Company.

Tabor, M. E. (1913). *The saints in art* (2nd ed.). New York: E. P. Dutton.

Tadd, J. L. (1901). *New methods in education: Art, real manual training, nature study*

194

(Student's ed.), Springfield, Mass.: Orange Juddo.

Takasaki, M. (1980, Summer). A hare and a tortoise. *Chit-chat*, *14*, 30-34.

Tall, L. L., & Davidson, I. (1921). *Course of study* (1921 revision, Baltimore county, Maryland, public schools, grades I to VIII). Baltimore: Warwick & York, Inc.

Tatsutomi, Y. (1997). Changes teachers' consciousness from 1871 to the present in Japan: From coercion to laissez-faire, inducement to freedom. In A. A. Anderson & P. E. Bolin (Eds.), *History of art education: Proceedings from the third Penn State international symposium* (pp. 285-291). University Park, PA: The Pennsylvania State University.

Thistlewood, D. (1991). Editorial: Modernism and modernization of the curriculum. *Journal of Art & Design Education*, *10* (2), 125-128.

Toku, M. (2001). What is Manga? The influence of pop culture in adolescent art. *Art Education*, *54* (2), 11-17.

Tomhave, R. D. (1992). Value based underlying conceptions of multicultural education: An analysis of selected literature in art education. *Studies in Art Education*, *34* (1), 48-60.

Trembath, P. (1989). The rhetoric of philosophical "Writing": Emphatic metaphors in Derride and Rorty. *Journal of Aesthetics and Art Criticism*, *47* (2), 169-173.

Tuita, Y., Itarashiki, S.. & Iwasaki, Y. (1978). *Jissenrei niyoru zokeiasobi no pointo* [Teaching materials of play activity]. Osaka: Sanko Syobo.

Turner, V. (1974). *Dramas, fields, and metaphors: Symbolic action in human society*. Ithaca: Cornell University Press.

Ue, S. (1967). Sozo no purosesu [Creativity and Creative process]. In S. Ue & K. Okatsu, *Bijutsu kyoiku no kozo* [Structure of art education]. Tokyo: David Sya.

Ueno, H. (1981). *Geijutsu kyoiku undo no kenkyu* [Study of the Arts Education Movement]. Tokyo: Kazama Shobo.

Ueno, K., Iwasaki, Y., Okazaki, A., Okumura, T., & Hino, Y. (2007). Curriculum development of art appreciation through meaningful dialogue. *Proceeding of InSEA regional congress 2007* (pp. 398-407). Seoul: Seoul National University.

U.S. Department of Education (1987). *Japanese education today*. Washington, DC: U.S. Government Printing Office.

Wachowiak, F. (1985). *Emphasis art: A qualitative art program for elementary and middle schools* (4th ed.). New York: Happer & Row.

Wang, W., & Ishizaki, K. (2002). Aesthetic development in cross-cultural context: A study of art appreciation in Japan, Taiwan, and the United States. *Studies in Art Education*, *43* (4), 373-392.

Washburne, C. (1932). *Remakers of mankind.* New York: The John Day.

Watson, R. I., & Evans, R. B. (1991). *The great psychologist: A history of psychological thought* (5th ed.). New York: Harper Collins.

White, M. (1987). *The Japanese educational challenge: A commitment to children.* Tokyo & New York: Kodansha International.

Wilber, K. (1977). *The spectrum of consciousness.* Wheaton, IL: Theosophical Publishing House.

Williams, B. L. (2013). Japanese aesthetic influences on early 20th-century art education: Arthur Wesley Dow and Ernest Fenollosa. *Visual Arts Research, 39* (2), 104-115.

Wilson, B. (1974). The other side of evaluation of art education. In G. Hardiman & T. Zernich (Eds.), *Curricular consideration for visual arts education* (pp. 247-276). Champaign, IL: Stipes.

Wilson, B. (1989). Amerika to nihon niokeru modanizumu no bijutsu kyoiku [Modernists art education in America and Japan: Seasons of shaped beliefs and prophecies for the postmpdern ear] (M. Nagamachi, trans.), *Ato Edukeishon* [Japanese Journal of Art Education], *1* (3), 7-18.

Wilson, B. (1989, March). Modernist art education in America and Japan: Seasons of shared beliefs and prophecies for the postmodern era. Paper presented at the annual meeting of Bijutsuka Kyoiku Gakkai [Japanese Art Education Association]. Yokohama, Japan.

Wilson, B. (1999). Becoming Japanese: Manga, children's drawings, and the construction of national character. *Visual Arts Research, 25* (2), 48-60.

Wilson, B. (2008). The end of child art and the emergence of adult/kid collaborative conjunctions in three pedagogical sites. *Proceedings* of the *32nd InSEA world congress 2008 in Osaka, Japan* (CD, Wilson-0805), The Organizational Committee.

Wilson, B., Hurwitz, A., & Wilson M. (1987). *Teaching drawing from art.* Worcester, MA: Davis. (The Japanese edition published under the title, *Bijutsu karano byoga sido* [M. Keitoku, A. Okazaki, & T. Abe, trans.]. Tokyo: Nihon Bunkyo Syuppan, 1998).

Winslow, L. L. (1928). *Organization and teaching of art: A program for art education in the schools.* Baltimore: Warwick & York.

Wygant, F. (1983). *Art in American schools in the nineteenth century.* Cincinnati: Interwood Press.

Wygant, F. (1985). Art structure: Fundamentals of design before the Bauhaus. In H. Hoffa and B. Wilson (Eds.), *The history of art education: Proceedings from the Penn State conference* (pp. 158-162). Reston, VA: National Art Education Association.

Wygant, F. (1993). *School art in American culture* 1820-1970. Cincinnati, OH: Interwood Press.

Yamada, K. (1992). The development of art courses of study in Japan. In P. Amburgy, D. Soucy, M. A. Stankiewicz, B. Wilson, & M. Wilson (Eds.), *The history of art education: Proceedings from the second Penn State conference, 1989* (pp.118-125). Reston, VA: National Art Education Association.

Yamada, K. (1995). Development and problems of art education in Japan. In H. Kauppinen & R. Diket (Eds.), *Trends in art education from diverse cultures* (pp. 64-71). Reston, VA: National Art Education Association.

Yamada, K. (2003). Evolution in qualitative factors used to evaluate Japanese students. *Journal of Aesthetic Education, 37* (4), 50-57.

Yamagata, Y. (1967). *Nihon bijutsu kyoiku shi* [The history of Japanese art education]. Nagaya, Japan: Reimei Shobo.

Yamamoto, K. (1921). *Jiyuga kyoiku* [Education through free drawing]. Tokyo: Arusu.

Yashiro, Y. (1969). *Suibokuga* [Ink painting]. Tokyo, Japan: Iwanami Shoten.

Young, M. W. (1969). Six principles of Chinese painting. In B. S. Meyers (Ed.), *McGraw-Hill dictionary of art* (Vol.5) (p. 191). New York: McGraw-Hill.

Yuasa, N. (1966). Introduction. In M. Basho, *The narrow road to the deep north and other travel sketches* (N. Yuasa, trans.) (pp. 9-50). New York: Penguin Books.

Yukawa, N. (1965). Art education of Japan (O. Muro, trans.). *Kyoiku Bijutsu* [Art in Education], Special Issue, 1-9.

Zurmuehlen, M. (1991). Kenneth Beittel: A re-interpreting presence in art education. *Visual Arts Research, 17* (1), 1-11

Index

A

A Celebration of Art and Consciousness (Beittel & Beittel), 164-165, 171, 176

Abe, Toshifumi, 149, 179, 196

Ability to draw, 85

Abstract symbolism, 57

Academism of art, 137

Adams, J., 6, 173

Aesthetic: appreciation, 114, 125, 143, 151; awareness of tone sensibility, 122; choices, 151; Education Program, 48, 168, 173, 186; imagination, 106; way of life, 165

Aesthetics 101-02: and beauty, 155

Akagi, Rikako, 9, 173

Akutsu, Hisashi, 11

Alschuler, L. B. W., 44

Alternatives for Art Education Research (Beittel), 93, 159, 174

Amae as a sense of dependence, 154-155

Amburgy, Patricia M., 79, 180-181, 186, 189, 196

American: art, 127; art education, 72-74, 134, 150; art education Odyssey, 150; art program, 95, 98; Board Mission, 141; contemporary art, 53; elementary schools, 74; Influence, 63, 64, 79; Minimal Art, 57; models, 106; Occupation, 41, 42; sources, 82, 85; way, 165

American Drawing Book (Chapman), 35, 65, 177

America's impact on art education in Japan, 42

Anderson, Albert A., 159, 173, 176, 182, 188, 190, 194

Anderson, R. S., 33-34, 173

Ando, Kyoichiro, 173

An Ipswich Hill (Dow), 113

Analyzing Children's Art (Kellogg), 47

Anatomy, 101-102

Applied Art (Lemos), 81, 107, 185

Applied Arts Book (now *School Arts*), 105

Appreciation of beauty, 101

Approach to Art in Education (Chapman), 35, 177

Arai, Koji, 43, 173

Archives of American Art, 130, 178-179

Arita (Japan), 160, 162, 170

Art, 94, 99, 102: and handicraft, 12, 109; appreciation, 101, 104-106, 114; as Things, 119; curriculum, 101, 108; education, 113; for daily life, 43; in Dress, 85; in Handwork, 85; in Home, 85; 82,108; lesson plan, 104; Student's League, 129; Supervisors, Art Specialists and Art Teachers, 19; Teacher Preparation at a College of Education, 16; textbook, 60; training for children, 144

Art and the Child (Richardson), 31

Art Education (Bailey), 36, 83, 102, 173, 192

Art Education in the Public Schools of the United States (Haney), 85, 182

Art in Secondary Education (Winslow), 43, 196

Art in the Schools (Boas), 82, 108, 176

Art Today (Faulkner & Ziegfeld), 43, 180

Arthur Wesley Dow and American Art & Crafts, (Green & Poesch), 146, 182

Artistic: design, 134; expression, 109; importations, 111; or poetic reconstruction, 167; process as imagination, 119

Arts, 12: and Crafts Movement, 104, 136

Art-to-School Program, 54, 55

As if Play, 57

Assisi Church, 142

B

Bailey, Henry T., 36, 37, 66, 83, 85-87, 111, 173, 192

Barbosa, Ana Mae, 22, 173

Barkan, Manuel, 48, 173

Barnes, Earl, 42. 88

Barzun, J., 170,173-174

Basho Matsuo, 165-166, 171-172, 176, 174, 197

Battiata, M. L., 3, 174

Bauhaus, 42

Beasley, W. G., 24, 25, 80, 99,

Law, 15

F

G

Education through Art (Read), 31, 45, 191

Factor analysis of creativity, 161

Gado Yoketsu (A Key to the way of Painting), 118

Educational: imagination, 80; policy-making, 96

Fairbrother, Trevor, 140, 180

Farnum, Royal Bainley, 81, 87-89, 106, 181

Gardner, Howard E., 47, 160, 169, 181

Educational Problems (Hall), 42

Faulkner, Ray, 43, 182

Gauguin, Paul, 108

Efland, Arthur D. 88, 111, 114, 127, 140, 149, 179

Feeding Her Birds (Millet), 79, 81, 107

Geido (aesthetic way of life), 165

Ehlers, Yohannes, 49

Fenollosa, Ernest, 36-38, 49n1, 72, 115, 120, 123-124, 129, 139, 181, 183

Geijutsu Kyoiku Undo (Arts Education Movement), 26, 99

Eisen Keisai, 147, 131, 143-144

Gerald, H., 181

Eisner, Elliot W., 2, 6, 20, 28-29, 32-33, 46-48, 50n9, 80, 90-91, 96, 98, 110, 149, 153, 167, 177, 179-180

German Bauhaus system, 46

Fenollosa-Dow system, 115

Giotto, di Bondone, 142

Fenolllosa, Marry, 115, 181

God, 163

Figure-ground relationship, 8, 29-32, 53-54

Good Housekeeping, 84

Elementary school majors, 17

Governmental and Non-governmental Educational Efforts, 96-97

Empirical-scientific researches on creativity, 161

Finding the Great Tradition, 165-167

Enlightened eye, 165

Fine arts, 12: education, 39

Göze, Karl, 88

Enyeart, James L. 128, 129. 137, 140, 145, 147, 180

Fisher, R. Michael, 7, 181

Gradual Process, 7-9

Flectcher, F. M., 89, 181

Grans of Grit into Pearls, 60-61

Epochs of Chinese and Japanese Art (Fenollosa), 115, 180-181

Formal Schooling, 152-154

Graoian, Charles, 54, 181

Foster, Mary S., 29, 56, 96, 140, 159, 181

Graphic design, 104

ERIC, 173-174, 176, 186, 192: Clearinghouses, 48; database, 2, 11, 113, 189-190, 194

Grauer, Kit, 182

Free: drawing, 88; expression, 99, 109; Hand Drawing, 66

Gray, James U., 169. 182

Gray rock garden, 57

European: and American progressive movement, 25; artists, 108; modernism, 4, 9, 31, 60; modernist art, 5, 21; Painting Program, 101

Free drawing movement, 5-6, 21, 24, 26-31, 40, 42, 46, 76, 80, 91, 99, 100-101

Great tradition, 166-167, 170

Green, Nancy E., 127-128, 140, 182, 191

French Impressionism, 100

Froehlich, Hugo D., 36, 38, 39, 67, 69, 70, 71, 81, 85, 181, 194

H

Evans, Rand B., 162, 196

Haboku (splashed ink), 136, 146

Examination for Employment, 18-19

Haga, Toru, 38, 72, 182

From the product to the child, 88

Hall, G. Stanley, 42, 44, 86, 88, 182: child study movement, 85

Expressive value, 76

Fujie, Mitsuru, 149, 179, 181

External and Internal Modes of Curriculum Development, 28, 97-98

Fukumoto, Kinichi, 149, 180, 181

Hamm, Glenn B., 167, 182

Hammitzsch, Horst, 168, 182

Handicrafts, 102, 102

Eye-hand-mind, 165

Handwriting, 102

value, 115

O

Okada, Hiroshi, 189

Okada, Masashi, 189

Okakura, Kakuzo, 49n1, 72, 116, 121, 124, 157, 168, 189

Okamoto, Yasuaki, 189

Okatsu, Keiichiro, 195

Okazaki, Akio, 4-9, 12, 21, 24, 26-27, 29, 50n9, 60, 65, 79, 91-92, 97, 100, 110-111, 113, 126, 137, 141, 149, 159, 166, 175, 180, 189-190, 195-196

O'Keeffe, Georgia, 136, 146

Okumura, Takaaki, 9, 195

Ollman, Leah, 140, 128, 190

Open: ended approach, 100; tracking system, 162

Oriental: art, 116, 126, 139, 156, 165; cultural tradition of art, 114

Ornaments, 104

Osaka Asahi Simbun, 127, 131, 177

Osaka Mainichi Simbun, 127, 132, 178

Ott, Robert W., 29, 96, 196

Outdoor, 30: drawing, 21; sketching class, 100

Out-of-doors, 41,100, 110

P

Painting, 94, 101, 103-104, 106

Painting and Personality (Alschuler & Hattwiek), 44

Parpenheim, Karl, 88

Participant observer, 170

Partridge, Sophia, 88

Passin, Herbert, 33, 77, 190

Pedagogy of Drawing (Hall), 42, 86

Penn State: Conference, 63, 79; International Symposium, 159, 173, 188, 190, 194

Pepper, Stephen C., 156, 179, 191

Perez, Bernard, 88

Perry, Matthew C., 33, 156

Philosophy and Civilization (Dewey), 178

Picture Study, 75, 105, 107: Movement, 114

Picturesque, 125

Pilgrim: -artist-researcher, 172; -poet, 166, 171

Pilgrimage(s), 7, 166-170, 172: to others, 167; or silent dialogues, 171; the process of, 166

Plaster model, 75

Play activities, 9, 60: in Japanese Art Textbooks, 55, 56; into the National Guidelines, 59-60

Plotinus, 164

Poesch, Jessie, 127, 140, 182, 191

Porcelain-making apprenticeship, 162

Post-impressionism, 4, 30, 31, 60

Pottery, 104, 151

Power and mystery, 125

Prang text books of art education, 68

Prang's book, 36, 64-65; of art education, 82

Pratt Institute, 115, 129

Preparation for Art (McFee), 47

Present Open System of Teacher Preparation, 14-15

Primary word, 93

Principles of painting, 75

Principles of Secondary Education (De Garmo), 87, 178

Printmaking, 104

Product desigh, 104

Project "Do", 57-59

Psychoanalysis, 108, 109

Public School Class, 66

Pure experience, 168

Q

Qualitative: immediate present, 170; research, 161

Quan, Roy, 54, 181

Quantitative research, 161

R

Raphael, 107

Rational reconstruction, 167

Raunft, R., 169, 190

Read, Herbert, 31, 45, 156, 191

Readings in Art Education (Eisner & Ecker), 47, 180

Real art world, 58

Realism, 120

Reconstruction of Philosophy (Dewey), 40, 98

Regard for: construction, 105; the material, 104; the tool, 105; the use, 105

Reischauer, Edwin O., 24-25, 40, 191

Repetition, 140
Representation, 121
Representatism, 124
Representative work, 106
Research in art education, 161
Rhead, G. W., 89, 191
Rhetoric deconstruction, 167
Rhythm of Things, 116
Rhythmic vitality, 118
Ricci, Corrado, 88
Richardson, M., 31
Rimer, J. Thomas, 167, 191
Romans, Mervyn, 5, 191, 194
Rorty, Richard, 167, 191
Rosenberg, Harold, 153, 191
Rosenfield, John. M., 21, 34, 49n1, 191
Rouma, G., 42
Rubin, Edgar John, 8, 53
Rubinger, R., 97, 191
Runes, D., 177
Ruskin, John, 104

S

Sakazaki, Shizuka, 118, 191-192
Salem Normal School, 63, 66
Sanieman Gallary, 140
Sargent, Walter, 89, 192
Saunders, Robert J., 82, 89, 122, 192
School: curriculum, 96; drama, 99
School and Society (Dewey), 40
School Art in Japan, 12-14
School Arts Book, 107, 111
School Arts Magazine, 81
Schneewind, J. B., 191
Schrikel, H. G., 177

Scroll painting, 151
Sculpture, 94, 104, 106
Secondary school majors, 17
Seidensticker, Edward G., 188
Seiga Shinan (Guide to Western Pictures), 21-22. 33-34, 184, 187
Seki, Mamoru, 36, 41. 42, 192
Self : -analysis, 108, 109; -expression, 25, 40, 162
Self-aid Cyclopedia for Self-taught Students (Burn), 21, 34
Sense: of dependence, 166; of reality, 162; of stained quality, 124
Sesshu, 81, 107, 113, 123, 131-132, 136, 143, 145, 147
Shading, 125
Shadow, 125
Shield, James J. 60, 191-192
Shimoda, Seishi, 31, 36, 38-40, 79-92, 94-96, 98, 100-110, 113, 173, 182, 192-193
Shimoda's: Art Program, 81, 104-110; Curriculum Development, 80-82; Studies of Theory and Practice in American Art Education, 82-91
Shin Kyoiku Undo (New Education Movement), 25, 99
Shinn, Milicent W., 88
Shintei Gacho (New Textbooks of Drawing), 21, 23, 27, 37-38, 69, 103, 187
Shirahama, Akira, 2-4, 7, 23, 35-39, 63, 65-70, 73-77, 113, 136, 193

Shirahama's: Transformation, 67-72; Study in America, 64-67
Shively, Donald H., 72, 182, 182, 191, 193
Shorts, E. G., 169, 175, 193
Shoso Hakkei, 143
Shubun, 131-132, 136, 143-145, 147
Silverman, R. H., 39, 70, 193
Single subject of modernist art, 100-103
Skinner, Q., 191
Smith, J. B., 90, 193
Smith, May, 3, 63, 193
Smith, Peter J. 35, 49n3, 114, 127, 139-140, 193,
Smith, Walter, 22, 34, 36, 193: industrial drawing, 85
Snow, Bonnie E., 36, 69, 70, 71, 81, 85, 194
Social: and cultural awareness, 101; reconstruction, 135
Soucy, Donald, 79, 180-181, 186, 189, 194, 197
Sound of running water, 151
South Kensington System, 5
Space relation, 73
Spectrum of Consciousness (Wilber), 164, 195
Spirit consonance, 117
Spiritual: expression, 145; injunction, 163
Spiritualism, 121, 124
Spry, W., 89, 188
St. Francis' Mercy, 141
St. Francis Preaching to the Birds (Giotto), 141
Stained quality, 145